Special Praise for *They'll Never Be the Same*

"I believe it is important that parents, teachers, and healthcare professionals become informed about the psychological impact of trauma on young and, especially, very young children. *They'll Never Be the Same*, by one of the key figures in the field, helps to do this."

Justin Kenardy, PhD
University of Queensland
Australia

"Dr. Mike Scheeringa lays out for parents what they need to know about trauma, PTSD, and effective treatments. It is based on solid scientific research—his own and that of other experts. At the same time, he is grounded in the true-life experiences of traumatized children and illustrates this with vivid clinical examples from his own clinic. He is speaking directly to parents so that they are empowered to act as educated consumers in getting the best care for their children. Clinicians seeking to help traumatized children would do well to read this book so they, too, understand the science of trauma and PTSD and are prepared to deliver treatments that work."

Lucy Berliner, MSW
Harborview Center for Sexual Assault and Traumatic Stress

"Children *do* recover from PTSD; Dr. Scheeringa's book provides parents with a wealth of information about this disorder and practical guidance for finding effective treatment."

Judith Cohen, MD
Professor of Psychiatry
Allegheny Health Network
Temple University School of Medicine

"Perhaps my highest endorsement of *They'll Never Be the Same* is that despite having studied pediatric PTSD for over twenty years, I still learned from reading it (e.g., the history of the controversy surrounding Lenore Terr's initial work). While researchers will continue to debate many of the ideas presented in this book, it is an excellent resource for the public to become educated about PTSD in children and youth. Moreover, there is no one better suited to present this information than Dr. Michael Scheeringa, one of the preeminent leaders in this field. From the case examples to the technical details of what symptoms to look out for, Dr. Scheeringa's explanations are accessible to a wide range of readers."

Carl Weems, PhD
Professor and Chair
Human Development and Family Studies
Iowa State University

They'll Never Be the Same

They'll Never Be the Same

A Parent's Guide to PTSD in Youth

Michael S. Scheeringa

CENTRAL RECOVERY PRESS

LAS VEGAS

Central Recovery Press (CRP) is committed to publishing exceptional materials addressing addiction treatment, recovery, and behavioral healthcare topics.

For more information, visit www.centralrecoverypress.com.

Publisher: Central Recovery Press
            3321 N. Buffalo Drive
            Las Vegas, NV 89129

23 22 21 20 19 18   1 2 3 4 5

Library of Congress Cataloging-in-Publication Data
Names: Scheeringa, Michael S., author.
Title: They'll never be the same : a parent's guide to PTSD in youth /
   Michael S. Scheeringa.
Other titles: They will never be the same
Description: Las Vegas : Central Recovery Press, [2018]
Identifiers: LCCN 2017048089 (print) | LCCN 2018001382 (ebook) | ISBN
   9781942094623 (ebook) | ISBN 9781942094616 (pbk. : alk. paper)
Subjects: LCSH: Post-traumatic stress disorder in children. |
   Teenagers--Mental health. | Post-traumatic stress disorder in
   children--Treatment.
Classification: LCC RJ506.P55 (ebook) | LCC RJ506.P55 S3918 2018 (print) |
   DDC 618.92/8521--dc23
LC record available at https://lccn.loc.gov/2017048089

Photo of Michael Scheeringa by Jeffery Johnston. Used with permission.

Every attempt has been made to contact copyright holders. If copyright holders have not been properly acknowledged, please contact us. Central Recovery Press will be happy to rectify the omission in future printings of this book.

Publisher's Note: This book contains general information about posttraumatic stress disorder (PTSD) in childhood and youth. It represents reference material only and is not intended as medical advice. This book is not a replacement for treatment or an alternative to medical advice from your doctor or other professional healthcare provider. If you are experiencing a medical issue, professional medical help is recommended. Mention of particular products, companies, or authorities in this book does not indicate endorsement by the publisher or author.

CRP's books represent the experiences and opinions of their authors only. Every effort has been made to ensure that events, institutions, and statistics presented in our books as facts are accurate and up-to-date. To protect their privacy, the names of some of the people, places, and institutions in this book may have been changed.

Cover design and interior by Deb Tremper, Six Penny Graphics.

To the one in the many who got it and inspired me.

Table of Contents

Preface

Thirty-nine years ago, pioneers in the field of psychological trauma recognized a new disorder called posttraumatic stress disorder (PTSD) that formally recognized the psychological injuries of victims of war, violence, abuse, accidents, and other life-threatening events. The formalization of this disorder fueled the explosion of research that followed. Since then, there has been a tremendous growth of knowledge covering the impact on emotional, cognitive, and biological domains and the treatment of this type of problem.

Despite these advances in understanding and treatment for trauma-related problems, we, as clinicians and scientists, have failed the consumers whom we are trying to help. PTSD still goes undetected in most individuals who have it. Clinicians who consider themselves experts miss the diagnosis the vast majority of the time. Parents are often inappropriately blamed for their children's problems because of misinterpretations of the research data. Patients are being told extraordinary stories that trauma has damaged their brains. Treatments that work are being ignored by clinicians.

In short, we cannot depend solely on professionals to get the right information to patients. Our current model of relying on professionals to be well-informed and to use the best practices must be given a respectful burial. For the most rapid, most efficient, and highest-quality help to reach those who need it, the information must go straight to the consumers. What has become exceptionally clear to me after twenty-three years of clinical practice and research in this field is that appeals to clinicians produce slow changes in practice, and more often than I like to see, produce no changes at all. I have personally trained hundreds of clinicians, written dozens of articles, and given dozens more professional lectures, and while I have enjoyed baby steps of progress, I know the impacts are small, and I am ready to leave that career behind.

The last straw for me was in January of 2013. Jeremy was fourteen years old. From the ages of five through eleven his stepfather physically abused him. After six different medications from doctors and weekly psychotherapy counseling with a psychologist for another two years, his problems were not getting better. In fact, they had been getting worse. Jeremy was irritable and easily annoyed, which caused him to argue with classmates and teachers. The school tolerated his spats, sulking, and disobedience until he vaguely threatened to burn the school down, at which point the school expelled him. The defiance and outbursts were frequent at home, too. He would leave home for hours without telling his father where he went.

Jeremy's PTSD symptoms had not been recognized, so the treatment he had received was wrong. Jeremy was referred to my clinic, and after four months of the right treatment his symptoms markedly improved and he was back in school for the first time in three years. This outcome was enormously satisfying to Jeremy's father, to the therapist who treated him, and to me. After I had seen hundreds of youths in my research studies, this was why I started the clinic in the first place—to fill a gap for children who were being misdiagnosed and inappropriately treated. If I could not have much impact by appealing to clinicians, perhaps I could have a bigger impact by talking straight to the consumers; hence, my decision to write this book. I've turned down previous offers to write books aimed at professionals. I think I always felt the best way to disseminate information was to get it directly into the hands of consumers. Let's see where this takes us.

Acknowledgments

Much of the material in this book comes from my research studies, and I am grateful to the many people who have worked on those studies. Because there are so many people to thank, it is impossible to list all of them. There have been twenty-one research assistants, plus twenty-seven volunteer student interns, along with all of the community agencies (nineteen agencies in just one of the studies!) that allowed us to recruit their patients and clients for the studies. Also, these have required the work and patience of many staff at Tulane University School of Medicine, where I have worked since 1998.

I am also grateful to the National Institute of Mental Health, which funded most of my studies, and the anonymous grant reviewers who found some merit in them. Frank Putnam, MD, and Charles Zeanah, MD, offered their advice on the design of many of these research studies. Of special note are Ruth Arnberger, LCSW; Emily Roser, LCSW; Alison Salloum, LCSW, PhD; and Allison Staiger, LCSW, who conducted much of the work on these studies as therapists, and Carl Weems, PhD, who provided valuable consultation on many aspects. These colleagues, however, shoulder no responsibility for the opinions expressed in this book, as my opinions on some things have changed over the years.

I owe a debt of gratitude to my agent, Jill Marsal, who guided me through this process and gave me good counsel. My editor, Nancy Schenck at Central Recovery Press, made many suggestions to make my meanings clearer and soften my tone.

Much support has been provided by my remarkable wife, Claire Peebles, PhD, who makes me feel like I picked the right one to be in the foxhole with.

Chapter One
Paths to Acceptance: A Beginning

"Grant me the serenity to accept the things I cannot change, courage to change the things I can, and wisdom to know the difference" is an old saying that suggests wisdom is hard to acquire. When children and adolescents have been through severely stressful, traumatic experiences, they are changed and they are frustrated, and parents recognize it. Parents want to know how their children have changed and how to help them. Some changes are obvious. Some changes are mysterious. Some changes are hidden from view. No one knows children better than their own parents, but the nature of post-traumatic stress reactions are such that parents cannot know everything by observing them or waiting for them to talk. Knowing that something is wrong is intuitive, but knowing the full picture of post-traumatic stress problems and knowing what to do about them requires some assistance.

As a parent, it is up to you now, but you have little idea what to do. I am quite familiar with post-traumatic stress in all its manifestations and complications, as I have spent the past twenty-three years in clinical practice and conducting research with children and adolescents who have these issues. The main syndrome that follows from traumatic events is posttraumatic stress disorder (PTSD), which is unique among all psychiatric conditions because there is a known cause: PTSD follows immediately from a life-threatening event. One day individuals do not have PTSD, and then the next day—the day individuals experience life-threatening events—they suddenly have PTSD. No other disorder in psychiatry has such a sudden, bewildering, and terrifying onset.

These immediate changes cause massive and wide-ranging destruction in the lives of the victims. Not only the youths, but also the parents and other family members must deal with the wreckage. There are many new questions to consider. What are the signs and symptoms? What is the right diagnosis? What does the future hold? When to seek help? How to find good help? This book is a guide to choose a path within the wreckage.

First, parents must recalibrate their expectations. Trauma is a game-changer for both parents and their children. To someone who has never had PTSD, it is difficult to describe what it is like. Life is harder, permanently. It is as though suddenly a judge has handed down a sentence stating, "You must live a different life now." The new task for survivors and their loved ones, as well as what must be done sometimes to survive, is to try to understand the new normal.

"My life changed. I'll never be the same. I mean I
used to be happy and a positive person, and now I'm
never happy. And I can't really tell anybody."
Fourteen-year-old trauma survivor

That sounds challenging enough, but it gets worse. Compare this to an example of another type of sudden change in life. Nearly all of us have had the experience of using a computer or a smartphone and then, after using one of these devices for months, one day the screen suddenly looks different than it looked yesterday. Some commands for touching or clicking have been moved to different locations on the screen and cannot be found. Perhaps the background colors and physical appearance of the layout have changed, too. The typical reaction of users is bitter frustration at the software developers who made these changes without our permission. The anger is softened considerably, however, because we are also confident that eventually we will find the commands that have been moved, and we will get used to the new layout.

Not so with PTSD. When one's mind and body have suddenly been changed, as with the onset of PTSD, the anger and bitter frustration start at low levels because those individuals tend to believe the change will fade with time. As with scratches and bruises on the skin and bad memories that fade with time, they think things will pop back to normal. But when weeks pass and then months pass and things have not popped back to normal, there is often an indescribable *sense of loss of control*. The anger and frustration increase with time rather than fade. It cannot be overstated how frightening this can feel when you realize you have lost control of your own mind and body.

Throughout the healing process, it usually will be up to parents to make sure the questions about children's problems get answered correctly. It is up to parents now because most clinicians do not know what they are doing. Parents need to accept this reality as surely as death and taxes. Most clinicians do not know what they are doing due to a variety of reasons. One reason is that they are poorly trained. Another is that the profession of mental health is inherently complicated and messy. Another is that clinicians make a lot of their treatment decisions based on their personal beliefs instead of research data. Much more will be said about this later in the book.

But let's start with some general descriptions of post-traumatic stress reactions using real cases. All of the children described in this book are real. They were patients with PTSD whom my team or I assessed and/or treated. The names and details have been changed to protect their privacy. They were selected from over 500 children and adolescents I have seen over the years with post-traumatic stress reactions.

Lisa: Hurricane Katrina Survivor

The case of Lisa is a good case to begin with because it illustrates the important point that far too often it takes far too long for children to get diagnosed and get the help they need. This case also illustrates how the symptoms of PTSD can severely impair children in their daily lives.

Lisa, who was thirteen years old when seen in our clinic, had been seven years old when she lived through a terrifying series of events in the Hurricane Katrina disaster of 2005. As the hurricane approached their home near New Orleans, her mother and father had made the same ill-fated decision as thousands of others and chose not to evacuate.

Actually, the mother and father felt the choice was more or less made for them because Lisa's grandfather was extremely frail. They thought an evacuation would cause more harm to him than toughing it out at home through a hurricane. They were wrong.

They lived in one of the low-lying areas of the New Orleans region that would never have been settled by more cautious developers. Their house and the houses of thousands of their neighbors were below sea level and, it turns out, protected by earthen levees constructed by the Army Corps of Engineers that were far too low. The storm surge produced by the hurricane easily flowed over the levees with enormous force and flooded the streets. As the wall of water hit their house and started rapidly filling up the downstairs, the family scrambled into the attic. Their house had no second floor. If they had had a second floor, they might have been able to get Lisa's grandfather to safe ground.

Lisa's dad coaxed the eighty-eight-year-old grandfather onto the attic ladder. The old man's steps were unsteady, his grip was weak, and the ladder was steep and slippery. He slipped and fell into the cold, salty water. Lisa's dad fished him out and shoved him halfway back up the ladder. By now the water was about seven feet deep and still rising. Lisa's dad was treading water and holding on to the ladder. Lisa was watching from the attic through the hatch for the ladder.

Her grandfather would not make it. It must have gone through her grandfather's mind that this wasn't going to be worth it. Perhaps he had survived in his attic during Hurricane Betsy in 1965 and already knew what was in store for them. He said, "I quit it," and dropped into the water. The water was almost at the ceiling. The father tried but couldn't pull the grandfather up this time.

As the father pulled himself into the attic, the water kept rising. The power was out and it was pitch dark in the stifling, humid heat. The water reached the attic and began to spread over the floor of the attic. The father had had the foresight to tell his wife to take an axe with her into the attic (as strange as that may sound, it is fairly common knowledge in New Orleans to take an axe into the attic if the "big one" hits). He chopped an escape hatch through the roof. Once the hatch was big enough, everyone was lifted through it and onto the roof. It was there, on a sliver of the roof that remained dry, that Lisa, her father and mother, and her sister heard the screams of their neighbors. Those who did not have axes in their attics drowned. The frantic screams stopped eventually, replaced by less frequent yells for help. Some of the yells continued; some did not.

Several hours later some neighbors began making rounds through the neighborhood in their boats. They focused first on the yells for help. The men in the boats chopped holes in the roofs—sometimes they were in time, sometimes they weren't. When the screams stopped, the boatmen began plucking the living off the roofs.

As Lisa floated in a boat through the floodwaters with her family and another family, she saw a few bodies bobbing in the water. But the snakes slithering through the water scared her the most. Once she and her family reached the elevated highway, they stepped off and started walking. She didn't know where they were walking, but at least it was dry.

When we evaluated Lisa, she had been living through frequent bouts of terror for the last six years. During heavy downpours, whether Lisa was at home or at school, she became so violently panicked that she went to the bathroom to vomit. She was deathly afraid of water— any water in large quantities. She refused to take baths and took quick, panicked showers. She would prefer to take a shower only once a week, but her parents forced her to shower more often. She would no longer go swimming. But rain was the worst, especially heavy rain with thunder. She checked the weather report every morning. Lisa didn't just check the weather as you or I might casually do each day. She checked it with panic. Her thought wasn't *I wonder if it will rain today*. Her thought was *Please God, please God, please God, don't rain today*. She had frequent nightmares. She could no longer stay in her own bed through the night most of the time. She jumped at the slightest unexpected noise. Whenever she heard a creak in their new house, she asked her parents what had caused it. She became less outgoing and rarely wanted to leave the house to see friends. She became a different child, yet it had taken six years to get help.

A Very Brief History of PTSD in Children

Some of the earliest cases in written history of individuals who were psychologically affected by trauma were from adult soldiers in the American Civil War in the 1860s and adult victims of train accidents in the 1870s. When PTSD was first recognized as an official diagnosis in 1980 in the *Diagnostic and Statistical Manual of Mental Disorders, Third Edition (DSM-III)*,[1] there had been no published studies that systematically tested the diagnostic criteria in any age group of children or adolescents, so it was not known whether the diagnostic criteria fit well with youths or not. When the Fourth Edition of the *DSM* was published in 1994, there still had been no published studies on diagnostic criteria in any age group of children or adolescents.

The lack of any published studies on diagnoses of PTSD in children at that time in history makes the early 1990s a good place to start when talking about what is known about trauma-related problems in children and adolescents. While research had been accelerating with adult populations for ten to fifteen years by then, only a handful of systematic research studies had been conducted with youths.

As of 1993, there had been only four published studies of youths that used systematic assessments of PTSD, and three of them involved natural disasters—a bushfire in Australia,[2] the Buffalo Creek dam collapse,[3] an Armenian earthquake,[4] and concentration camp-like experiences in Cambodia.[5] These early studies helped to establish the notion, extremely novel at the time, that children and adolescents could be affected by trauma just like adults, but these studies did not go so far as to test the actual diagnostic criteria in the youths. There had been no systematic assessments or longitudinal follow-ups of children who had suffered sexual or physical abuse, acute injuries, or man-made disasters, or who had witnessed domestic or community violence. Researchers had no idea whether the diagnostic criteria that had been developed for adults were suitable for children.

And there had been no randomized controlled treatment studies. Because there had been so little research with children and adolescents, many, if not most, clinicians did not yet accept the idea that youths could even develop PTSD.

Children Can Develop PTSD: "Your Data Must Be Wrong."

Lenore Terr, MD, deserves credit as one of the first child psychiatrists to publicly talk about PTSD in children and adolescents. One of her earliest and most memorable contributions came from data she meticulously collected about a group of twenty-six children who had been kidnapped in 1976 while they were on their school bus.[6] The children, five through fourteen years of age, were from a small town in California called Chowchilla. A group of three kidnappers took control of the school bus, forced the children off the bus and into two vans, drove the children around without food or water or restrooms for nearly eleven hours, and then forced them into an underground pit they had constructed. The pit was actually a truck trailer that had been driven into the pit that had been dug in the middle of nowhere in rural California. They covered the top of the truck trailer with dirt. The children were basically buried alive.

Fortunately, after sixteen hours of being buried underground, they were able to escape. They had been able to reach the hatch in the ceiling of the trailer, and they were able to remove the lid over the hatch that had been weighted down with two 100-pound batteries. One of the older boys then dug with his hands through several feet of dirt and created a tunnel to the surface. By the time the children were reunited with their families, it had been a terrifying two days.

The three kidnappers, young men from nearby areas of California, were quickly found, arrested, and sentenced to life in prison. Their intentions were never clearly known. It is suspected that they intended to ask for a $5 million ransom, but it is unclear why they picked the town of Chowchilla.

Physically, the children seemed fine. In 1976 few people thought to ask about their psychological well-being. There was at least one person, however, who *was* interested in their psychological well-being. One hundred fifty miles away in San Francisco, child psychiatrist Lenore Terr had read a newspaper story about the kidnapping, and she was very interested in learning about how children deal with trauma. Dr. Terr called one of the mothers of the children mentioned in the newspaper story and arranged a meeting. Starting five months after the kidnapping, Dr. Terr began making trips to Chowchilla to meet more and more of these families and offer her help to them as she evaluated the children. Over the next five years, she collected unprecedented historical and observational follow-up assessments with all but a few of the children, and these data would constitute the first-ever in-depth, longitudinal examination of the psychological reactions of children who had experienced terror.

In the early 1980s, Terr presented her findings in a lecture at a professional meeting with her peers in which she described the intense and long-lasting psychological symptoms of the survivors, many of them resembling PTSD. The reaction of one of the other speakers and some of her peers in the audience was described by an independent audience member as initially mocking and then openly hostile.[7] The assigned discussant, described as a normally mild-mannered, polite colleague, became enraged. He assaulted Dr. Terr's methods and accused her of overpathologizing. Members of the audience joined in with the hostility.

As this independent audience member puzzled over this unusual reaction from the audience, it struck her that this was not really unusual at all. Both our field of professionals and the public in general had a long history of denying the reality that children can be victims of trauma. Most civilized societies did not begin to recognize the widespread problem of child sexual and physical abuse until the 1970s.

We have made a lot of progress since then toward the acceptance of PTSD in youths, but it is unfortunate that I am still familiar with this type of experience two decades later. Many health professionals who work with children every day are still walking blindly in the dark when dealing with children who have PTSD.

My Beginning: Young Children and the PTSD Diagnosis

The story for me begins with diagnosis, too. When I was young doctor in my mid-thirties and naïve, I wanted to rid the world of child abuse and thought we could create prevention programs that would eventually get us to that goal. As a young researcher, I had to accept the fact that it was not realistic for me to start a grandiose and groundbreaking program to prevent child abuse (although I thought I had some really cool ideas). I needed to start with smaller, incremental steps to build my skills and reputation in research. With input from my mentor at the time, I decided to start small and tackle the diagnostic criteria for PTSD in very young children. While investigations of post-traumatic problems in very young children were not what I had dreamed of doing, it was close enough to be interesting to me. (It would take about ten years and lots of lessons learned the hard way before I would come to grips with the idea that prevention of child abuse is not currently feasible.)

As nearly everything about how children and adolescents are treated hinges on what we believe about diagnoses, tackling the diagnostic criteria was not only a good place for me to start in my career; this type of new information was also much needed by other professionals in my field. The diagnostic criteria for all ages of children, from the very young to teenagers, needed to be investigated (remember, at that time, in 1993, there had never been any tests of the accuracy of diagnostic criteria in children of any age), but given my partiality in the area of prevention, I started to investigate the criteria for very young children. As I dug into the problem of diagnostic criteria for young children, I became rapidly convinced of two things. First, young children most definitely develop PTSD just like adults. Second, the diagnostic criteria that existed at that time were grossly insufficient. I became terribly concerned that the large majority of young children with PTSD were being missed.

The Case of Tommy: "I Want My Boy Back."

Tommy is an example of a very young child with PTSD. Tommy's mom brought him to my research study four months after they had been involved in a motor vehicle accident. Prior to the accident, Tommy had been a fun-loving four-year-old boy with dishwater-blond hair and brown eyes. Tommy's mom had driven her car, with Tommy in the backseat, on Highway 47 just outside New Orleans. They were going up a steep incline on a bridge that spans a commercial waterway that feeds into New Orleans. The car stalled. Traffic was not heavy, which explains why the vehicles behind them were going fast. For an unknown reason, a black pickup truck did not see them stopped on the highway and slammed into the back of the stalled car. Glass crashed. The ripping of aluminum shrieked. The rear of the car crumpled in over the backseat.

The impact whiplashed the mom's neck, slammed her head into the headrest, and briefly knocked her unconscious.

Tommy was trapped in the backseat. The car was leaking gas. Mom, relieved that her immediate fear that they would both die had not happened, staggered out of the car and called to Tommy to try to keep him calm. Cars stopped in all lanes. Several men stopped their cars and got out to help. They eventually wrenched the back door open with their bare hands and managed to squeeze Tommy out, and then they waited for the ambulance.

Tommy and his mother were rushed to the Level I Trauma Center at Charity Hospital. Fortunately, neither of them had serious injuries. I was not part of the trauma team, but as part of my research study I was allowed to carry a special pager that alerted me when pediatric victims were en route to the emergency department. When I arrived at the ER, I found Tommy alone on a gurney in the corner. His mother, strapped into a neck brace, was on a gurney in a hallway about thirty feet away, waiting for an x-ray of her spine. After talking with his mother about our study, I hung out with Tommy until his father arrived.

Several months later, we evaluated Tommy in our clinic. Since the accident, he had developed many symptoms of PTSD. Horrific images of the accident kept intruding into his mind. When he had to go somewhere in a car, he balked about being strapped into his car seat and he insisted on knowing exactly where they were going. If he felt they were going over that bridge again, he would refuse to get in the car. Often he seemed to go into a trance during car trips no matter where they were heading, with his head turned, trying to look behind, staring silently out the back window. As the car sat at every stop sign or red light, he froze in vigilance, as it reminded him of the sensation when the car had stalled just before they were rammed by the pickup truck.

Tommy was different at home, too. He refused to be left alone in any room in the house. One of his parents had to lie with him to get him to sleep. His entire demeanor seemed to change. He was less affectionate and seemed less happy. He wasn't the same child anymore, his mom said, and she wanted help. She told me, "I want my boy back."

Tommy had multiple symptoms of PTSD, but to make a formal diagnosis, remember, the *DSM* also requires evidence of functional impairment. Tommy did indeed have significant functional impairment. Because of his refusal to ride in the car, this markedly disrupted his ability to function routinely in public places. Because of his refusal to sleep alone, this caused a negative change in his relationship with his mother, who, despite being incredibly sympathetic, eventually became frustrated and worn out as her sleep and nighttime routines were disrupted by his demands.

Very Young Children Do Indeed Develop PTSD

The excellent work of Dr. Lenore Terr in the 1980s helped to show that children and teens could indeed develop severe and long-lasting post-traumatic stress symptoms. Yet, after experts conceded that children and young teens could develop PTSD, it was still doubted that *very* young children could develop PTSD. Experts seemed to believe their intuition, quite wrongly, that very young children could not remember and/or understand the nature of things that happened to them. This intuition was likely grounded in other life experiences of a related nature. For example, as adults, most people cannot remember any specific personal memories of events that occurred when they were younger than five years. Like a dog that looks in a mirror and cannot comprehend that what he sees is actually his reflection, many people believed young children could not comprehend the concept of danger. If it is believed that young children can neither remember events that occurred to them nor comprehend the concept of danger, then this reinforces the intuition of experts that young children cannot possibly develop PTSD. Intuition, though, turns out to be an imperfect guide, and we now know that children as young as three years of age can develop PTSD.

At Tulane University in New Orleans, we conducted the first long-term study of PTSD symptoms in very young children. In 1999, we started with sixty-two children—one through six years of age—who had experienced a wide range of different types of traumatic experiences.[8] At the beginning of the study, 26 percent of the group met the full criteria for PTSD and had an average of 6.1 PTSD symptoms. After one year of follow-up, 23 percent still met the full criteria for PTSD, and after two years of follow-up, the rate was still 23 percent, with no significant decrease in the number of PTSD symptoms.

You Do Not Recover from PTSD on Your Own

"Time heals all wounds" is a common saying, but time does not heal most post-traumatic stress reactions. Bruises on skin go away after several days. Broken bones heal in about one month. Unpleasant memories, such as embarrassing moments of public speaking, fade with time. Because this is our normal experience with unpleasant events, our intuition is that PTSD symptoms from traumatic events will also fade away on their own. The hard evidence, though, is quite clear that we must accept that time alone does not heal this particular wound.

Psychologist Richard Meiser-Stedman and colleagues in London conducted the second long-term study of PTSD symptoms in very young children. One month after motor vehicle accidents, 6.5 percent met the criteria for the PTSD diagnosis. When they were reassessed six months later, the proportion diagnosed with PTSD had actually increased, almost doubling to 10 percent.[9]

The research on the long-term course of PTSD indicates that about 50 percent of adults with PTSD show some natural recovery and about 50 percent have a chronic course. There are even recorded cases that have not improved much over thirty or forty years. But even the 50 percent of adults who show some natural recovery do not show total recovery. Complete recovery to the level of zero PTSD symptoms is fairly rare. It is more appropriate to think of PTSD as being in the same class as other chronic diseases like diabetes, cerebral palsy, and back pain.

Several notable studies that followed children and adolescents for a long time found that their symptoms are even more persistent compared to symptoms in adults. In the largest study ever conducted on trauma-exposed children, Alexander "Sandy" McFarlane studied 808 Australian schoolchildren (mean 8.2 years old) following a bushfire. When he reexamined their PTSD symptoms more than two years after the fire, there was no significant decrease in their symptoms.[10]

Even when researchers find significant decreases in PTSD symptoms over time, they still find massive amounts of severe and chronic problems. For example, researchers followed thirty six- through eleven-year-old children after Hurricane Andrew.[11] Twenty-one months after the hurricane, the children's symptoms had decreased at the level of statistical significance, which sounded promising. Yet 70 percent of them were still in the moderate to severe category of post-traumatic stress symptoms. Not a hopeful picture for symptoms going away on their own.

These data appear, however, to be difficult for people to accept. PTSD is a disorder that was not there one day, then a life event happened that caused PTSD, and then PTSD was there the next day. What other experiences in everyday life are like that? Bruises, cuts on your skin, and unpleasant memories of embarrassing situations are some of the most common. Bruises, cuts, and unpleasant memories go away on their own after several days or weeks. Because the everyday experiences of life are that bruises, cuts, and unpleasant memories go away on their own, I think nearly everyone believes, or at least hopes, that PTSD goes away on its own as well.

The Long Shadow

PTSD is unique because it is the only major psychiatric disorder that by definition must follow after a life event. Depression, anxiety, schizophrenia, and antisocial behaviors—none of these disorders carry the requirement that the symptoms follow after a life event.

The connection to life events shrouds discussions about PTSD in the long shadow of the eternal debate about whether we become who we are due to nature or nurture. The belief that nature determines who we are means that our genes determine our personalities and abilities; we are basically wired at birth to become who we will eventually become. The belief that nurture determines who we are, on the other hand, means that our life experiences can determine our personalities and abilities. The life experiences can come from parents, teachers, chronic living environments, chance events, and, of course, life-threatening traumatic events. Philosophers, scientists, and nearly every parent of a child throughout time have wondered whether the successes or failures of individuals were due to nature or nurture.

The requirement for a life event to cause PTSD uniquely opens the door for one's personal beliefs, biases, and intuition about the nature-versus-nurture debate to influence how one thinks about many issues related to PTSD. These biases are nasty fellows, and they have a strong hold on many so-called experts. We will have some figurative fistfights with these experts and their biases on the following pages. But once one accepts that there is a problem and we can put a name on it, such as PTSD, then we have the start of a path past the biases and toward healing. When Tommy's mom said, "I want my boy back," she had made a good start.

Recap

- PTSD is well documented to occur in children as young as three years of age.
- PTSD does not go away on its own.
- Parents often wait far too long to seek help. I have seen cases where children suffered for up to seven years before finally getting help.
- PTSD is chronic.

For Parents to Do

- The first step is to familiarize yourself with the symptoms of PTSD so you know what to look for.
- A handout of tips for parents and other adults on how to talk with and help children following trauma is in the Appendix.
- After your child has experienced a traumatic event, you ought to be on the alert for any new problems that appear. Two cases were described in this chapter—Lisa and Tommy—to illustrate what to look for. More cases will be presented in the following chapters.

Chapter Two
Life Threat Is Trauma

PTSD became official in 1980. That was the year the diagnostic criteria were first published in the manual that professionals use in practice to make diagnoses, officially called the *Diagnostic and Statistical Manual of Mental Disorders.*[1] That being the Third Edition, the manual was called *DSM-III* (pronounced "DSM three"). Since then, the bedrock definition of traumatic events has coalesced into a clear expectation that the experiences associated with PTSD be *life-threatening.* For rather obvious reasons, life-threatening experiences are those that are most likely to lead to the development of PTSD. Among these types of life-threatening experiences, some of the most obvious are war, sexual abuse, rape, and motor vehicle accidents.

Trauma Is Sudden, Unexpected Moments of Life-Threatening Panic

The two major classification systems of psychiatric disorders in the world have actually been quite clear and consistent on the matter of how to define traumatic events. The *DSM* is the system used in the United States. The *DSM-III-R* in 1987, the *DSM-IV* in 1994, and the *DSM-5* in 2013 are all explicit that the definition of traumatic events are those that are life-threatening or a serious threat to one's physical safety or that cause fear for the lives or safety of loved ones. A list of the most common types of traumatic events is in Table 2.1.

The system used in many other countries is the *International Statistical Classification of Diseases and Related Health Problems* (ICD). The latest edition of the *ICD* in common use, the Tenth Edition, defines trauma in a manner that is consistent with the *DSM-5* as "a stressful event or situation (either short or long lasting) of exceptionally threatening or catastrophic nature" (*ICD*-10).[2]

Table 2.1. Traumas Are Life-Threatening Events

Natural disasters (hurricane, typhoon, flood, tornado)
Man-made disasters (fire, war, bombing)
Sexual abuse
Physical abuse
Witnessing domestic violence
Animal attacks
Motor vehicle accidents and other severe injuries
Invasive medical procedures
Near drowning

It is a consensus, thus, that the essential elements of events that are most likely to cause PTSD are moments of terror that come upon individuals suddenly and unexpectedly. The following three cases are examples of such events.

Joe: Combat Trauma

Joe was sent to fight in Vietnam in 1969 when he was nineteen years old. He had been in Vietnam several months but had not yet seen much heavy combat with his platoon. However, Joe felt the tension in the air because he heard the stories of combat from the veterans and was drilled by his commanders to be prepared for close-quarters gunfights in the jungles. One morning, his platoon was sent out to secure an area in which there had been reports of enemy activity. Without warning, the enemy opened fire with machine guns into Joe's platoon before they could take cover. The fire seemed to come from several directions. The jungle around them exploded in fire and the entire platoon got hit at once. As Joe fell to the ground after taking a bullet in the leg, he was nearly certain he was going to die. When he lifted his head to look around, ears ringing and heart thumping, he was staring at a grotesque body lying on the ground with no head. As he scrambled back to safety, he saw severed arms, legs, and other unidentifiable body parts lying around. Joe had experienced sudden and unexpected fear for his life and had felt an overwhelming moment of panic.

Yvonne: Sexual Trauma

Yvonne's parents were divorced and she occasionally spent weekends at her father's house. During some of these visits, Yvonne was raped by her father when she was eleven years old. He raped her at least twice. The sexual acts themselves were not the most terrifying. Yvonne described them to her therapist as more confusing than anything. It was after the sex that her father whispered in her ear that if she told anyone he would kill her mother, then kill her sister, and then kill her. That was the moment when Yvonne felt the clearest moment of panic that she and her family could be killed and that her father, the man she thought had loved her, could actually be her murderer.

Carl: Motor Vehicle Trauma

Carl was fifteen years old when he was in the front passenger seat of his older brother's car. His brother was driving them home from movie night at their local high school. The country roads were empty and the night seemed quiet and peaceful. As they rounded a sharp curve, his brother slid the car over into the lane for oncoming traffic in order to take the curve faster. Seemingly out of nowhere, the headlights of a car appeared, coming straight at them. The other car was also coming fast and had veered outside of its lane. There was just enough time to swerve so that the rear of the car took the brunt of the impact. The sound of metal screeching against metal and glass shattering triggered instantly in Carl the thought that this must be what it sounds like to die in a car crash. His head was whipped to the left and rammed into his brother, and then they were whipped back in the other direction. His body slammed against the door and his head crashed against the window. He momentarily blacked out. When he woke up, his heart was pounding in his chest, his hands were trembling, and his survival instinct kicked in, warning him to get out of the car before they got hit by another car.

Joe, Yvonne, and Carl: three radically different types of traumatic events. The common element among all three was the *sudden* and *unexpected* moments of sheer *terror*.

> *"I have, indeed, no abhorrence of danger, except*
> *in its absolute effect—in terror."*
>
> Edgar Allan Poe

Trauma Is Different from Stress. There Really Are Not Many Exceptions.

The distinction between traumatic, life-threatening traumatic events and nontraumatic, non-life-threatening stressful events lies in the sensations of sudden and unexpected terror. The distinction is unambiguous and the relations of each to PTSD are clear. I frequently encounter my fellow professionals in the field who believe there are exceptions to this rule. When I give lectures or trainings, audience members almost invariably state that they believe neglect, living with a mother who abuses drugs, and being separated from one's parents and placed in foster care easily qualify as traumatic events, and they have examples from their work to prove it. When we walk through their examples, however, it becomes clear that they have failed to separate discrete traumatic events from the larger stressful events.

Let us walk through a discussion I had with a colleague, which is typical of these encounters. This colleague discussed the case of a nine-year-old boy who was removed from the custody of his parents because both parents were being arrested on drug charges and was then immediately placed in a foster home. Typically, an arrest is not life-threatening. The boy was distressed to watch his parents being handcuffed and led away by police officers, but there was no violence reported. Also typically, arrival at a new foster home is not life-threatening, either.

So far, nothing has occurred in this story that was life-threatening, so I was comfortable saying to my colleagues that it was extremely unlikely the boy would develop PTSD from this experience. Many of my colleagues disagree because they say they have seen cases exactly like this and the children had PTSD. For the sake of argument, I say, let us agree that you conducted a good assessment for PTSD symptoms and the boy actually does have PTSD. Let us look at the event more closely.

I ask what happened when the police showed up at the house. Did they break down the door at midnight and everyone in the house mistakenly believed they were being robbed? Did the father physically fight with the police? Was anybody hurt and bleeding? Let us say my colleague replies that indeed the boy's father refused to cooperate with the police and a struggle ensued. The police tackled the father to the ground. The father's nose was smashed against the ground and blood ran down his face. A policeman screamed repeatedly, "Stop fighting or I WILL tase you!" The mother screamed at the police, "Get off him! You're going to kill him!" The boy now believed his father's life was in danger. The initial description of the so-called separation event was not traumatic. But upon closer examination, the father's fight with the police was life-threatening. The boy did not have PTSD from parental separation. He had PTSD because of his father's fight with the police.

Even after walking through the example, audience members were still confused and persisted in believing the separation from the parents was indeed traumatic.

"See?" one person said. "The separation was traumatic just like he told you."

"No," I would reply, "the event was not traumatic until the father fought with the police. The father's fight with the police was a separate incident. That was a fight, not a separation from parents."

The person replied, "But I still think the separation was traumatic."

Maybe I am deficient in the skills of persuasion. Maybe some people believe what they want to believe.

A Very Short History Lesson: 1867–1980

A brief history of how trauma has been defined is helpful for understanding the current-day definitions about traumatic events and why it matters to you. Perhaps the first description of psychological problems that developed after traumatic experiences was a book published in 1867 about passengers on trains who had been involved in collisions.[3] Their syndrome was called **railway spine**. As a group, they had no obvious physical injuries but exhibited a strange variety of nervous reactions. These passengers became known mainly because they were pursuing legal cases against the railroad companies and wanted compensation for their injuries.

This also foreshadowed one of the main controversies about PTSD that would arise in the 1980s when attorneys started to use PTSD as the foundation for many lawsuits. The quest for monetary compensation and fighting these battles in courtrooms would become a recurring theme in the history of trauma reactions.

Curiously, the definitive publication on railway spine was a book written by a surgeon, not a psychiatrist. Sir John Eric Erichsen was a British surgeon who, in addition to being a worldwide-recognized expert on surgery, rose to become the surgeon-extraordinary to Queen Victoria. Perhaps it was logical that a surgeon wrote this treatise; surgeons were the ones seeing these "sort-of" injured patients, and psychiatry didn't really exist as much of a specialty in the 1800s. At the time, railway spine was considered to be a neurological condition. In fact, doctors seemed to be completely missing the point that people could have psychological reactions to these types of life-threatening events. It would not be until quite a bit later in the twentieth century that it was recognized as a psychiatric condition.

Soon after railway spine was described, another surgeon, Jacob Mendes Da Costa, published a paper in 1871 on the strange afflictions of soldiers in the American Civil War.[4] He described soldiers who showed signs similar to heart disease—chest pains, palpitations, and fatigue—but physical examination showed no signs of abnormalities. Da Costa called it **irritable heart**. But the condition became known as "soldier's heart" because he based his description of the symptoms on his observations of over 300 soldiers. It was also known as Da Costa's syndrome. Da Costa speculated at length about the possible causes, of which he focused on fevers, "hard field service," wounds, rheumatism, scurvy, sunstroke, and tobacco. He focused on physical causes, and at no point did he show any strong indication that emotional fear was a cause.

Scholars have suggested that railway spine and soldier's heart were the forerunners of PTSD, but, truth be told, they little resembled any of the definitions of modern PTSD. Neither railway spine nor soldier's heart described clearly the psychological symptoms that would later be recognized in PTSD. It seems possible that these early conditions were indeed quite similar to PTSD, but doctors did not know what questions to ask or what to listen for to detect the symptoms.

Eventually, as psychiatry as a profession grew, psychiatrists helped to connect the dots that trauma causes psychological problems for people. Sigmund Freud, an Austrian neurologist but basically a practicing psychiatrist, catapulted trauma into a prominent place in one of his earliest theories. In 1896, Freud published his theory that unconscious memories of sexual molestation in early childhood were the root of the problems of some of his adult female patients.[5]

When the *Diagnostic and Statistical Manual,* First Edition, or *DSM-I,* was published in 1952, it contained a post-traumatic syndrome called **gross stress reaction**.[6] The stress events that could be involved were identified simply as either "combat or civilian catastrophe," with no other details provided. This was modified in *DSM-II,* published in 1968, to a disorder called **adjustment reaction of adult life**, with a more liberal definition of what could count as possible stressors.[7] For example, a mother dealing with an unwanted pregnancy was listed as one of the examples for this new disorder. Once again, neither the 1952 nor the 1968 syndrome much resembled the later definition of PTSD. As with most of the psychiatric diagnoses of that era, the definitions of the disorders were vague and could mean vastly different things from one doctor to the next.

1980: The *DSM-III* Changed Everything

The definition of trauma changed dramatically in 1980 when the *Diagnostic and Statistical Manual,* Third Edition, was published.[8] This edition, known as *DSM-III,* was a landmark shift in the field of psychiatry for all disorders. The *DSM-III* changed almost everything about the diagnosis of psychiatric disorders. The definitions of disorders in *DSM-III* were simply clearer than they had ever been. A menu of distinctly defined symptoms described each disorder. When a symptom is described in simple and precise language, it is said to be **operationalized**. For example, in the earlier version, *DSM-II*, depressive disorder was described in a single sentence as "an excessive reaction of depression." This was not a well-operationalized syndrome. In contrast, in the *DSM-III*, depression was described as at least four out of eight possible symptoms, such as "loss of interest or pleasure in usual activities" or "loss of energy." This was well operationalized. It was clear and precise. Clinicians could now talk to each other and to patients with some reliability.

The importance of the new philosophy in the *DSM-III* and the way PTSD was defined cannot be overemphasized. The way post-traumatic reactions had been defined and diagnosed prior to the *DSM-III* was insufficient for a number of reasons. Clinicians could not agree from one to the next on how to diagnose patients. The absence of reliable agreement between professionals meant that understanding the disorder could not advance much. And without a reliable way to communicate about the disorder, new and better treatments could not be easily developed. With the creation of PTSD in the *DSM-III*, the problem of reliable communication between professionals was largely solved. Once a doctor in New York could reliably diagnose the same syndrome as a doctor in Los Angeles, then apples could be compared to apples with reliability—a very basic tenet of medicine that, prior to *DSM-III*, simply did not exist in psychiatry. Understanding of PTSD grew in spectacular fashion. New methods were developed to diagnose it. The neurobiology of the disorder was studied. Many new treatment methods were tested.

Because of this newfound reliability in diagnosis, the impact on research was tremendous, and the volume of research exploded in psychiatry after *DSM-III*. The reason for this was simple. Now that a researcher knew what PTSD was, because it was well operationalized by the symptoms, he or she could study it. Once you can literally or figuratively put your fingers on a thing, you can do things to it. You can count the number of cases of PTSD. You can count the risk factors that may lead to PTSD. You can use different treatments on PTSD and determine which ones work and which ones don't work. And researchers did this in droves. Notwithstanding the controversies about PTSD that I'll discuss later, PTSD is one of the most well-validated disorders in all of psychiatry.

The event that probably had more impact than anything for the recognition of PTSD was the Vietnam War. In the 1960s and 1970s, thousands of soldiers had been coming home from the war with serious psychological problems. The operationalization of PTSD in 1980 was extremely helpful for victims, who could now more easily get monetary compensation for psychiatric disability. Indeed, my first personal experience with PTSD was performing disability compensation exams on Vietnam War veterans in the late 1980s. During my psychiatry residency training in Indianapolis, Indiana, I took an extra job on the weekends to perform exams at the local Veterans Administration hospital. On Saturday mornings, a couple of other trainees from my residency program and I would each interview three to four veterans to determine whether they would receive disability checks from the federal government because of their military service. I would have to ask each veteran what happened to him, his rank, the name of his unit, the city or region where the incidents happened, and the names of his commanding officer and some other members of his unit. This information could be used by a senior officer to corroborate his story, in case the veteran was trying to deceive the government in order to get a disability check. Whether or not thousands of soldiers could qualify for disability based on PTSD had consequences for huge amounts of money.

Trauma Is a Sudden, Life-Threatening Event

Despite the groundbreaking shifts created by the *DSM-III* in 1980, the definition of traumatic events back then was not exactly as it is today. The *DSM-III* definition of trauma was vague, defined as a recognizable stressor that would evoke significant symptoms of distress in almost everyone. By this time it was apparent that many different types of scary experiences were recognizable stressors that were likely to cause PTSD, such as domestic violence, rape, sexual abuse, physical abuse, motor vehicle collisions, and natural disasters. Many people thought this definition of recognizable stressors was too broad and allowed people who did not really experience trauma to claim that they had PTSD. What one person might recognize as a recognizable stressor could be quite different from what another person might recognize.

Therefore, in 1987, when the *DSM-III* was revised to become the *DSM-III-R*, the definition of a traumatic event was narrowed so that the traumatic events had to be *life-threatening*. The framers of the *DSM-III-R* still left the door open for non-life-threatening events to cause PTSD with an additional statement that an event at least had to pose a psychological threat to well-being. Nevertheless, the definition of trauma in 1987 had become narrower and clearer. With only minor tweaks, the requirement that traumatic events be life-threatening or pose a serious threat to one's physical well-being was maintained in the *DSM-IV* in 1994 and the *DSM-5* in 2013.

Encounters with Very Young Children

Some of the first cases described in print of very young children with true post-traumatic stress reactions involved attacks by dogs[9] and a leopard.[10] Large animal attacks are life-threatening to young children for the obvious reasons that young children are smaller, weaker, and more vulnerable to these attacks. As these attacks likely would not have been perceived as life-threatening by teenagers or adults, this nicely makes the point that the perception of "life-threatening" is in the eye of the beholder. Even when individuals are of the same age, what can be perceived as life-threatening can differ from one person to the next.

In 1995, I published the first study of PTSD in a group of very young children. Since then, PTSD has been documented in young children who have been exposed to abuse,[11,12] have witnessed domestic violence,[13] or have been involved in motor vehicle accidents,[14,15,16] natural disasters,[17] or conditions of war.[18,19] Children are also likely to perceive disasters as more life-threatening because they have fewer ways to remove themselves from harm's way and are less strong to fight against debris or swim through water. My research team and I relearned this in a surprising new way after the Hurricane Katrina disaster.

In 2003, I began a study on a research grant from the National Institute of Mental Health (NIMH) to assess the largest-ever sample of very young children (three through six years of age) who had been exposed to traumatic events. I work at Tulane University School of Medicine in New Orleans. When Hurricane Katrina struck in August of 2005, we were in the middle of that study. For the remainder of the study, we were then able to collect the largest sample of very young children who had been exposed to a disaster.

Within this sample of disaster-exposed children, we divided the children into two groups based on the type of traumatic events they had suffered. One group had stayed in the city during the hurricane and experienced the wind and the subsequent flooding and horrors of trying to survive and flee the city. The second group had evacuated the city safely before the storm and then returned after authorities allowed citizens back into their homes.

The children who had evacuated before the storm had not been in harm's way. The evacuated children had not experienced a life-threatening event, so they should not have developed PTSD. Yet we found that 44 percent of this evacuated group that had, we thought, never been in harm's way met the full diagnosis of PTSD.[20] This was, needless to say, an unexpected finding. However, when we interviewed the parents about the start of the PTSD symptoms for these children, we found the answer rather clearly. Nearly all of the parents stated that the symptoms started when the families returned to see their devastated homes. As the young children got out of their cars and stood on their old sidewalks, or what was left of their sidewalks, and saw their homes, or what was left of their homes, for the first time, those were clearly the times when the children's symptoms of PTSD started. The homes were barely recognizable. The yards were cluttered with debris. Cars were in trees or on rooftops. Walls were caked with smelly, black mold. Hardly any possessions were salvageable. And every home for blocks and blocks around was similarly ravaged. These were scenes of end-of-civilization destruction one would only see in movies.

Still, why should this cause PTSD? The development of PTSD requires a moment of panic when individuals fear for their lives. What went through the minds of those young children, and what caused their moments of panic as they stood on the sidewalks and saw their homes for the first time? Something caused panic in their minds when they stood on those sidewalks, and it was different from adults because we did not see the same development of PTSD for the parents when they visited their homes. This is exactly what we mean when we say that trauma is in the eye of the beholder. It is probable that when the young children could see the devastation firsthand, the danger finally became real to them, and they realized for the first time just how close to harm they had come. If their parents had not gotten them out of there before the storm, they now fully realized they could have been killed.

Recap

- PTSD is one of the few psychiatric disorders that requires the patients to have experienced an event. There is both agreement and considerable disagreement among experts on how to define the types of events that can cause PTSD.
- The agreement has been that traumatic events are events that are life-threatening or a severe threat to one's physical safety; also, they tend to be sudden and unexpected. The overall effect is of producing a moment of sheer panic that one is going to die.
- Stressful events are distinct from trauma events in that stressful events are not life-threatening and they do not typically cause PTSD.

For Parents to Do

- During evaluations by clinicians, monitor to see whether the clinicians asked about all of the main types of traumatic events. The questions can be either verbal or written. The clinicians should not ask a single generic question such as "Has your child been in a traumatic event?" How do you know what he or she means by a traumatic event? How does he or she know what you mean by a traumatic event? If that generic question is the only question your clinician asks about traumatic events, fire that clinician.

- You should expect, because of the poor quality of training that most clinicians receive, that most clinicians will not be this thorough. You, as the consumer, may have to shop around until you find acceptable clinicians.

- Traumatic events are those listed in Table 2.1. Free interviews and questionnaires about traumatic events can also be found easily on the internet. My questionnaire, the Child PTSD Checklist, is available for free at my Scheeringa Lab website: http://medicine.tulane.edu/departments/psychiatry/research/dr-scheeringas-lab.

- If your children are at least seven years of age or older, the clinicians should also ask your children about these events.

Chapter Three
Not All Stress Is Trauma

Often when I give lectures, I have been known to note the curious case of a sixteen-year-old female who, having just broken up with her boyfriend, believed this was the most traumatic event in her life and, furthermore, was the only traumatic event in her life. It was curious because she had experienced other events that most individuals would have considered quite traumatic. She was being assessed for possible participation in one of my recent treatment studies of seven- to eighteen-year-old children with PTSD. Prior to the assessment, her mother had told us over the phone that her traumatic events had been the accidental death of her brother and the recent suicide attempt of her sister, who had cut her wrists rather deeply.

We were utterly surprised, then, when, during the assessment, the teenager did not consider her brother's death or her sister's suicide attempt to be traumatic. She did, however, consider her own recent breakup with her boyfriend to be traumatic. She endorsed six symptoms of PTSD related to the breakup, and she was clearly enormously distressed by these symptoms. She met enough criteria for the diagnosis of PTSD, but because the breakup event did not meet the definition of a life-threatening traumatic event, I would not enroll her in our study, and I did not believe she had PTSD.

There are deep divides among experts on this issue. If you were to ask ten psychiatrists (or psychologists or social workers) today to define a traumatic event, you would likely get ten fairly different answers. Many of the events that many psychiatrists believe are traumatic are stressful, but not in the slightest degree considered to be life-threatening. That makes for some interesting barstool discussions; however, it poses some serious consequences for consumers. So you need to ask, How is stress different from trauma? And why does it matter?

Stress is not the same as trauma. Everyone feels stress nearly every day. Trauma is different from stress primarily in that trauma is life-threatening. By the nature of life-threatening events, traumatic events are also often sudden and unexpected. This combination of life-threatening, sudden, and unexpected is what creates moments of intense panic in which people fear for their lives. Stress, on the other hand, is not life-threatening and is usually predictable.

Let us start with an example that was published in a scientific journal. A British psychologist published a paper in which he concluded that divorce could cause PTSD in youths. This psychologist and his team conducted a survey of 427 youths who were eleven to sixteen years old and recruited from six schools in England. Of those who reported that their parents had separated or divorced, an amazingly high percentage reported a high enough severity of PTSD from that specific event to have probable PTSD diagnoses.[1] A whopping 29 percent of males and 39 percent of females appeared to have PTSD because they had suffered through the divorces of their parents.

Even more astounding was that these rates of probable PTSD were higher than the rates of PTSD for those individuals who had experienced a direct life threat to themselves, witnessed an attack on someone else, or lived through a disaster. In an astonishing act of detachment, the researchers wrote absolutely nothing in the paper to try to explain this extraordinary finding, stating simply that the PTSD scores related to parental divorce were among the highest for any type of event. The only caveat they presented was that "we would note the study has limitations."[2] What are we to make of this?

"Too much of a good thing" is a saying that fits this situation nicely. When PTSD was made an official diagnosis in 1980, it immediately bestowed the definition of trauma with a new formality and official status. The definition of what counts as a traumatic event instantly acquired new importance because an authorized diagnosis was tied to it. Since PTSD appeared in the *DSM-III* in 1980, the diagnosis has become extremely popular, has been validated in hundreds of studies, and has become part of our everyday lexicon. As PTSD became more and more popular, advocates of special causes that are not life-threatening realized they could get more attention by linking it to PTSD. For someone wishing to draw attention to his or her cause (or to his or her career), linking the cause to PTSD has obvious advantages. Because of this arbitrary overuse, the meaning of trauma has become diluted. What I make of it is an enormous problem that leads to unnecessary confusion among clinicians and bad advice for parents.

"Hey, Pay Attention! I Think This Causes PTSD!"

Published studies by researchers that have appeared to link other events similar to divorce that were stressful but not life-threatening have become a common method of basically shouting, "Hey, pay attention! I found something else that causes PTSD!" I am not always sure whether they are trying to get attention for themselves and just desperate to get a paper published or they are trying to get attention for a pet cause. An important question, nevertheless, is how to think about the whole range of adverse life events, from those that were simply stressful to those that were clearly traumatic and life-threatening.

Gulf Oil Spill

Nearly everyone is familiar with the Hurricane Katrina disaster that affected New Orleans and the surrounding region in 2005. Over 1,000 people were killed and tens of thousands of people were directly in harm's way; however, a very different kind of disaster affected New Orleans and the surrounding region in 2010. In April of that year, there was an explosion on the Deepwater Horizon oil rig in the Gulf of Mexico and the rig sank. The explosion killed eleven crewmen on the rig. There were another 115 crewmen who made it to safety. Before the underwater oil well could be capped, oil gushed into the ocean for eighty-seven days. It is estimated that 210 million gallons of oil spewed into the ocean, and it is considered the largest-ever oil spill.

The amount of oil was so massive that it shut down commercial activity in a huge swath of the Gulf of Mexico, which affected the employment of thousands of workers and thereby indirectly affected their families. Shrimp fishermen were banned from shrimping. The supporting industries of processing plants, packagers, and transporters were also severely affected. Drilling on thirty-three nearby rigs was ordered shut down in a six-month moratorium. The recreational fishing lodges lost nearly all of their business. The supporting infrastructure jobs for all of these businesses were affected in a domino effect. In total, tens of thousands, if not hundreds of thousands, of persons were economically and psychologically impacted. Unlike the Hurricane Katrina disaster, these individuals were never in harm's way and never experienced a life-threatening event. The sudden loss of income caused by the aftereffects of the Deepwater Horizon oil spill instead caused substantial distress as families wondered how they were going to feed their children and how they were going to keep paying loans. These fears were coupled with the anxiety of not knowing if or when they would ever be able to resume business.

A couple of weeks after the explosion, a conference call was held with relevant scientists of Tulane University and Tulane's lobbyists for Congress to pull together a plan of what areas would need help and how much money to ask for from the federal government. I was in one of the conference call rooms with the chairman of my department, a medical internist, and an assistant dean of the medical school. When the conversation turned to the psychological impact of the disaster on workers in the Gulf and their families, the internist asserted that we would see high rates of PTSD in these folks. I disagreed and replied that it was unlikely we would see PTSD in the folks who lived around the Gulf. Unless one was on the oil rig that exploded, it was highly unlikely that one would develop PTSD, and all of those shrimpers and all of those whose businesses were impacted were never in danger for their lives. Those businessmen and their families were more likely to develop anxiety or depression. By the absolute silence that followed, I sensed some disagreement.

Once the call ended, we stayed around the table a little while to chat. The internist then made it clear that he did not agree with me, and he brought up the studies on the people who were affected by the

1989 Exxon Valdez oil spill in Alaska. Until the Deepwater Horizon oil spill, the Exxon Valdez oil spill in Alaska had been the largest oil spill on record, with a spill of approximately thirty million gallons of oil into the sea. He noted that studies had shown high rates of PTSD after the Exxon Valdez disaster in those whose businesses and lives had been impacted by the spill.

There was indeed one study of 599 adult residents who lived around the Exxon Valdez oil spill, and the authors of the study wanted us to believe that it showed they had PTSD. The study, however, was dead wrong. A team of investigators had surveyed 599 inhabitants of thirteen Alaska communities around the Exxon Valdez oil spill of 1989.[3] Their ways of life, but not their actual lives, had been threatened by the loss of the fishery grounds, just like in the Gulf oil spill.

According to the researchers, 10 percent of those with exposure to the oil spill area had enough PTSD symptoms for the diagnosis. To cite just one of multiple flaws in their methodology, when respondents read the question, "Do you feel distressed by reminders of the event?" many of them responded yes to that item, so the researchers counted it as a PTSD symptom. Just because the respondents said yes to that item, however, does not mean it was a symptom of PTSD. We all have memories of distressing or embarrassing life events, but those memories are not the same as PTSD memories. I can still remember the discomfort of having to recite a Shakespeare sonnet in front of my high school English class more than thirty-five years ago, but I do not have and never did have PTSD from that experience.

Do Separations, Neglect, Divorce, and (Insert Your Own Life Problem Here) Cause PTSD?

For advocates of special populations of children and people affected by sociopolitical and environmental disasters, this muddling of the definition of trauma has opened the door for all sorts of speculation about non-life-threatening events that might cause PTSD. Does sudden separation from a parent count as "separation trauma"?[4] Can children of divorce have "divorce trauma"?[5] What about people who lose their pets? Does spanking count as a trauma? Does neglect while your parent is out on a drug binge count? What about just living in a bad neighborhood? Or a child living in a city that has had missiles shot at it, even though the child never saw a bomb explode? What about the death of a beloved grandparent who dies in old age from natural causes? Other unusual stressors are listed in Table 3.1. All of these things have been considered at one time as potential causes of PTSD.

Table 3.1. Unusual, Non-Life-Threatening Stressors That Are Not Traumas and Typically Do Not Cause PTSD

Separation/divorce
New parent moved into home
Child moved to a new home
Loss of home
Parental neglect (failure to provide adequate food, shelter, and emotional support)
Placed in foster care
Parent arrested and held in jail
Change of school
Loss of close friend through distance
Death of pet
Parent hospitalized
Bullying
Medical illness
Medical procedures and hospitalizations
Non-life-threatening injury
Suicide of teacher/neighbor/peer
Witnessed community violence
Vicarious exposure to violence or death (TV, news, gossip)
Witnessing a friend or family member getting hurt or mistreated (less serious than life-threatening domestic violence)

A group of researchers at Harvard University conducted a study with adult patients specifically to ask the question, "If you have experienced stress but not a life-threatening trauma, can you still develop PTSD?"[6] They measured PTSD symptoms of adult patients who were enrolling in treatment studies for depression. Patients were placed in three groups depending on the nature of their past life experiences. One group was the trauma group for those who experienced a true life-threatening traumatic experience. A second group was the nontrauma group for those who experienced no traumatic events. A third group was the equivocal group for those whom raters could not agree about. If one rater thought he or she experienced a traumatic event but the other rater did not, this would place him or her in the equivocal group.

The individuals in all three of these groups were asked about PTSD symptoms. The patients in the nontrauma group and the equivocal group were allowed to answer questions about PTSD symptoms in relation to a "proxy for trauma" by being asked about any "thoughts, worries, or fears that had troubled them." The researchers provided examples in the paper of some of the events that were used as proxies for the nontrauma group—a man who worried about his looks, a mother who worried about the safety of her children, and a woman who worried about losing her siblings. An example of a proxy event for the equivocal group was a man diagnosed with a heart-rhythm abnormality. Surprisingly, included in the equivocal group was a woman who had been approached sexually by a group of men in a locked room but then escaped and a boy who had been forced to fondle an adult man's penis when he was seven years old; most trauma experts would have considered those unequivocal traumas. All three groups had nearly 80 percent rates of PTSD.

This study's strength was its use of structured interviews with trained interviewers, as opposed to self-administered questionnaires. But the study had several serious flaws. First, the interviewers/researchers apparently did not ask when each of the symptoms started in relation to the nontrauma life events. For example, if a patient had difficulty concentrating, loss of interest in usual activities, and hypervigilance—all potential symptoms of PTSD—the researchers did not ask whether those were present prior to their life events or started after their life events. Second, the researchers did not ask about the quality of the distress patients felt from the triggered reminders of their life events. When patients with PTSD are confronted with reminders that trigger memories of their life-threatening traumatic events, they feel fear. When patients who have anxiety disorders but not PTSD are confronted with reminders of their past life events, they feel nervous, which is quite different from fear. Third, no attempt was made to grade comparatively the severity of distress within each of those groups. If they had measured severity, they might have found that the true traumas were associated with different and more severe outcomes than were the equivocal and nontrauma events.

There are other similar examples. PTSD symptoms have been reported in relation to financial problems.[7] PTSD symptoms were reported in a group of 661 Dutch farmers who had to put down their cattle due to foot-and-mouth disease; about half of them reported severe PTSD symptoms.[8] Returning to the Gulf oil spill, a group of researchers from the University of Southern Mississippi surveyed 588 inhabitants who lived around the Gulf of Mexico during the Deepwater Horizon spill of 2010.[9] About 28 percent supposedly scored above a cutoff for PTSD because their ability to make a living was disrupted. In all of these examples, the participants were never in sudden, life-threatening situations even though that is required for the definition of PTSD.

All of the studies mentioned above suffer from the same flaws as the study by the Harvard group. The researchers did not ask when each of these symptoms started in relation to these nontraumatic life events. Many patients with depression have loss of interest in their usual activities, for example, but if those symptoms started before they had their stressful experience, then their loss of interest cannot be tallied under PTSD. In addition, the researchers did not ask about the quality of the distress that patients felt from the triggered reminders of their life events. Many patients with anxiety have intrusive and unpleasant thoughts, for example, but they feel nervous, which is quite different from fear.

In my opinion, the main value of these studies is that they illustrate how conducting good research on PTSD is quite difficult. These studies fail by a large measure in their aim to show that stressful but non-life-threatening events can cause PTSD. How do I justify my opinion? I have personally been involved in rigorous assessments of over 600 youths who suffered truly life-threatening traumatic events. If that's not more than any other clinician, then it's close. All of these youths were assessed with the most careful and rigorous assessment methods of any research study or clinic in the world. In addition, I have seen hundreds of youths who have other diagnoses and who do not have PTSD. I have never seen a youth who I believed had PTSD due to events such as divorce, neglect, separation from parents, living in a bad neighborhood, or the natural death of a grandparent when there were no other mitigating factors. In contrast, I have seen hundreds of youths who have experienced those types of nontraumatic, stressful events and they never seek help for PTSD-like symptoms from those events. They seek help for other things. Individuals with nontraumatic stress experiences may endorse PTSD symptoms on self-report questionnaires, but they do not think the problems are serious enough to seek help, which marks a major difference from those truly suffering from PTSD.

The following is a good example of the rigorous assessment methods we use that help us differentiate true PTSD symptoms from other problems.

Gus: A Playground in Shambles

Within my sample of very young children who lived through Hurricane Katrina, I noted earlier that we divided the children into two groups: those who had stayed during the hurricane and those who had evacuated the city safely before the storm and then returned after the storm was over. Within this second group of those who had evacuated, they could be further subdivided into those whose homes had been utterly devastated and those whose homes had remained in good shape. In our evaluations of the evacuated children, we saw that those whose homes had been utterly devastated frequently had developed PTSD. But what about those whose homes had remained in good shape?

Gus was three years and nine months old when his family evacuated with him from New Orleans ahead of the hurricane. Their home had suffered minor damage from water that leaked in through a small hole in their roof, but otherwise their home and their neighborhood were in pretty good shape. The most distressing experience for Gus was that he had to live in a city that was an inconvenient mess. When we evaluated Gus eleven months after the storm, we interviewed his mother and asked her about all of the symptoms of PTSD. When we asked whether there were reminders of the experience that upset him, his mother had some difficulty deciding whether he had this symptom or not. The most distressing thing she could think of was that there was rubble in the playground in their local public park. The rubble consisted of tree limbs, roof shingles, pieces of wood, and trash that had blown about and collected on the ground.

His mom replied, "That's so hard to say, I mean, he has talked about the rubble when we're at the playground, but I don't know if he's reminded of the trauma of hearing about the storm or if it's just the day-to-day drudgery that he would rather go to a clean playground."

When asked if these things made him upset, the mother paused for several seconds, and said, "Yeah, I think they do. He's frustrated. But I don't know if it's abnormal. I think it's actually like a normal response. If he weren't frustrated the park was a shambles, that would be odder, I think."

Unlike the evacuated children in my study who developed PTSD when they returned to see their devastated homes, Gus did not have PTSD. Gus's case was a bit confusing, though, and it took careful interviewing, patience, and understanding of the issues to untangle it, which was not the evaluation technique used in the studies on the Gulf oil spill, divorce, foot-and-mouth disease in cows, and related studies.

Ignorance or Propaganda

Despite the consistent clarity for over thirty years that the definition of traumatic events that typically cause PTSD involve life-threatening experiences, many professional organizations and government agencies appear to be confused. For example, the Substance Abuse and Mental Health Services Administration (SAMHSA), which is the main government agency of the United States for promoting mental health services, stated on their official website that trauma includes withholding of food or clothing.[10] This was an attempt to include the concept of neglect, for which many children are taken into foster care by child welfare agencies.

The National Child Traumatic Stress Network (NCTSN), a national center funded by the United States federal government to promote awareness and intervention for trauma-affected children and adolescents, also included neglect as one of the types of trauma, which could include "neglecting the child's education."[11] The notion that our National Child Traumatic Stress Network considers neglecting a child's education as a trauma leaves me scratching my head. In contrast, the National Center for PTSD, which is the corollary national center for adults, makes no mention of neglect as a type of trauma; their definition of trauma is much more consistent with the life-threatening concept.[12]

If these national agencies are not confused, then they must truly believe experiences like neglect cause PTSD. Perhaps they are being over-inclusive on purpose. If so, it seems the success of the PTSD diagnosis has become its own enemy. Because so many people now understand the concept of trauma and PTSD, advocates of special populations cloak themselves in the garment of PTSD in order to gain attention for their causes. These advocates have ulterior motivations to define trauma in ways that meet their political needs. Perhaps these advocates know exactly what they are doing when they trivialize the definition of trauma. If this practice is not ignorance, then it surely seems like propaganda.

What's the Harm?
Is propaganda a bad thing? The propaganda comes from well-intentioned people who believe they are trying to help children. So, it would be a fair question to ask, What is the harm of lumping stress in with trauma in the discussions about PTSD?

Admittedly, the harm seems minimal. But it is only minimal if people are not taking this seriously. The world took little notice when a psychologist published a paper that concluded children whose parents divorced could develop PTSD. Similarly, few people know or care about published papers that associated PTSD with ranchers whose cattle died. None of those children or ranchers, as far as I know, were actual patients who were misdiagnosed or received the wrong treatment.

If we were talking about cancer or deadly infections, it would be different. It would be a serious problem for someone to be diagnosed with cancer and given chemotherapy when they did not really have cancer.

The harm, then, is mostly in a lack of precision. Equating stress with trauma is a problem only if one cares about being accurate in the terminology. The harm, such as it is, may arise in several areas.

First, accuracy in the terminology that all clinicians use is important for communication. To have a consensus about what is trauma and what is not trauma is important because it provides the common language for nearly all discussions about PTSD. The breakthrough of the *DSM-III* in 1980 is an excellent example in that it provided a common language for doctors, researchers, patients, and everyone else to be able to communicate with each other reliably about psychiatric disorders.

Second, it is important for research. PTSD is associated with biological stress reactions and increasingly clear brain pathways that are part of a fear-related neural circuitry. It is doubtful that the biological stress reactions and neural circuit patterns that occur when teenagers struggle with a romantic breakup are identical to those that occur with the overwhelming fear of death when others are trying to kill you. As scientists get closer to understanding the neural and chemical mechanism of the causes of PTSD, it is important that they study the right types of cases.

Third, it matters for evaluations. PTSD is one of the very few psychiatric disorders that requires an event for the diagnosis. Depression, anxiety, schizophrenia, autism, and ADHD—none of these require an event for the diagnosis. For that reason, the definition of what constitutes a traumatic event is extremely important because this determines who is eligible for the diagnosis. Diagnoses determine whether patients get identified, whether they get referred for appropriate treatment, and whether insurance companies pay for treatment (not to mention who can win lawsuits based on PTSD injuries).

The diagnosis is the starting point for much of what psychiatrists, psychologists, social workers, and other types of mental health clinicians do for patients. Having a clear definition of psychiatric disorders, whether PTSD or depression or schizophrenia, is like having a common frame of reference. It is the same reason that it is wise to have one type of money for everybody within a country. If your grocery store does business in dollars, but the drug store uses drachmas, and the gas station uses yen, it would be quite inefficient. Imagine one doctor telling you that your child has experienced a trauma and ought to be evaluated, and a second doctor telling you that your child has not experienced a trauma and does not have PTSD. Sounds simple and basic, but this is the kind of confusion parents currently face with many mental health providers.

Fourth, and perhaps most important, in order to determine the best treatment options, clarity is needed about stress versus trauma matters. The wrong diagnosis could mean a patient receives the wrong treatment. Part of my job at Tulane involves supervising doctors who are in training to become child and adolescent psychiatrists. The trainees are required to learn evidence-based psychotherapy by treating at least one child patient with a full course of cognitive behavioral therapy (CBT). A trainee met with me once to discuss a case she had been treating and to ask if I would supervise this as her CBT case. The child was a six-year-old boy who was in foster care because his mother was in jail on drug charges. When police entered the home, they also decided to charge the mother with neglect because this boy and his siblings were in the home unsupervised and without food. The trainee had assumed that the experiences of both neglect and being separated from his mother were traumatic. She interpreted his symptoms of stashing food, aggression, sleep difficulty, and lack of concentration as PTSD. The trainee had already conducted the first three psychotherapy sessions of the CBT protocol and hoped that I would help her on the remaining sessions. Instead, we backed up and reviewed the case. Based on what the trainee knew (and we were aware that we may not have known everything that happened to the boy), the child actually had never experienced a traumatic event. Furthermore, the child did not exhibit distress or avoidance of reminders of possible abuse or violence that might be clues for traumatic events we did not know about. If the trainee had continued with CBT, the therapy would have hit a dead end and valuable time would have been wasted on the wrong treatment.

The wrong treatment can be delivered on a much larger scale, too. As noted earlier in this chapter, discussions were held after the Deepwater Horizon oil spill in the Gulf of Mexico in 2010 among administrators at my university, lobbyists, and government agencies about what types of services and research might be implemented along the Gulf Coast and how much money might be requested from the federal government to fund those activities. In the usual money grabs that occur after disasters in the United States, these discussions happened at many other universities as well. If the internist in our group had had his way, the government would have funded a PTSD treatment program. This would have been a bad idea not only because there would be very few people with PTSD whom they could treat; it would be doubly bad because a PTSD treatment program would have siphoned off scarce funds that could have been used for something else that would have been truly beneficial.

Recap

- The major psychiatric classification system in the world agrees that PTSD is caused by traumatic events, not stressful events.
- Individual scholars, professional organizations, and government agencies constantly try to borrow on the legitimacy of PTSD to draw attention to their special populations.
- There is harm from lumping stressful events in with traumatic events.

Chapter Four
Symptoms

Clinicians in the field must hold two divergent facts in their minds that seem completely contradictory to each other, but both of which must be used to guide treatment. Individuals with post-traumatic stress problems are vastly different from each other, yet they are the same.

Individuals with post-traumatic stress problems are different from each other because there are twenty possible symptoms in the *DSM-5* definition of PTSD. These twenty symptoms are divided among four clusters: cluster B (re-experiencing symptoms), cluster C (avoidance symptoms), cluster D (altered cognitions), and cluster E (increased reactivity). A person does not need all twenty symptoms for the diagnosis. Instead, a person needs one or more symptoms from each of the four clusters, so there is a wide variety of ways one can qualify for the diagnosis. Patient #1 may have two cluster B symptoms, one cluster C symptom, three cluster D symptoms, and two cluster E symptoms. Patient #2 may have the same two cluster B symptoms, one cluster C symptom, and three cluster D symptoms just like the first person, but then have three instead of two cluster E symptoms. Researchers have calculated that there are 636,120 different ways an individual can meet the diagnostic criteria for PTSD.[1] This makes it unlikely that any two patients with PTSD will have exactly the same collection of symptoms and ensures that individuals will be vastly different from each other. I will discuss these differences in Chapter Seven.

Yet Patient #1 and Patient #2 are the same in that they both have PTSD and both probably should receive the same treatment. In this chapter, I will focus on how all patients are the same by focusing on the diagnostic criteria.

The Diagnosis of PTSD

"What's in a name? That which we call a rose by any other name would smell as sweet." As written by William Shakespeare, these are the immortal lines Juliet spoke to argue that it did not matter to her that her Romeo came from the wrong family and had the wrong family name. In contrast, in psychiatry, the name is of great consequence.

The name in psychiatry is the diagnosis, and it determines nearly everything that needs to happen in the treatment. The right diagnosis determines whether treatment is needed at all. The right diagnosis determines whether the wrong type or the right type of treatment is given.

The symptoms to look for that make up the diagnosis of PTSD are about twenty core symptoms that can be organized into four types. To qualify for the diagnosis, individuals must have a minimum of six symptoms in a specific pattern from these four types of symptoms according to the official diagnostic guidelines used in the United States, the *Diagnostic and Statistical Manual*, Fifth Edition (*DSM-5*). Individuals must have at least one re-experiencing symptom, at least one avoidance of stimuli symptom, at least two altered cognitions symptoms, and at least two increased arousal symptoms. In addition, patients must have both symptoms and impairment to formally qualify for a diagnosis.

(1) *Re-experiencing Symptoms*

Distressing memories. Unwanted memories of the traumatic events burst into their minds. These memories are always distressing, and patients find it difficult to control them and make them go away.

Nightmares and highly distressing dreams. Young children usually call out for their parents when they have nightmares. Adolescents may handle them on their own and not tell their parents. Sometimes the dreams do not cause the youths to wake up, but they are highly distressing, and the youths can be seen thrashing around or calling out in their sleep. Dreams often are by nature symbolic in the sense that the events and characters in dreams are not the real events and characters that the sleeping mind is thinking about. In order to count as a symptom of PTSD, the content does not have to be about the traumatic events.

Dissociation. Individuals can become temporarily so overwhelmed by their thoughts and feelings that they break from reality in what are called **dissociative reactions**. These episodes are usually brief—on the order of a few seconds to several minutes. There are two types of dissociative reactions. In the classic reaction, called a **flashback**, persons feel like they are back in the traumatic events and they act accordingly. For example, I was providing medication management for a nine-year-old boy who had been physically abused by his father. He was also receiving weekly psychotherapy with a female therapist in our clinic. During one of his psychotherapy sessions, he suddenly stood up and started backing into a corner of the room and screaming, "Stay away from me! Get away!" He put his arms up to defend himself from blows, but his therapist had been seated and calmly talking with him. Something, however, had triggered him and he felt like he was back in the moment when he had been beaten by his father and then thought the therapist was his father. After a few minutes, he calmed down and recognized where he was.

In the second and far more common type of dissociative reaction, persons freeze and stare straight ahead into space for a few moments. These reactions usually last less than a minute. Most of these episodes probably go completely unnoticed because the children do not cause any disturbance.

Psychological distress when triggered by reminders. The triggers are specific to the traumatic events that the individual experiences. The triggers can be places, people, objects, sounds, music, smells, or thoughts. For example, I treated a boy who had developed PTSD after being in a motor vehicle accident. The boy would become distressed every time he had to be strapped into his car seat because it instantly reminded him of the accident.

Physiological distress when triggered by reminders. Typical reactions include heart racing, hands shaking, "butterflies" in the stomach, dry mouth, lump in the throat, sweating, and stuttering. More severe reactions may involve dizziness, nausea, and vomiting.

(2) *Avoidance of Stimuli*

Avoidance of internal triggers of the traumatic events. This symptom can be difficult to tell apart from psychological distress when triggered by reminders. The difference is that psychological distress when triggered by reminders occurs after the individual has already been exposed to the reminder, whereas avoidance of triggers occurs before the person has been exposed to the trigger. The distinction can be subtle. Examples of internal triggers include memories, thoughts, feelings, or conversations associated with the trauma.

Avoidance of external triggers of the traumatic events. External triggers usually involve activities, places, people, or conversations associated with the trauma. Looking back on the example of the boy who had been in a motor vehicle accident, the child would insist on knowing exactly where they were going because he wanted his mom to avoid driving back to the place where the accident occurred. His refusal to get in the car when he knew they were going to drive on the road where the accident occurred was avoidance of the trigger before being physically exposed to the trigger.

(3) *Altered Cognitions*

Loss of interest in activities that they used to enjoy. Adolescents drop out of their after-school activities and stop going out with friends. Younger children stop playing favorite games or refuse to go outside to play.

Feeling isolated and disconnected from loved ones and friends. Youths keep to themselves and avoid interaction with their families and loved ones.

Inability to display their emotions. This is most notable when youths show fewer positive emotions such as pleasure and happiness.

Loss of hope for the future. Patients stop making plans for the future because they have lost motivation to believe the future will be better.

Inability to remember the trauma. This symptom is rare, but it is so remarkable that it deserves mention. Doctors have published cases of individuals who appear to have forgotten entirely that they had experienced traumatic events. The theory is that the individuals have not truly forgotten, but that traumatic events were so overwhelming that the patients' brains reacted defensively to block all memories of the events.

(4) *Increased Arousal*

Irritability and anger. This appears as either constant irritability throughout the day or explosive outbursts of anger.

Hypervigilance. Individuals are on a constant lookout for danger, looking over their shoulder and expecting danger nearly everywhere.

Exaggerated startle response. Individuals startle easily and have difficulty calming down when they are surprised by unexpected noises or other sudden stimuli.

Difficulty concentrating. Patients have trouble concentrating on their work, academics, or anything that requires prolonged attention to one thing.

Sleep difficulty. Sleep patterns are disrupted and individuals have difficulty falling and/or staying asleep.

Impairment, also known as functional impairment or disability or incapacity, is the loss of the ability to perform adequately some functions needed for routine daily living. For children and adolescents, functional impairment is usually seen as disruptions in school, social activities, and family relationships.

Symptoms and impairment are different. An individual can have symptoms but not show any impairment, although the symptoms would usually have to be mild. An individual can have only a few severe symptoms and have impairment. Usually, the more symptoms one has and the more severe the symptoms, the more severe the impairments.

The diagnosis of PTSD also requires that the symptoms be present for at least one month. This is a common requirement for disorders in the *DSM-5* in order to ensure symptoms are not temporary blips that resolve rapidly on their own.

Jade: A Girl on the Edge of Suicide

The following case describes how difficult it can be for parents to recognize the existence of PTSD, the severe impairments in daily functioning that can ensue, and the real potential for suicide.

Jade, now twelve, had been raped by her uncle over the last two years. The abuse was discovered when, seeing the family's pediatrician for a school physical, Jade asked the pediatrician for a pregnancy test. Puzzled, the pediatrician asked Jade why she might need the test. Jade told the doctor that her uncle had been having sex with her and, quite naturally, she wondered if she might be pregnant. The doctor called the mom into the room to find what, if anything, she knew about this. They called child protection investigators immediately, which quickly led to the uncle going to jail for many years.

The mother was stunned and shocked, but, fortunately for Jade, appeared to believe her allegations against the mom's brother. Jade had been holding her secret for the past two years because the uncle had told her that if she told anyone he would kill her mother, then kill her brother, and then kill her. When Jade had asked the pediatrician for the pregnancy test, she rationalized that she really hadn't told anyone, and would not trigger the cascade of murders upon her family. She was just asking for a simple pregnancy test. If the pediatrician asked her why, well, she was just answering the doctor's questions.

After the child protection investigation, Jade promptly fell apart. The strain of holding in her secret for the last two years had been tremendous. Of course, she hadn't always been successful at holding in her emotions over those two years. The emotional turmoil and panic had leaked out of her anyway during that time. In retrospect, the mother said, "I wondered why she had been pulling her hair out." She also admitted she wondered why Jade's grades had fallen from As to Cs. The mom rationalized that the classes were getting harder with each year of school and Jade was just having trouble keeping up. In addition, the mother had wondered why Jade had begged her mom not to leave her with her uncle in the evenings or on weekends. Also, Jade had become more irritable and withdrawn. Now that she didn't have to hold it together anymore, the leaks became a flood.

Jade's mom felt like she had lost her daughter. Now that the story was out, Jade couldn't sleep in her bedroom anymore. She insisted that she either be allowed to sleep in Mom's bed or Mom had to sit in the living room where Jade could see her from her bed. She quit going out with her friends and basically never left the house except to go to school. Jade felt she was like nobody else at her school. She was "damaged goods." None of her friends could understand her, and she was too embarrassed to tell them what had happened to her to try to make them understand. At school, the intrusive memories of the rapes swamped her brain to the point where she missed parts of her teachers' lectures and couldn't concentrate on exams. Her grades fell further to Ds and Fs. Because she couldn't block out the memories and the anguish, she began to contemplate suicide. Finally, one night when she broke down crying while trying to concentrate on her homework, she told her mom that she didn't think she could go on.

PTSD can be deadly. These thoughts of suicide are what finally compelled Jade's mother to seek treatment and to bring her to my clinic. It is fortunate that Jade found help and did not try to commit suicide, but if she had, she would have been one of thousands of individuals who attempt suicide every year as they suffer from PTSD.

There has been a tremendous amount of attention lately on the higher-than-average suicide rates among military veterans since approximately 2008. A leading theory is that many of these veterans were overwhelmed by the suffering they experienced from combat-related PTSD.[2] This would not mark the first time suicide and PTSD have been linked in military veterans.[3]

We do not have good research that tells us how often PTSD leads directly to suicide in children and adolescents. It is an enormously difficult topic to study because many, if not most, people who commit suicide are not being seen by mental health specialists or they commit suicide spontaneously before discussing their plans in depth.

Enrique: Exhausted by What He Saw

Enrique's case emphasizes that youths do not need to be the direct victims of traumatic events for them to develop PTSD. Being witnesses to violence can cause all of the same post-traumatic stress reactions as being the direct victims.

Enrique, twelve years old, had many of the same symptoms as Jade, but he reacted to his symptoms in a different way. He had watched his father beat his mother in a violent, drunken rage. This was the first time his father beat his mother, but prior to that violence there had been years of threats, insults, cursing, and screaming by his father. Enrique's mother took herself and the children to a battered women's shelter immediately after she was abused.

Once the family moved back home, Enrique reacted by becoming the man of the family. He felt responsible now for protecting his mother and for disciplining his two younger siblings. At the slightest sound of cars stopping outside the house or strange noises, Enrique leapt into action to investigate. Heart racing, knees shaking, and hands sweating, he looked out windows, checked to make sure doors and windows were locked, and raced through the house to make sure he knew where everyone was. He lost sleep and was chronically tired, which led to difficulty concentrating at school. While he was at school, his mind raced with intrusive thoughts about whether his mom was safe. His grades suffered.

These symptoms were not hidden, but his mother did not recognize these behaviors as symptoms of a disorder and did not take him to a doctor or therapist. After six months of this, however, he was exhausted. Realizing finally that he had become someone different and he could not control it, Enrique asked his mom to take him to counseling.

Post-trauma Symptoms in Very Young Children

My research has focused on very young children who were six years of age or younger, which includes the largest study every conducted on children who were exposed to trauma in this age group. So I feel quite confident in saying that I have personally seen or supervised the in-depth assessment or evidence-based treatment of more young children with PTSD than anybody else in the world. Through a programmatic series of studies that I and my coauthors published in 1995, 2001, 2003, 2008, and 2012, plus studies by investigators at other sites, we established the guidelines for how to diagnose post-traumatic problems in these very young children with developmentally sensitive methods.

The main developmental challenges to the assessment of young children consist of a double whammy of circumstance. The first whammy is that many PTSD symptoms exist primarily within the brain as thoughts or feelings. For example, intrusive thoughts about traumas that are extremely upsetting exist only inside the brain. There is no external, visible signal that individuals have these disturbing thoughts. This is what psychiatrists call **internalized symptoms**; that is, they are thoughts or feelings that are going on internally, inside a person's skull. Internalized symptoms can be known to others, such as parents or doctors, if the individuals can verbalize what is going on inside, which depends on language skills.

Thus, the second whammy is that language skills are just developing in very young children. Most children are just learning to put enough words together to form sentences when they turn three years old. Internalized symptoms that depend on verbalizations from individuals can be quite tricky to detect in this age group.

An additional obstacle is that the capacity to know that something is wrong with your thoughts and feelings, and hence even needs to be reported to an adult, requires the ability to think about your thinking. As adults, we take this for granted. We think about our thinking without even knowing we are doing the thinking. But this type of metacognitive awareness is still developing in young children.[4] In fact, researchers do not even try to interview children about their own psychiatric symptoms until they are at least seven years old, when they have reached the proverbial "age of reason" and we can send them off to first grade where they can begin systematic learning.

The diagnostic criteria for PTSD in very young children have been scientifically validated in nearly a dozen studies.[5] *In fact, the criteria for young children have now been so thoroughly tested that they have been validated better than the diagnostic criteria for adults.* Because of the overwhelming evidence in favor of these criteria for young children, a new category was created in the *DSM-5* called "PTSD in children six years and younger." This was the first ever—and so far the only—developmental subtype of a major psychiatric disorder to appear in the *DSM* classification system.

There are seven developmental differences in the symptoms for very young children:

(1) The most important change was to reset the rules for how many symptoms are required for the diagnosis. The rule for the usual diagnosis of PTSD is that at least three of the "avoidance of stimuli" and "altered cognitions" symptoms are required. There are seven possible symptoms of these types (two symptoms of avoidance and five symptoms of altered cognitions). These symptoms, however, are exactly the type of internalized symptoms that are difficult for young children to talk about. Some of these symptoms, such as "loss of hope for the future," are not even possible in young children. My coauthors and I quickly figured out that a requirement of three of these symptoms was too many, and the requirement should instead be only one symptom in total from the avoidance and altered cognitions clusters.

(2) For the usual symptom of intrusive recollections of the traumatic events, it is required that the recollection be distressing to the individual. From the very first study that we conducted with young children, we met children who clearly had PTSD but did not appear upset when they had the intrusive recollections. In our largest study, in which we assessed 284 three- through

six-year-old trauma-exposed children, we found more than one-third of those with the symptom of intrusive recollections appeared either excited (22.6 percent) or happy (3.8 percent), or showed no effect (11.3 percent) during their intrusive recollections.[6]

(3) Loss of interest in their usual activities is a symptom that is evident in older youths by their loss of interest in school, sports, or hobbies. It is evident in adults by their loss of interest in work, family, and social activities. Very young children do not have school, sports, hobbies, or work yet in their lives. The primary usual activity in the day-to-day lives of young children is play. Hence, the wording of the symptom for young children was changed to be clear that loss of interest in play counts as a symptom.

(4) The usual symptom of feeling abnormally distant from people is worded as a "feeling of detachment or estrangement," which is known for certain only when individuals verbalize these thoughts or feelings. Because young children cannot yet verbalize their thoughts and feelings well, it is challenging to know if they are feeling detached or estranged. My coauthors and I agreed that the wording of this symptom for young children should be changed to instead reflect observable behaviors. We changed the wording of the symptom to describe young children who isolate themselves and withdraw to be alone.

(5) The symptom of having blocked from memory the entire traumatic event is a remarkable symptom that appears to occur in a relatively small number of individuals. We have looked diligently but, having never observed a case of this in very young children, probably due to developmental differences in cognitive capacities, this symptom is not included even as a possibility for young children.

(6) The usual symptom of a sense of hopelessness about the future includes the lack of motivation to study or work, or even not to want to live. This symptom is developmentally inappropriate for young children because their sense of the future is "this afternoon" or "tomorrow." We have looked but never observed this symptom in young children, so it is not in the list of possibilities.

(7) The usual symptom of irritability or outbursts of anger is observed in older youths and adults as flashing eruptions of anger. In very young children, these tend to be described as temper tantrums, so a simple change was made to include "extreme temper tantrums" in the wording of the symptom.

Young children show other symptoms following traumatic experiences that are not often seen in older children or adolescents. These symptoms are not part of the diagnostic criteria (and do not need to be):

- Loss of previously acquired developmental skills, such as toileting and language.
- New onset of physical aggression.
- New separation anxiety.
- New onset of fears that are not obviously related to the traumatic event. The most common are fears about going to the bathroom alone and fear of the dark.

Special Considerations for Seven- to Twelve-Year-Old Children

Developmental psychologists have stated that seven years of age is the "age of reason." New skills come on line such as better abilities to tell right from wrong, moral reasoning, advanced logic, and new abilities to compare oneself to others. It is not by accident that this is the age when proper schooling begins, which, in the United States, is first grade. With these new skills, it now becomes possible to obtain reliable information from the children themselves about their symptoms.

Seven- to twelve-year-old children—I'll call them older children from here on—have many more thinking skills than very young children, but they have not gone through puberty and all of the cognitive developments that occur during adolescence. In terms of PTSD symptoms, are older children more like very young children, or are they more like adolescents? Do they need special diagnostic criteria like the young children, or do the usual criteria work just fine for them?

The research data on this age group are a bit thin, with only three studies conducted, but the findings appear pretty consistent. When the diagnostic criteria that were created for very young children are used, older children can be diagnosed with PTSD two to three times more compared to when the usual criteria are used.

My co-investigators and I were the first ones to find this in a study we published in 2006. In a group of youths who we recruited from an emergency department, 9 percent met the PTSD diagnosis with the usual criteria, but 18 percent met the diagnosis when using the criteria for young children.[7] A group in London led by psychologist Richard Meiser-Stedman found nearly the identical result, with 19 percent diagnosed with PTSD by the usual criteria, but 40 percent diagnosed by the young child criteria.[8] Lastly, a group in Queensland, Australia, led by psychologist Greg Iselin and colleagues conducted a similar study at the University of Queensland and found that 4 percent qualified for PTSD by the usual diagnosis while 13 percent qualified by the young child diagnosis.[9]

These three studies do not settle the question of which diagnosis is correct, but they provide some pretty strong early evidence that we need special considerations for older children or we risk missing the diagnosis.

When to Seek Treatment? One Month of Watch-and-Wait Is Long Enough

Nearly 100 percent of individuals will have some post-traumatic stress symptoms following life-threatening events. But research has also shown that those symptoms go away during the first month for about 70 percent of individuals. It is only about 30 percent of trauma victims who have enduring symptoms after the first month.

Thus, if symptoms of PTSD persist more than one month following the traumatic event, parents should seek treatment for their children. As described in Chapter One, PTSD is chronic and time alone does not heal these wounds.

Even when the symptoms of PTSD are obvious in youths, many parents and professionals still believe, rather amazingly, that they do not need treatment. The mother of Enrique, described at the start of this chapter, clearly saw his symptoms, but did not think enough of them to get him to treatment until he asked for it. Jade's mom ignored all of the signs for more than two years. The mother of Lisa, who was introduced in Chapter One, knew about her child's symptoms for six years before something finally caused her to seek treatment. Those children suffered needlessly because they should have received help after the first month. The question of why it takes so long to get help is the topic of the next chapter.

Recap
- Very young children and seven- to twelve-year-old children have some different symptoms to diagnose PTSD.
- PTSD is often severe.
- Relatively more children have functional impairment even when they do not have the full PTSD diagnosis.

For Parents to Do

- Because we know that most PTSD is chronic and does not go away on its own, no purpose is served by waiting longer. If problems persist for more than one month, it is time to seek help.
- Start asking around for good therapists for PTSD in children and adolescents. The best therapists are usually found through word-of-mouth and they often have waiting lists.

Chapter Five

Seven Reasons Why PTSD Is Under-Recognized

It is likely to come as surprise to most people to hear that most diagnoses of post-traumatic stress are missed. I have seen it happen so often and the research data are so convincing that I believe PTSD is the most difficult problem to diagnose in all of psychiatry. This goes on even though some of the clues are right under our noses. The training that professionals receive to recognize PTSD is completely inadequate in most training programs. The following case is a perfect example.

The Girl Who Wouldn't Cross the Street

In 2005, I gave a lecture to a group of pediatricians in New Orleans on the recognition of PTSD in very young children. The group was gathered in the banquet room of a New Orleans restaurant. After I gave my talk about the developmental differences in how young children react to trauma, a pediatrician near the front raised his hand to ask a question. He had seen a five-year-old girl and her mother in his practice several months after the girl had been struck by a car. She had been crossing a street in her neighborhood when a car sped toward her. She could not see the car because cars parked on the curb blocked her view. She bounced off the grill of the car and landed about forty feet away in the neighbor's front yard. She broke a leg and had extensive soft tissue bruises. Now that the bone was healing and her massive bruising had disappeared, it appeared that she would make a full physical recovery. The pediatrician felt this little girl was enormously lucky.

The mother, however, had asked him a pointed question one day in his office. The mother told the pediatrician that now the girl was afraid to cross the street. In fact, she seemed terrified. The mother asked the eternal question that pediatricians hear every day: "Should I be worried?"

My impression of this pediatrician was that he was excellent. This particular pediatrician struck me as relatively more sensitive to the psychological issues of his patients. The fact that he was posing this question to me at all was a sign of his recognition of psychological issues. In addition, that a mother apparently felt she could trust him well enough to impose her agenda in the 6.4 minutes allotted to an average pediatric visit suggested to me that he might be more attuned to psychological problems than the usual doctor.

So I thought he was going to tell me next that he immediately identified the girl's terror as a sign of PTSD and that he sent them off with a referral to a mental health clinic. I was almost sure that was why he was bringing up this story in front of his fellow pediatricians.

Instead, this pediatrician reported that he had told the mother not to worry. "Put the notion of PTSD out of your mind," he told the mother, hoping to reassure her. He went on, saying to the mother how being scared of crossing a street after getting struck by a car was just normal caution following a bad experience. The pediatrician then asked me, "Should I have been worried?"

Was the girl's fear of crossing the street just a bit of healthy caution learned from experience? His reasoning was that if children suffered any harm from past experiences, such as being hit by a car while crossing a street, then their fear of similar situations, such as crossing any street, is logical and appropriate. In other words, it is not a symptom. What this reasoning fails to acknowledge is that caution is normal for children when crossing busy streets, but terror is not. Fear is not developmentally normal for everyday situations. Fear is almost always abnormal. This girl was fearful—so absolutely fearful that she was frozen on the sidewalk, unable to do something as simple as cross a street in her neighborhood even though no cars were near. The experience of almost losing her life had been burned into her mind. While it is wishful thinking that such PTSD symptoms, like a cut or a bad memory, should go away with time, they do not. I gently scolded the pediatrician, "Yes, the mother was right to be worried."

The Miele and O'Brien Study

That pediatrician was not a mental health expert, so perhaps we (i.e., all professionals and loved ones who care about children) ought not be too worried. Highly trained and experienced mental health clinicians do better at recognizing PTSD, right? Unfortunately, no, they do not do better at recognizing PTSD. A stunning research study by Andrew Miele, a student at Marywood University in Scranton, Pennsylvania, and his professor, psychologist Edward O'Brien, captured the massive incompetence of mental health experts. Miele and O'Brien conducted a study at two mental health programs for children and adolescents in Pennsylvania.[1] The researchers reviewed the charts of the patients at the beginning of the study and found that the rates of diagnosis of PTSD were 2 percent at one site and 5 percent at the second site. This represented the recognition of PTSD when mental health clinicians used their usual methods of practice.

Miele and his professor then did their own evaluations on all of those patients with a standardized diagnostic interview for PTSD. This time they found the rates of diagnosis of PTSD were actually 48 percent and 45 percent at the two sites. Trained and licensed mental health clinicians were missing the diagnosis of PTSD a whopping 90 percent of the time!

Even more disappointing is that Miele and O'Brien found hardly any change when they revisited one of the sites ten years later. Despite the results of the study being made public and increasing awareness of trauma and PTSD over those ten years, the program was still not using a standardized diagnostic interview, and the rate of diagnosis was back down to only 11 percent.

Maybe the Miele and O'Brien study was just a freak occurrence, you may think. Maybe Miele and his professor knew beforehand that these two programs had shady reputations and that is why they studied them, to "pick the low-hanging fruit" because they already knew what they would find. Perhaps. But the pattern of missed diagnoses is so easy to find that I believe the Miele and O'Brien study is the norm, not a freak occurrence.

For example, a group of doctors at the University of Stellenbosch in South Africa conducted a similar study on an inpatient unit for adults with anxiety and mood disorders.[2] Before the study, the rate of diagnosis of PTSD on the unit was 6 percent. This represented the recognition of PTSD when mental health clinicians used their usual methods of practice. To avoid any bias in how they studied the patients, the researchers then selected forty patients at random from the inpatient population over a period of six months. Using the gold standard diagnostic interview for adults, the Clinician Administered PTSD Scale, they found the rate of diagnosis of PTSD was actually 40 percent—amazingly similar to what Miele and O'Brien found. Again, trained and licensed clinicians were missing the diagnosis of PTSD a whopping 90 percent of the time.

It seems that individuals who are suffering from the horrors of PTSD may appear quite different on the surface. They live in a foreign world, which we can pass through only with great effort and an experienced guide.

Seven Reasons Why PTSD Is Under-Recognized

Parents trust expert professionals who work with children to be able to accurately diagnose their children's problems, but they likely would be wrong to possess such trust. The professional training of pediatricians, psychiatrists, psychologists, social workers, and other mental health counselors is tragically inadequate with regard to PTSD. Parents and their children do not have time to wait for training programs to get better. It is up to parents to recognize PTSD.

To become better at recognizing the symptoms of PTSD, it helps to know the reasons why the symptoms are so difficult to detect. The following is a list of the seven main reasons PTSD is under-recognized.

   1. **Etiological event is required.** PTSD is one of the rare disorders in the *DSM-5* that requires an etiological event. That is, life events had to happen before the symptoms could appear in the patients. Before the clinicians ask about a single symptom of PTSD, they must take the time to ask about the traumatic event.

Furthermore, researchers have learned that many, if not most, children who have experienced a traumatic event have experienced more than one traumatic event. For example, in a community representative sample of 1,420 children, 37 percent had been exposed to more than one traumatic event.[3] To be thorough, clinicians must take the time and go through a menu of all possible types of traumatic events.

Next, in order to make sure the symptoms are due to the traumatic events, clinicians must determine whether the symptoms were present before the events or they arose after the events. Each and every one of the twenty PTSD symptoms has to be tied back to an event and date of onset. It is insufficient to establish that only one of the twenty PTSD symptoms developed immediately after a traumatic event. This process also poses unique technical challenges. Many of these inquiries require multistep connections for both the interviewer and respondent: identify the symptom, connect it back in time to a past event, and recognize that the current manifestations are similar to the past experiences. These processes take time, precious time, and most clinicians will cut corners on this in order to save time.

2. Avoidance. Talking about trauma is, to put it mildly, uncomfortable. Many clinicians believe, quite mistakenly, that asking about traumas will make the youths excessively uncomfortable and cause tension in their relationships with patients. Contrary to popular opinion, I believe the real reasons clinicians avoid talking about trauma is that it makes the clinicians feel uncomfortable, not the patients.

Liam is the youth introduced in Chapter One. He was a fourteen-year-old who was seen by a psychologist for several years for attention problems, oppositional behavior, and academic failure at school. His trauma exposure and PTSD were not recognized by the psychologist. Liam avoided the topic and did not volunteer this information to the psychologist because he did not want to think about those experiences. The psychologist avoided the topic as well and did not ask about traumas. Luckily, the psychologist referred Liam to a psychiatrist for possible medications, and the psychiatrist conducted a thorough review of the boy's trauma history and discovered that he had experienced many frightening events since he was a toddler, including times when he witnessed his mother being beaten by boyfriends and passed out from drugs.

Another patient showed avoidance in a different manner. Rose was raped at the age of thirteen by a stranger in a parking lot. She developed nearly every symptom of PTSD, including the avoidance symptoms. Rose avoided talking to her parents about her symptoms because it was too painful and embarrassing. In order to avoid the memories of the rape that kept barging into her mind, she would stay busy to distract herself. She would never stay home where it was quiet and boring and the memories could overwhelm her. Instead, she went out with her friends, drank alcohol to numb herself, and had sex with boys she barely knew.

And then there is Jade, whom I introduced in Chapter Four. Jade had shown many clues of her symptoms, but her mother avoided putting the clues together. There had been multiple obvious clues, such as pulling out her hair, begging her mother not to leave her with her uncle, and so on. It is not entirely clear why Jade's mother did not react to the clues, but it was likely due, at least in part, to her own avoidance. Her mother may have wanted to avoid the difficult topic of trauma and thought that if she asked about trauma it would upset Jade, or herself, or both.

Memories of trauma feel like things to be avoided. In fact, avoidance of reminders of traumatic events is part and parcel of the PTSD syndrome. Two of the symptoms of PTSD are that the patient tries to avoid thoughts or physical things that remind the patient of past events. This avoidance makes it more difficult to conduct a good assessment. The tricky job of doctors is to solicit descriptions of events that patients would like to forget. When patients are asked if they try to avoid reminders of their trauma, patients are often known to reply, "I don't want to talk about it" or "I don't think about it." Those replies could mean that they simply do not have the symptom and there is nothing to talk about, or they could mean that they have such tremendous avoidance that they cannot bear to talk about the events. The doctor, when faced with these types of replies, has to ask more questions to get to the truth. This can be unpleasant and, again, it takes more time.

3. Many symptoms are internalized and get overshadowed by better-known syndromes. Internalized symptoms are those that exist primarily as thoughts or feelings inside patients' heads. That is, they are not flagrantly manifest by behaviors to the outside world. Internalized symptoms are difficult to observe for parents and difficult to express for children who have developing language and narrative skills. These types of PTSD symptoms include avoidance of internal reminders of past traumas, inability to recall past events (due to psychogenic blocking of painful memories), sense of a foreshortened future, feeling of detachment or estrangement from people, certain types of psychological distress to reminders of traumas, physiological reactivity to reminders of traumas, dissociative experiences, intrusive recollections, and perhaps nightmares. For the doctor to probe patiently, gently, and thoroughly with questions about the existence of these symptoms takes time, time, and more time.

Luke: PTSD Mistaken as ADHD

Luke was a young boy who was in his grandmother's legal custody because of Luke's mother's drug abuse and neglect. Luke was four and a half years old when his preschool teacher told his caregiver that she ought to get him evaluated for attention-deficit/hyperactivity disorder (ADHD). His caregiver took Luke to his pediatrician who agreed with the diagnosis of ADHD but said he was not comfortable prescribing ADHD medication to such a young child, so he referred Luke to a child psychiatrist.

Luckily for Luke, the pediatrician punted on the ADHD medications. The child psychiatrist fortunately picked up the trail of clues the pediatrician missed. Luke's grandmother expressed her concern that Luke asked her frequently why the boyfriend beat up his mommy. With a little bit of probing, the child psychiatrist discovered that Luke had witnessed dozens, probably hundreds, of episodes of domestic violence between his mother and her various boyfriends. The worst episode that he remembered was when his mom had been punched in the face and developed a black eye.

The child psychiatrist then referred Luke to our research study, where, using a structured diagnostic interview with the grandmother, our assessment revealed that Luke actually qualified for five different diagnoses: PTSD, ADHD, oppositional defiant disorder, major depressive disorder, and separation anxiety disorder. We could not be certain whether he truly had ADHD that existed prior to his traumatic experiences or he had trauma symptoms that mimicked PTSD, because his grandmother had not known him well enough before the traumas. But the main point is that Luke's PTSD had been missed at least in part because the internalized symptoms of PTSD had been overshadowed by the in-your-face ADHD symptoms.

> **4. Developmental differences.** Many symptoms of PTSD look different in children compared to teenagers and adults because of their developmental differences. For example, the symptom of intrusive recollections is shown by school-age children almost entirely by what they say, but it is shown by many preschool-age children by how they play because they are still learning how to talk about their thoughts and feelings. Other PTSD symptoms, such as avoidance behaviors, restricted range of affect, diminished interest in activities, detachment from loved ones, difficulty concentrating, and outbursts of anger may also have systematic differences in presentations by age. This requires awareness on the part of the doctor about developmental differences and requires patience and flexibility to gather this history.

Do not misunderstand this point. It does not mean children cannot get PTSD; it means children show their symptoms of PTSD in different ways sometimes, and this makes it more difficult for professionals to stay on their toes to recognize the symptoms.

PTSD is particularly under-recognized in very young children. The first-ever published case report in the world's scientific literature of a very young child with PTSD was also a very memorable case. A father had taken his three-year-old boy to visit a pet store with an unusual attraction: the pet store had a real, live leopard on display. While they were in the store, the leopard made a sudden leap to the top of the cage. There was a gap between the top bar of the display cage and the ceiling of the display room. The leopard squeezed through the gap as the father watched in horror. The leopard attacked the boy, perhaps because he looked like smaller prey, and bit him on the neck and head before the father managed to beat the leopard away.

Five months later, the father took his boy to see child psychiatrist George MacLean in Montreal, Canada. MacLean seemed to know that he had on his hands an extraordinary case of a very young child with post-traumatic symptoms, and he published the case report in the *Canadian Psychiatric Association Journal* in 1977.[4] The term *PTSD* was not officially coined until 1980, so MacLean's diagnosis was "traumatic neurosis." Nevertheless, the symptoms described in the case report seem clearly to describe the first published case report of PTSD in a child under seven years of age.

Since then, detailed case studies have been published on very young children who survived witnessing a father murder a mother,[5,6] frightening medical procedures,[7] physical abuse,[8] attack by dogs,[9] kidnapping,[10] sexual abuse,[11,12] plane crash,[13] and motor vehicle accidents.[14] The developmental modifications for the symptoms that apply to very young children were described in Chapter Four.

5. Memory complicates things. Memory is so important to the development of post-traumatic stress problems that a whole chapter is devoted to memory later in this book. Memory is a critical part of PTSD in a way that is unique from any other disorder. Memory of a traumatic event is required for the disorder, and memory to connect present symptoms to past experiences is needed in order to discuss any symptoms in an evaluation.

The chief barrier this presents in an assessment is that it takes additional time for respondents to retrieve their memories, and time is the enemy for busy clinicians. I teach my clinicians and research assistants to sit quietly and count to six in their heads each time they must wait for respondents to retrieve memories.

Philosophical problems arise also in conjunction with memory. For a long time in human history, most people believed that young children had no ability to remember things. I have personal experiences to make me think this is still believed by many people even today. After Hurricane Katrina, I ran advertisements for young children in New Orleans television and radio media for my research study. A parent of one of my son's classmates saw me later at a school function. This father, who was a computer programmer by profession, told me that he saw my advertisement in the newspaper. He told me point blank that he did not believe children could develop PTSD. He seemed convinced that young children could not remember dangerous experiences like adults do.

At first I thought he was joking and he was just trying to needle me and have some fun. After I realized it was *not* a joke and more of a lecture to me than a conversation to exchange different opinions, I muttered something about there being pretty good research that children develop PTSD just like adults, and then I acted quite interested in something else until he went away.

6. Time-consuming. If it has not been obvious from the first five reasons that time is a crucial factor in a good assessment for PTSD, here is some more evidence. There are twenty possible symptoms in the *DSM-5* PTSD criteria. This is more than double the number found in nearly all other disorders, with a few exceptions. It more than doubles the amount of time to conduct an assessment per disorder. We timed how long it takes to interview for PTSD compared to other common disorders. In our assessment study funded by the National Institute of Mental Health, parents of three- to six-year-old children who had suffered traumatic experiences were interviewed with a systematic diagnostic interview. The average time it took to evaluate for PTSD was 52.4 minutes. The average time to evaluate for major depressive disorder was 25.6 minutes, for ADHD was 13.3 minutes, for oppositional defiant disorder (ODD) was 10.3 minutes, for phobias was 8.0 minutes, for separation anxiety disorder (SAD) was 6.5 minutes, and for generalized anxiety disorder was 4.3 minutes.[15] It took almost as much time to evaluate PTSD as it did for six other disorders combined.

7. **Frame of reference.** When dealing with children and adolescents, at least half of the information we need must come from the parents. If parents have never had PTSD themselves, they have no frame of reference for what the symptoms look like and they can have a difficult time understanding the questions. Parents must be educated as to what the symptoms look like before they can answer the questions accurately.

Not too long ago, I was at a party and started talking with an old acquaintance I barely knew. In trying to make some conversation, I asked, "What do you do for a living?"

"I'm a chemical engineer, you know that," my acquaintance replied.

"Oh, yes, sorry, I had forgotten," I replied. I did not know what to say next because I had little idea of what a chemical engineer does. I had no frame of reference for being a chemical engineer. After hearing the words "chemical engineer," I had hoped that he would take the lead and describe for me spontaneously what he did without me having to ask. But he did not. He just smiled and nodded slightly. Actually, it looked like he was enjoying my discomfort.

I stood there, frozen. I thought twice before saying another word. It seemed that I already might have offended him by forgetting that he was a chemical engineer, so I worried that if I asked for more details I might offend him again by revealing my ignorance about what a chemical engineer does. I also worried that if he told me what he did I would not understand much of it, which would leave me bored and regretful I had ever asked. So, I changed the topic.

This is similar to the situation of parents who have never had PTSD themselves. Because they have never had PTSD, they do not know what to ask or how to answer questions.

Contrast this to other types of psychiatric syndromes, such as depression, ADHD, or oppositional defiant disorder. Nearly everyone intuitively understands and recognizes the sadness of depression, the hyperactivity of ADHD, and the defiance of oppositional defiant disorder; these are easily observable and require little in the way of verbalization and self-recognition from children for caregivers to be aware of them.

When interviews are conducted properly, the doctors first educate the parents as to what the symptoms are before it can make sense for the doctors to ask if the symptoms exist. This process, which I call "educational interviewing," takes extra effort and time.

The frame of reference problem is not just a problem for parents. The frame of reference problem is a problem for clinicians, too, if they have never had PTSD themselves or have never treated a case of PTSD or have never received proper training about PTSD. Understanding this issue, as the story about Dr. Lenore Terr in Chapter One illustrates, makes a bit more sense. At the time Dr. Terr stood before her colleagues as a pioneer in the early 1980s and was openly ridiculed by her colleagues, there were only about a half dozen rigorous studies in existence—all of them in adult samples—and the diagnosis of PTSD had only just been formally described in 1980 in the *DSM-III*. The first systematic studies of PTSD in groups of trauma-exposed children would not appear until

1986 with a small study that described the symptoms of forty-six youths, fourteen to twenty years of age, who were refugees from Cambodia living in the United States,[16] and in 1987 with the description of symptoms of 251 six- to thirteen-year-old children who witnessed a sniper attack on their school playground.[17] Experts in the field were just getting their own frame of reference as they were beginning to grapple with the developmental issues that made PTSD more obvious in children.

PTSD Is Common

The problem of missing the diagnosis of PTSD is no small potatoes. The occurrence of PTSD is common, and the experience of trauma is even more common. In one of the largest epidemiology surveys ever conducted on youth in the United States, it was discovered that more than two-thirds of individuals had experienced at least one potentially life-threatening traumatic event by the age of sixteen years.[18] These experiences included a wide variety of traumatic events, such as motor vehicle accidents, disasters, accidental injuries, dog bites, physical abuse, sexual abuse, witnessing of domestic violence, frightening medical procedures, and others.

Of those who experience traumatic events, about 30 percent will develop full PTSD. Doing the math, if 30 percent of the two-thirds who experienced such events actually develop PTSD, we ought to see the frequency of PTSD in the general population at around 20 percent. Yet, in the National Survey of Adolescents, investigators interviewed 4,023 adolescents (twelve to seventeen years) using a structured diagnostic interview, and they found only 4 percent of boys and 6 percent of girls qualified for PTSD in the past year according to *DSM-IV* criteria.[19]

The results were about the same in a similar type of study conducted in Switzerland. Again, with recruitment methods to carefully represent the population of their country, 6,787 teenagers completed self-administered questionnaires.[20] Fifty-six percent of respondents reported that they had experienced at least one life-threatening traumatic event in their lives. They found that only 2 percent of boys and 6 percent of girls qualified for PTSD.

I think there are two likely explanations for why these national surveys found only 2 percent to 6 percent with PTSD instead of the expected 20 percent. One reason is that these studies used only the children's self-reports. The researchers did not gather parental reports. There is strong evidence I will describe later that you need the reports from both children and parents to have the most accurate picture of PTSD. The second reason is that I suspect the interviewers in the American study were not trained to ask the right types of questions with enough patience to obtain the most accurate answers. The Swiss study relied on a self-administered questionnaire that left the door open for even more potential misunderstandings because there was no interviewer available to educate the respondents about the symptoms. The proper method to assess for post-traumatic stress problems is the topic of the next chapter.

Recap
- PTSD is fairly common.
- Professionals have been slower to acknowledge that PTSD can exist in youths compared to adults because of skepticism as to whether children can remember traumatic events and/or be affected by the events.
- For a variety of reasons, PTSD appears to be vastly under-recognized in children and adolescents and, particularly, in young children.
- Children and adolescents with PTSD may be misdiagnosed as having ADHD, oppositional defiant disorder, anxiety, or depression.
- Interviewers have to "lead the witness" with "educational interviewing" to obtain full and accurate information.
- Clinicians have been too quick to suspect that parents lie about their children's symptoms.
- You cannot tell who has PTSD by simply looking at them.

For Parents to Do

- You may have to be a strong advocate to get doctors to recognize PTSD. If you believe your children have been affected by traumas but your clinicians did not conduct a thorough review of traumatic experiences or PTSD symptoms, you ought to bring this up or switch clinicians.

- Be a good watcher of your children. Look for triggers that may bring out symptoms of PTSD. When doctors conduct evaluations of your children, they will depend heavily on your information.

- Is it possible you have underestimated the severity of your children's problems following traumas? It may be a good time to recalibrate. Download the Child PTSD Checklist questionnaire for free on my Scheeringa Lab website. Pick the questionnaire that is appropriate for the age of your children. If the score is above the cutoff for clinical concern, start looking for a good therapist. Do not wait a little while longer to see if the behavior problems will go away. Collect your own data and act now.

- Is it possible your children's clinicians have underestimated the severity of your children's problems? If your children have already been evaluated by clinicians, did the clinicians "lead the witnesses"? The clinicians should have followed up general questions with more specific questions and used examples that were specific to your children's traumas. If clinicians did not use this type of interviewing technique, they may have underestimated the severity of your children's symptoms. If you believe this has happened, collect your own data with PTSD questionnaires and give them to the clinicians.

- Do you think your children's clinicians dismissed your information? Again, data may be your best weapon. If your children are seven years of age or older, have them fill out PTSD questionnaires, and you do the same. Ask to meet with the clinicians to go through the questionnaires side-by-side to discuss discrepancies in the responses. For example, if a child denied the symptom of psychological distress at reminders but you know examples of the symptom, you can discuss these openly to resolve the differences of opinion.

Chapter Six
Proper Assessment

"Don't ask, don't tell" became the official policy of the United States in 1994 with regard to military service by gays, bisexuals, and lesbians. The policy lasted until 2011 when being openly gay or lesbian was finally allowed in the military. It is unfortunate that "don't ask, don't tell" also has been the de facto method of practice for many mental health professionals with regard to trauma because they avoid the topic.

"Do ask, do tell" is the method of practice that ought to be used with regard to trauma. Based on my experience and the research data, there are four basic pillars of proper assessment to achieve that practice.

1. "This Is Our Business" Approach
It seems almost too obvious to say it. Questions about traumatic events and post-traumatic stress symptoms have to be asked. Patients are not usually going to volunteer this information.

The manner in which one asks is vitally important. The way we do it in my clinic is that the very first thing parents do when they arrive for their first appointment is sign the treatment and privacy consents. The second thing they do is fill out five brief, standardized questionnaires about their children, one of which is about traumatic events and possible post-traumatic stress symptoms. We use the Child PTSD Checklist that I developed, which is available for free at my website. The other four questionnaires—also all free and in the public domain—cover depression, anxiety, disruptive behaviors, and global impairment in functioning.

The parents complete these standardized, evidence-based measures of symptoms in the waiting room before we ever start the interviews. We never get pushback from parents about this because, I believe, we do it in way that makes them feel like we know what we are doing and they are in good hands. I call this the businesslike approach. It sends the message that "This is what we do here. We know what we're doing and this is how we do it." We make no apologies for this highly matter-of-fact approach. We have never had anyone complain about this.

The countervailing argument against this straightforward, businesslike approach stems from the fear that asking questions about trauma will be harmful. Isn't it going to bring up bad memories and make them worse? David Finkelhor, a sociologist at the University of New Hampshire who is known for his research on child sexual abuse, conducted a research study to ask that exact question. Finkelhor and his team interviewed over 2,000 children by telephone, asking them if they had ever suffered life-threatening traumatic events.[1] They asked specific questions about sexual abuse, physical abuse, injuries, disasters, witnessing of violence, and so forth. Then they asked if the interviewees had suffered any of the symptoms of PTSD following those events. Then, at the end of the interviews, they asked the children if answering these questions made them feel distressed.

The results, published in 2014, ought to put permanently to rest any fears that asking children about trauma is harmful. Only 4.6 percent of the children reported any level of distress from the interviews. More importantly, only 0.3 percent of the children responded that they would not participate in the interview if they were asked again. And within that 0.3 percent, only one child reported the nature of the questions as the reason he would not participate again.

2. Standardized Questionnaire

I have memorized the twenty post-traumatic stress symptoms that are in the *DSM-5* diagnostic criteria, but that is only because I write about or study PTSD in some form nearly every day. Very few clinicians are familiar enough with PTSD to have all of the symptoms memorized. So, as noted earlier, we ask parents and youths to complete standardized questionnaires that cover a menu of twelve different types of traumatic events and the twenty possible post-traumatic stress symptoms. We do this also to be comprehensive, and it saves time in the following interview.

You Cannot Tell Who Has PTSD by Looking at Them

I have conducted numerous workshops and supervised many trainees, and clinicians have frequently told me they do not need to give a questionnaire to every patient because they can tell who needs one and who does not. They believe they can conduct their clinical interview first and make their own determination of who has suffered significant trauma. Well, I tell them, I am truly amazed by their skills because I have personally seen over 600 youths who suffered trauma exposure and I could not tell by looking at them whether or not they had PTSD.

We give my standardized Child PTSD Checklist to the parent of every child who walks through our door even if they did not indicate that trauma was a problem during the telephone intake. That could appear excessive to a lot of people. It even took me a long time to come around to doing it this way. It should be self-evident by now, though, that there are multiple reasons for doing it this way, such as the seven reasons PTSD is vastly under-recognized that were discussed in Chapter Five.

It seems many people, clinicians and parents alike, still possess quaint notions that PTSD should be easy to see. The children with post-traumatic stress would "act out," "act up," or say things that would make it obvious they were distressed. I think these clinicians and parents believe this because they wish to believe it, not because it is true. Psychologists call this "confirmation bias." These folks either hold the personal belief that post-traumatic stress reactions are rare or hold a desire that they prefer not to deal with post-traumatic stress problems. To keep convincing themselves of their personal beliefs, they see only the information that supports their beliefs and they ignore the evidence that contradicts their beliefs.

In Chapter Four you met Enrique, whose symptoms went unrecognized by his mother for six months, and Jade, whose symptoms went unrecognized by her mother for two years and were unrecognized by her pediatrician until she asked for a pregnancy test. You also met Lisa (in Chapter One), whose symptoms went untreated for six years after Hurricane Katrina. In Chapter Five you met the girl who wouldn't cross the street and whose PTSD was missed by her pediatrician even after her mother asked him about it. And in the next few sections I'll introduce Liam, whose symptoms of PTSD were missed by his psychologist. No, you cannot tell who has PTSD simply by looking at them.

3. Educational Interviewing. You Must "Lead the Witness."

Here is a little secret. During the training years of health professionals, especially for medical students, trainers and supervisors put an enormous amount of emphasis on the principle that clinicians should never supply the possible answers to questions. They should never suggest what a physical reaction could be to a test during a physical examination. They are taught to never "lead the witness."

Dr. House, the famous doctor from the American television show *House*, once said, "I don't ask why patients lie, I just assume they all do." It is either implied or explicit that a large swath of patients are prone to either lie or exaggerate in order to inhabit the sick role, wheedle pills out of doctors, or hide a dark secret. The results of examinations are thought to be more valid if the information from patients is obtained with Sherlock Holmes–like detective sleuthing and produced by the patients without undue prompting by the clinicians. These well-meaning doctors are taught to stand back in their Dr. House–style detachment and observe as the signs and symptoms flow out of the patients, free from the suggestive biases. I always thought this was nuts.

Contrast this approach to that of a trial lawyer. In a jury trial, attorneys know exactly the outcome they want at the end. In order to achieve that outcome, attorneys know exactly what they want their witnesses to say on the stand. Attorneys frame their questions to drive the witness to the exact answer they want and freely put words in the witness's mouth.

For the evaluation of PTSD, the interview method needs to be less like the medical school model of not leading the witness and much more like the trial attorney model of leading the witness. Every doctor reading this is cringing and probably thinking something like "That idiot Scheeringa went too far again," because the model of not leading the witness has nearly sacrosanct status in the medical world. Because this is such an important issue in order to get the right diagnosis, I will make the case again that the medical model of not leading the witness is completely and absolutely wrong for PTSD.

For the assessment of PTSD, clinicians *have to lead the witnesses* for several reasons.

1. There is a frame of reference problem. In child and adolescent psychiatry, we need to gather assessment data from both the children and the parents. If the parents have never had PTSD themselves, then they do not have a frame of reference from firsthand knowledge of what the symptoms look like. Everybody knows what hyperactivity and depression look like, but most people do not know what a dissociative flashback looks like.

2. Avoidance is part and parcel of the PTSD syndrome. Patients will not typically volunteer to talk about symptoms without very direct and focused questions.

3. Many PTSD symptoms are simply more complicated than the symptoms in other disorders. For example, consider perhaps the most common PTSD symptom: psychological distress at reminders of the traumatic event. In order to be able to report this symptom to clinicians, what is required is a three-step process in which patients must recognize that they have psychological distress in response to cues in the environment, that the cues resemble aspects of past events in their lives, and that the past events were life-threatening experiences. For example, one would have to connect that an internal sensation of fear triggered by a mundane kitchen knife reminded a person of the knife that was in the hand of her father two years ago as he stabbed her mother to death, while at the same time the person is trying to block that painful memory.

Here are some examples of the wrong way and the right way to ask about all types of traumatic events.

WRONG WAY: "Has your child experienced any traumatic events?" There are no follow-up questions and no specific examples are given.

RIGHT WAY: "Has your child experienced any life-threatening traumatic events? For example, has he been in a serious car accident?"

Wait for the answer. If the interviewee has not responded and appears to be thinking, be quiet and count to six in your head.

"Has he ever been attacked by someone?"

"Has he ever seen you get attacked or hurt?"

"Has he been in a disaster like a flood or tornado?"

"Any scary medical procedures?"

"Attacked by a dog?"

If any of these traumatic events happened, the clinician should go through each of the specific PTSD symptoms.

Here's another scenario: A girl was the first person to discover her father's dead body in their home after he died from a heart attack.

WRONG WAY: "Does she have any symptoms from that traumatic event?" There are no follow-up questions and no specific examples are given.

RIGHT WAY: "Does she get upset when there are reminders of what happened? For example, is she nervous about living in that house? Does she get nervous about being in the room where she found him? Is she bothered when she's around other sick people?"

In this instance, specific examples are given that could be related to her individual event.

"Is she what we call hypervigilant—she always seems to be 'on guard' and looking over her shoulder for danger?"

In asking this question, additional details are provided about what hypervigilance might look like.

Specific questions like these should be posed for most of the twenty PTSD symptoms.

There is a huge difference between the wrong way and the right way to assess for PTSD. In the wrong way, the clinician asked relatively vague questions. These are called open-ended questions. In the right way, the clinician asked leading questions. The clinician's questions teach the respondent what the symptoms might look like so that the respondent can answer the questions most accurately. This is what I call "educational interviewing."

The Misjudgment of Parents

The concern about "leading the witness" is that patients might bamboozle the clinicians. Patients might convince clinicians that they have all sorts of symptoms and problems they do not really have. If clinicians tip them off with descriptions of symptoms, then patients will learn how to fake it. During training programs for young doctors and psychologists and counselors, it is not difficult to convince these clinician trainees that patients lie. Clinicians, perhaps especially medical doctors, see themselves, somewhat rightly and somewhat wrongly, as where the buck stops. Doctors are a self-selected group who are independent and do not like to take orders. They see themselves as the last wall between death's door and rare diseases, between the evils of drug abuse and prescription drug addicts, and between taxpayers' money and disability cheats, and they will be damned if they are going to be bamboozled. The actual number of patients who lie, however, is probably rather small, although those are the patients whom trainees remember most acutely.

There is a particularly repugnant type of suspicion of lying that is reserved for parents. This type of lying involves either parents who markedly exaggerate their children's symptoms to make them appear more disturbed than they really are, or parents who markedly downplay their children's symptoms to make their children appear less disturbed than they really are.

Let us take, for example, a lecture about PTSD that I give every year to child psychiatry doctors in training. I show them the graph in Figure 6.1 that shows the frequencies of PTSD diagnoses for children based on children's self-reports and parental reports. These data were taken from a study I conducted with thirteen- through eighteen-year-old youths who had been treated in a Level I trauma center for injuries.[2] I explain to the trainees that when using only the youths' reports about themselves, the frequency of the diagnosis for PTSD was 8 percent. When using only the parents' reports about the youths, the frequency of the diagnosis for PTSD was 4 percent. But when information from both the youths and the parents is combined, the frequency of the diagnosis for PTSD skyrockets to 38 percent. Then I ask the trainees, "What do you think explains these big differences?"

Every year, there is a trainee who says, "The parents lied about their children's symptoms." An explanation that parents lied about their children's symptoms does not help to explain the data in the figure, but amazingly, it is the trainee's knee-jerk response. The trainee is wrong. The correct answer is that youths know certain things about themselves that parents do not know (see item 2 about avoidance and item 3 about internalizing symptoms on page 77), and parents see certain things about youths that youths do not see so easily. Neither children nor parents are lying. They each are able to report different information.

Figure 6.1. Frequencies of PTSD diagnoses for youths, thirteen to eighteen years (n=24), based on children's self-reports, parental reports, and combined child-parent reports.

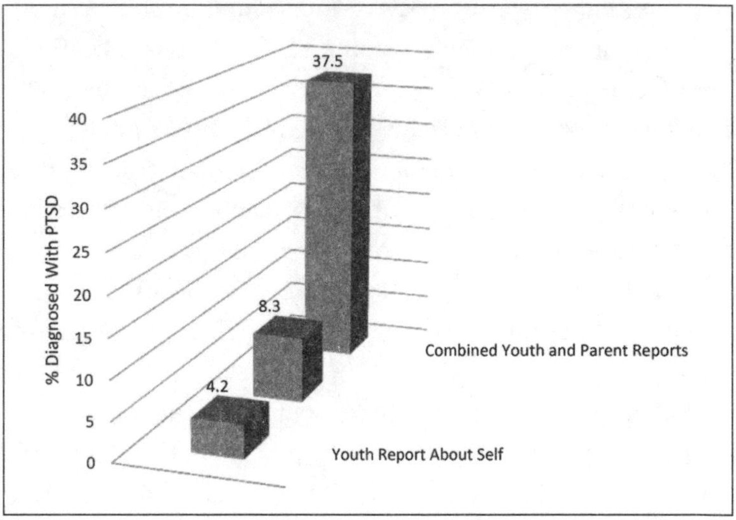

Data from Michael S. Scheeringa, Mary Jo Wright, John P. Hunt, and Charles H. Zeanah, "Factors affecting the diagnosis and prediction of PTSD symptomatology in children and adolescents," *American Journal of Psychiatry* 163 (2006): 644–51.

Let us take another example from my same lecture to the young doctors. I explain to them a fascinating study conducted with a group of children who were in the World Trade Center in New York City during the first terrorist bombing attack on one of the towers in 1993. Harold Koplewicz, MD, and his colleagues asked the parents about their children's PTSD symptoms three months after the bomb explosion and then repeated the questions with the parents nine months after the explosion.[3] The fascinating thing Koplewicz did, though, was that he also asked the parents about their own PTSD symptoms even though none of them were in the tower with their children during the explosion.

Three months after the explosion, there was no association between the children's PTSD symptoms and the parents' PTSD symptoms. Nine months after the explosion, however, there was now a significant correlation between the children's PTSD symptoms and the parents' PTSD symptoms. By nine months after the explosion, the children with the most PTSD symptoms had parents with the most PTSD symptoms, and vice versa. Then I ask the trainees, "What do you think explains this change in symptoms over time?"

Every year, there is a trainee who says, "The parents lied about their children's symptoms." The trainee believed that parents perceived their children to be more like themselves as time passed regardless of whether this were true or not. The trainee believed that parents who had more symptoms of PTSD themselves saw PTSD symptoms in their children that were not really there. Also, the trainee believed that parents who had fewer PTSD symptoms themselves failed to see PTSD symptoms in their children that really were there. The trainee was wrong.

Like myself, Dr. Koplewicz and colleagues believe the parents were not lying. What they believe happened is that parents who had children with more PTSD symptoms became more and more distressed over time because they were concerned, and rightly so, about their children. The parents who had children with fewer PTSD symptoms became more and more relaxed over time because their children were doing better. Parents were being affected by their children, not the other way around, which is an enormously important point that will be discussed more in Chapter Nine.

4. Patience

My father was a doctor. He was a general internist who specialized in cardiology before the specialty of cardiology had been invented. One day he was complaining about the way doctors were being treated, and he said, "You know, doctors are manual laborers, just like a farmer. If we're not seeing patients, we're not getting paid."

He was right. Time is money for clinicians, and insurance companies have been doing all they can to cut into that money. Because time is money, clinicians feel pressured to spend as little time as possible with each patient so that they can pack in more patients.

However, as I described in Chapter Five, an overarching factor for why PTSD is underrecognized is that the assessments take a long time compared to all other disorders. Clinicians must be patient and allow themselves time to conduct a thorough assessment and allow patients time to access their memories. The pressure to spend less time with patients clashes head-on with the need to spend more time on assessments for PTSD.

So far I have been discussing only the straightforward and uncomplicated cases of post-traumatic stress reactions. But as the next chapter illustrates, straightforward and uncomplicated cases are relatively rare. Time and patience will be in even more demand to manage the more complicated cases.

Recap

- Clinical interviews in mental health ought to be educational at the same time they are data gathering. This is what I call educational interviewing; the interviewers educate the respondents with what they are asking about so that the respondents can respond with accurate information.

For Parents to Do

- After this type of evaluation, you ought to ask the clinician how he or she is thinking about the issue of trauma in relation to your children's experiences. Your children may have nontraumatic experiences that the clinicians believe are trauma, and then the wrong treatments get applied. Or your children may have truly traumatic experiences that the clinicians are missing.

Chapter Seven
Complex Problems

For over 100 years, it was thought to be practically a law of nature that no two snowflakes are alike. With a complex crystalline structure of ice that has six arms, each of which grows independently, there are nearly an infinite number of ways that snowflakes can form. Then Nancy Knight, an employee at the National Center for Atmospheric Research, published a paper in 1988 with photographs of two identical snowflakes.

There are multiple ways that post-stress reactions can be complex. One way is through a nearly endless combination of symptoms of PTSD. A second way is through the co-occurrence of other disorders. A third way is through the overlap of symptoms between two or more disorders.

Combinations of Symptoms of PTSD
Post-traumatic stress reactions are a lot like snowflakes. As noted in Chapter Four, researchers calculated that there are 636,120 different ways that an individual can meet the diagnostic criteria for PTSD.[1]

Yet it is more complex than that. There are additional symptoms that can develop following trauma that are not included in the diagnostic criteria. For example, young children can develop fears of the dark and the bathroom, which are not in the PTSD criteria. When these post-trauma symptoms are also considered, the number of ways to have PTSD increases even more.

Co-occurrence of Other Disorders
Actually, it is much more complex than that. Persons who have PTSD will also have at least one other psychiatric disorder 70 to 90 percent of the

time. This is one of the most consistent of all findings in PTSD research. The official jargon that doctors use for this is called **comorbid disorders,** but I'm just going to call it co-occurring disorders. For example, if an individual has depression and anxiety disorders in addition to PTSD, then the individual has three co-occurring disorders.

The high rate of co-occurring disorders with PTSD has been found across all age groups, races, and types of traumas. In adults, the co-occurring disorders are usually major depressive disorder, generalized anxiety disorder, and alcohol and/or other drug abuse. The data from one of the larger adult studies are shown in Figure 7.1. In a survey of 1,127 adults,[2] researchers found that patients who were currently diagnosed with PTSD (as opposed to being diagnosed at any point in their lifetime) also currently had major depression 69 percent of the time, generalized anxiety disorder 38 percent of the time, and panic disorder 23 percent of the time.

In very young children, the co-occurring disorders are different because of their different developmental level. We conducted the first study on PTSD and co-occurring disorders in very young children (six years of age and younger). We found that the most common co-occurring disorders were oppositional defiant disorder and separation anxiety disorder.[3] The young children diagnosed with PTSD also were diagnosed with oppositional defiant disorder 75 percent of the time, separation anxiety disorder 63 percent of the time, and attention-deficit/ hyperactivity disorder 38 percent of the time (Figure 7.2). In contrast to the findings with adults, depression was also diagnosed only 6 percent of the time.

Figure 7.1. Of Adults Who Have PTSD, What Is the Percentage Who Also Have a Co-occurring Disorder?

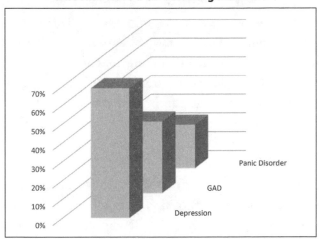

Note: Of those adults who had PTSD, they also had major depression disorder 69 percent of the time, generalized anxiety disorder (GAD) 38 percent of the time, and panic disorder 23 percent of the time. From Brown et al., "Current and lifetime comorbidity of the *DSM-IV* anxiety and mood disorders in a large clinical sample," *Journal of Abnormal Psychology* 110 (2001): 585–99.

Figure 7.2. Of Very Young Children, Three to Six Years, Who Have PTSD, What Is the Percentage Who Also Have a Co-occurring Disorder?

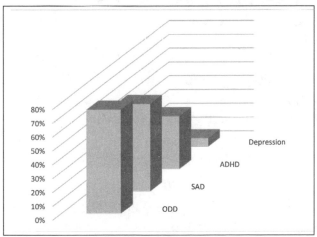

Note: Of those young children who had PTSD, they also had oppositional defiant disorder (ODD) 75 percent of the time, separation anxiety disorder (SAD) 63 percent of the time, attention-deficit/hyperactivity disorder 38 percent of the time, and major depression disorder 6 percent of the time. From Scheeringa et al., "New findings on alternative criteria for PTSD in preschool children," *Journal of the American Academy of Child and Adolescent Psychiatry* 42 (2003): 561–70.

Two persons could have exactly the same symptoms of PTSD, but one person may also have co-occurring depression whereas the second person does not have depression. They both have PTSD, but overall they obviously differ from each other on whether or not they have depression. The researchers who calculated that there are 636,120 different ways an individual can meet the diagnostic criteria for PTSD also calculated the number of different ways one can have these co-occurring disorders. They calculated that there are 227 ways to have depression and 23,442 ways to have panic disorder. Using the same methods, I calculated that there are 7,056 different ways to have ADHD and seventy different ways to have ODD. If one includes the co-occurring disorders of depression, panic disorder, ADHD, and oppositional defiant disorder, there are more than one quintillion ways to have PTSD plus co-occurring symptoms. That's what I mean when I say it is much more complicated.

These complications can make it more difficult for patients to get the right treatments because many clinicians and researchers are vexed by this complexity of PTSD symptoms and co-occurring disorders. Clinicians get distracted by the co-occurring disorders, which are usually easier to see, and then they lose sight of the PTSD, which, as discussed in earlier chapters, is usually more difficult to see. This vexation can cause diagnostic confusion and delays in appropriate treatment, as illustrated in the following cases.

Luke: PTSD Manifest as ADHD

I introduced Luke in Chapter Five. He was misdiagnosed with ADHD as a preschool child. Luke was a four-year-old white male who was on the verge of being kicked out of his pre-K–4 school because of his behavior. His teachers in day care had barely tolerated him the year before, and the same disruptive behaviors were repeating in pre-K–4 school in the current year. He was an extremely disruptive force in his class. He would hit students and teachers and have rages when angry. On his assessment with us, he qualified for the diagnosis of ADHD with thirteen of the ADHD symptoms: fidgets, difficulty remaining seated, runs or climbs excessively, always on the go, talks excessively, avoids tasks that require mental effort, difficulty concentrating, difficulty waiting his turn, often blurts out answers, and often interrupts. He also qualified for the diagnosis of oppositional defiant disorder with seven symptoms: rule breaking, disobedience, defiance, arguing, losing temper, annoying others, and spitefulness.

Luke's grandmother assumed legal guardianship when his mom lost her parental rights when Luke was four years and two months old. Luke had witnessed multiple incidents of domestic violence between his mother and her boyfriend. His grandmother described the same types of problems at home that the school had described. She was particularly distressed by his emotional meltdowns that lasted until he wore himself out by screaming, slamming doors, and throwing things.

We saw similar behaviors during his psychotherapy sessions as we attempted to treat his PTSD with cognitive behavioral therapy (CBT). Luke was not able to focus for very long in sessions. When the therapist tried to get him to cooperate with the therapy, Luke would often get mad and hit himself or throw markers.

Despite Luke's limited cooperation, the therapy was remarkably successful. By the end of twelve weekly CBT sessions, his PTSD symptoms had decreased from thirteen to one. His ADHD symptoms had decreased from seventeen to two. His ODD symptoms had decreased from eight to two. The critical part of therapy that seemed to turn things around was the CBT technique of confronting the painful memories of his trauma experiences.

Liam: PTSD Masked by Defiant Behavior and Inattention

Liam was misdiagnosed with oppositional defiant disorder and attention-deficit/hyperactivity disorder for years. He was a fourteen-year-old boy who had been in psychotherapy for over one year. The psychologist who was treating him had diagnosed him with depression and oppositional behavior but had completely overlooked his PTSD. Liam was close to being kicked out of his high school. The psychologist found no intellectual disability or learning disabilities that could explain his poor grades. In counseling, the psychologist focused on depression and family relationships. The school counselor who saw Liam also missed his PTSD. It was only after the psychologist referred him to a psychiatrist for an evaluation for medication to treat his attention problems that his trauma history was discovered. It was discovered that Liam had witnessed many frightening events related to his mother's drug abuse and domestic violence. Liam's PTSD from these events had gone unrecognized by licensed clinicians for years because they never asked about trauma and PTSD symptoms, or if they did ask, their interviewing techniques were rushed and sloppy.

When the psychiatrist interviewed Liam and his aunt about PTSD symptoms, she found that he had twelve of the seventeen possible symptoms. She referred Liam to one of our PTSD research studies and he improved substantially, without medication, within two to three months with CBT for PTSD. He continued to need longer-term supportive therapy for other issues. He continued to struggle with following rules and showed a profound self-destructive and antisocial streak that interfered with making friends and succeeding in school. His tendency toward depression and blaming others often set him back after making steps toward progress. However, by his senior year in high school he was set to graduate, and he had returned to live with his mother and was doing well. His mother wrote a note to the counselor that the PTSD treatment and the recognition of trauma in his life had been the turning point.

Overlap of Symptoms Between Disorders

Even the most famous psychiatrist of our country was vexed by the complexity of co-occurring disorders. Dr. Robert Spitzer, who passed away in 2015, was arguably the most famous modern-era psychiatrist in the world. Working mostly from the highly respected New York State Psychiatric Institute, he conducted a large number of important studies, but is known mostly for being one of the chief architects of the *DSM-III*, which revolutionized clinical and research work in psychiatry. In 2007, Robert Spitzer and two colleagues wrote a scathing article with the provocative title "Saving PTSD from Itself in *DSM-V*."[4]

In this article, Spitzer approached the concerns about co-occurring problems from a different perspective. He and his colleagues blasted the criteria for PTSD because five of the seventeen symptoms of PTSD (in the *DSM-IV* version) were symptoms that could also be found in depression and generalized anxiety disorder. They theorized that this overlap of symptoms in multiple disorders led to too many people being diagnosed with PTSD.

If these overlapping symptoms really belong to depression or anxiety disorders and aren't really PTSD symptoms, then PTSD is not as common as people think it is. Spitzer and his colleagues proposed modified diagnostic criteria for PTSD by eliminating those five overlapping symptoms from the diagnostic criteria for PTSD. However, they rather irresponsibly proposed this modification in the absence of data, so they couldn't report on how this actually changed anybody's diagnosis.

Fortunately, another group of researchers, led by Jon Elhai, PhD, at the University of South Dakota, decided to test Spitzer's idea. Elhai and colleagues reviewed the data of 5,692 participants in the National Co-Morbidity Survey Replication and found that Spitzer's recommendations made essentially no difference.[5] Spitzer's recommendations lowered the rate of PTSD only from 6.81 percent to 6.42 percent. Elhai and his group of researchers concluded that "little difference was found between the criteria sets in diagnostic co-occurring and disability, structural validity, and internal consistency."

This is important to note because it debunks Spitzer's claim that too many people are being diagnosed with PTSD because of a flawed taxonomy. In other words, the fact that some PTSD symptoms are also symptoms of other disorders such as depression and anxiety is not a problem for making diagnoses.

Doctor, Please Teach Me

"Round and round she goes, and where she stops nobody knows" is a popular saying used for spinning dials in games, song lyrics to describe the course of love, and existential musings on the seemingly random complexity of life. It may also appear appropriate for the massive complexity of post-traumatic stress reactions, which seems more like random mystery steered by the unseen hand of fate than the outcome of immutable laws of nature. Any attempt to understand the pattern to this complexity appears to be a delusional act.

Amid this apparent confusion, I think there are two things that parents and clinicians ought to keep in mind to keep from getting dizzied by the spinning dial. First, when one sees a clinician for post-traumatic stress problems, one should expect a decent level of education about the assessment. A decent level of education means talking about the complexity openly, including the uncertainties and gray areas.

The origin of the word for doctor is the Latin word *docere*, which means "to teach." To me, this always seemed a good first principle to keep in mind when meeting with patients. I think patients want above all to be educated about what is going on with them. If it can be fixed, that would be great, too. It seems, however, that many clinicians never learned that trick.

I have been unlucky enough to suffer from a fair amount of neck, back, and various nerve pains. As a consequence, I have visited numerous neurologists over the years. Neck and back pains can be tricky because so many different types of structures are packed together in tight spaces. Is the underlying irritation of nerves from bone, ligament, cartilage, or muscle? Depending on the answer, the treatment may be simply to rest or it may be injection or surgery. The accurate diagnosis would seem terribly important. I leave the visits feeling more satisfied when I've had a frank discussion of what these experts think than when they have just prescribed a treatment. I want the doctor to teach me.

You should expect the same clarity when you see a clinician. Is it depression? Anxiety? Or PTSD? Or all three? Is it mild or severe PTSD? Have you seen this before? Do you expect it to get better or not?

The Eye of the Beholder

In Aesop's famous fable "The Ugly Duckling," an egg from another bird was mistakenly laid in the nest of a mother duck. When this young bird hatched, it did not look like the other ducklings. Everyone thought it was the ugliest duckling they had ever seen. But by the time the bird matured into a graceful adult, it eventually realized it was a beautiful swan.

Just as beauty was in the eye of the beholder for the swan, I think the same is true when talking about complex post-traumatic stress symptoms. Confusion versus clarity is in the eyes of the beholder. People's brains seem to be wired differently with respect to how they are able to view complex situations. I think there are two types of people in the world in terms of how they embrace complexity.

One type of person is the Chicken Little of the village who always thinks the sky is falling. They see complexity as a story that needs to be reduced to comic book simplification. If complexity were a sound, to them it would be white noise. They are overly focused on the negatives in a complicated world. For them, monsters lurk in the shadows, molehills become mountains, and complexity is a threatening hive of buzzing confusion. I do not think they fear these things. Rather, I think they thrive on these things, but they lack the inclination to sort them out. Chaos and confusion are their oxygen.

The other type of person sees complexity as opportunity. For them, monsters are potential allies, molehills are small speed bumps, and complexity is like a light to a moth. They too thrive on complexity, but they wake up each morning to sort it out. Complexity is not a dense conundrum. Instead, complexity is like a friendly Godzilla that watches over us.

I am of the second type. I do not feel vexed by the complexity of symptoms from the co-occurring disorders. I think the level of complexity that we are aware of is just a good start, and that we are just scratching the surface of how complex things really are. Embracing the fact that complex, co-occurring, and overlapping problems are the norm and not a nuisance opens up our minds to a whole world of possibilities we wouldn't think of otherwise.

I don't find multiple diagnoses with overlapping symptoms in one individual terribly confusing. I'm not saying you need to think like me, and I'm not saying that one type of thinker is always better than the other. I'm saying I think part of the controversy about how to make diagnoses that never gets mentioned is what the critics or supporters bring to the table about themselves. That's an important consideration for you to keep in mind when you are reading criticisms and listening to clinicians. The critics are not blank slates.

So, despite the elaborate theories and elegant arguments put forth in scientific journals, I believe that much of this debate boils down simply to individual differences in the way different people think. The trick is in understanding that there are two types of people in the world writing and talking about this issue, and these writers and talkers are fundamentally different from each other. My contention is that how one writes and talks about the issue depends on the character traits of the individual doing the writing and talking.

This situation is sort of like the well-known "observer effect" in physics—sort of, but not exactly. The observer effect states that physicists can never know exactly the measurements of the small things they measure in physics because the act of measuring causes little changes in the system. In our situation, the observers do not cause changes in the system, but we do get different opinions depending on who the observers are.

The Chicken Littles say we're between a rock and a hard place with a hopelessly messy, confusing, buzzing, blooming situation of endless individual variations and co-occurring disorders. They insist on grand, unifying theories that organize ideas neatly; these Chicken Littles are simply confused by comorbidity because it doesn't suit how their brains work, and so many experts of this type have called into question the entire way we diagnose problems. They think our diagnostic system is all wrong, which is the topic of the next chapter.

Recap
- Individuals who have PTSD will also have at least one other psychiatric disorder 70 to 90 percent of the time.
- The type of co-occurring disorder differs for different age groups.
- The co-occurring disorders are often more apparent and easier to recognize than PTSD. This can lead to diagnostic confusion and the wrong treatments.
- The number of co-occurring disorders is probably just a good start.

For Parents to Do

- If new problems develop in your children following traumas, whether these look like depression, anxiety, or disruptive behavior, make sure they receive a competent evaluation for PTSD.

- Write down the dates of onset of each of the co-occurring disorders your children show. Determine which ones existed prior to traumatic events and which ones developed after traumatic events. Your therapist and doctors should have already done this, but probably did not, and if they did they probably will not share the information with you. This information can help you and your therapists determine sequential treatment approaches.

Chapter Eight
Facing the Disinformation Critics of the *DSM-5*

The starting point for all discussions about diagnoses of PTSD in the United States is the official definition in the *Diagnostic and Statistical Manual*, Fifth Edition (*DSM-5*). If the *DSM-5* definition of PTSD is a good definition, then we are on the right track to making the correct treatment decisions. If the *DSM-5* definition of PTSD is a poor definition, then we are on the wrong track.

I shall give my opinion at the start of this chapter. The *DSM-5* definition of PTSD is a good definition. It is perhaps the most well-validated set of diagnostic criteria in all of psychiatry. It is a very good definition for a lot of reasons.

Many clinicians do not share my opinion. In the daily course of their practices, these clinicians pay little attention to the *DSM-5* definition, and many of them do not even really know the criteria because they believe it is not worthy of their time. You will also be on the internet inevitably searching for information and you will run into massive amounts of criticism and disinformation about the *DSM-5*.

In this chapter, I address three of the biggest criticisms of the *DSM*.

1. Is the *DSM-5* inherently a badly flawed system for making diagnoses?
2. Do we give patients too many diagnoses? Is there a simpler or more accurate way to diagnose people to lead to more efficient treatment?

3. Do we need a new diagnosis to replace or complement PTSD for certain types of patients?

1. Is the *DSM* Classification System Inherently Flawed?

The short answer is no. The long answer is probably best approached with a look at why many people do not like the *DSM* classification system.

Criticism of the Categorical System

In a categorical classification system such as the *DSM*, patients are placed in categories. You have this disorder or you do not. Decisions about diagnoses are thumbs up or thumbs down, yes or no decisions. There is no middle ground, at least theoretically.

An alternative to a categorical classification system would be a dimensional classification system, says one group. A **dimensional classification system** would grade the severity of problems on a scale as opposed to the yes or no decisions of a categorical system. A dimensional classification system would reflect the reality that psychiatric problems exist on a continuum in the world. Some folks have mild depression, some have moderate depression, and some have severe depression, and so on.

The former head of child and adolescent psychiatric research at the National Institute of Mental Health (NIMH) edited a book that was published in 2006 called *Toward a New Diagnostic System for Psychopathology: Moving Beyond the DSM*.[1] The contributors to the book made impassioned pitches against categorical classification and described the perceived shortcomings of the *DSM*. Yet the most amazing thing in my view is that the book never offered an alternative classification system. The authors never offered a dimensional classification that could replace the *DSM*.

In fact, despite a chorus of critics against a *DSM*-style categorical classification system, no one has ever proposed a dimensional classification system to fully replace the *DSM*, and any dimensional classification that could be proposed would have its own set of flaws.[2] The *DSM* classification may have flaws, but the flaws are far outweighed by its strengths and by the fact that there is no better alternative.

Neurobiological Criticism

The *DSM* describes disorders by the ways individuals feel, think, and act. The *DSM* does it this way for the simple reason that the ways individuals feel, think, and act are the things that we can most easily measure. In other words, disorders are descriptions of collections of symptoms that go together. Our fancy professional word for descriptions of the way that individuals feel, think, and act is a **phenotype**. So, the phenotype of an individual with PTSD is that they have intrusive thoughts about their traumas, nightmares, loss of interest in their usual activities, exaggerated startle response, difficulty concentrating, and so on.

Yet it is widely agreed that the phenotype (that is, the symptoms) is simply the outward manifestation of underlying neurobiology. Feelings, thoughts, and behaviors all are possible only through underlying neurobiological processes. In short, everything is neurobiological; we just don't know enough yet to describe the neurobiology, and the neurobiology is extremely difficult to measure. Many experts nevertheless believe that our future classification system ought to define problems based on neurobiology.

This is exactly what the NIMH is trying to do with a project launched in 2013 called the Research Domains Criteria project. RDoC, as it is otherwise known, has been the dream of many scientists from the early beginning of classification systems, but in 2009 it was the director of NIMH who finally formalized the effort. With the director and the resources of NIMH behind it, the group of RDoC supporters is loaded with heavy hitters and lots of federal funding. The aim is to produce new types of research studies that look way beyond the clusters of symptoms that go together and instead investigate the underlying neural circuits that produce those symptoms. The dream is that eventually there will be enough information to completely revamp the way we make diagnoses. RDoC supporters would like to see the language change from mental disorders to brain disorders. For example, instead of PTSD, there will be a hypoamygdala-hyperfrontal neural circuit disorder. I am making up a somewhat silly name, but you get the idea.

At this point, it is difficult to disagree on principle with the aim of the RDoC project. But there are far too little data at this point to know whether it will have any better payoff for patients than the current *DSM* system. Without a single neural circuit disorder identified so far, it is premature for the RDoC method to claim superiority. Also, I wouldn't hold your breath for this to happen. There have been too many failed promises in the past about how our researchers were going to unlock the secrets of the brain or that we are on the verge, yet again, of a new dawn of discovery. I don't expect anything near completion of RDoC in my lifetime.

Existential Criticism

Others have criticized the *DSM* system on a much broader scale. There is a vocal group of critics who are against diagnosing in general. They have made it clear that they believe too many people are given psychotropic medications, too many people are diagnosed with psychiatric disorders in general, and too many people are diagnosed with PTSD specifically.[3] These critics seem bent on persuading us that humans are healthier than we think they are and that we overpathologize their problems.

These critiques are embedded in a much larger view of mental health through the lenses of anthropological and sociological contexts. The best I can describe these concerns is that they seem to come from an existential stance that there is some law stating human beings ought to be healthy (my words, not theirs) rather than acknowledging the data indicating that humans often dysfunction. Within this twisted logic, these critics actually have some interesting points. For example, they have noted that these differences in people's brains that we call mental disorders may actually be helpful to the species' adaptability in the long run because they provide variations in ways to adapt. Their underlying concern seems to be more that psychiatry as a field has underestimated the robust healthiness of individuals and pathologized normal behaviors by calling them disorders. When these critics say that way too many people are diagnosed with disorders, however, I suspect they have rarely worked in a clinic and really have not known many patients with real suffering. I don't recognize what planet they are talking about. In my daily world, I see patients who are truly suffering, have trouble functioning, and need help.

Despite their clever points, they are in the same boat as the respected critics who pine for dimensional and neurobiological classification systems in that none of them have been able to propose a better system to replace the *DSM*. As a parent, you may feel confident that even though the way we diagnose PTSD is not perfect, it is the best system yet that we've been able to figure out and has withstood many challenges from the best of the critics.

2. Do We Give Patients Too Many Diagnoses?

When the *DSM-5* was published in 2013, there were ample critics who loudly warned that psychiatry was diagnosing too many normal people with disorders. The *Huffington Post*, for example, reported that the *DSM-5* was ballooning and contained over 300 disorders.[4] Many of these critics were very prominent in the field. Allen Frances, MD, who led the team that created the *DSM-IV*, the predecessor to the *DSM-5*, has been one of the loudest and most persistent critics of the *DSM-5*. Apparently, in his retirement he has had second thoughts about his work on the *DSM* system.

Dr. Frances gave a series of interviews and wrote a bunch of high-profile articles for the popular press to try to lead a revolt against the *DSM-5*. Dr. Frances blogged that too many diagnoses were being created and this was causing what he termed "diagnostic inflation."[5] He claimed the new *DSM-5* would "take psychiatry off a cliff."[6] As Frances realized his revolt was not working, he even wrote a book with the super-scary title *Saving Normal: An Insider's Revolt Against Out-of-Control Psychiatric Diagnosis, DSM-5, Big Pharma, and the Medicalization of Everyday Life.*[7]

Despite Dr. Frances's frightening misinformation, the number of disorders actually may have declined with the *DSM-5*. The *Washington Post* quoted one of the leaders of the *DSM-5* committees as saying that there were only 157 specific mental disorders,[8] not the over 300 reported in the *Huffington Post*. One doctor reported that the number of disorders had actually decreased from 172 in *DSM-IV* to 152 in *DSM-5*, but it was not reported exactly how he counted them.[9]

Unable to find a consistent answer, I counted the disorders in *DSM-5* myself. The confusion comes from all of the subtypes. When you count all of the secondary causes of disorders and severity subtypes, there are actually 468 listings. I will call them listings and not disorders in order to avoid confusion.

Of these 468 listings, 198 of them are subtypes. For example, bipolar is counted as a single disorder, but if you have bipolar with psychotic features, that is a subtype. Bipolar that is caused by a medication reaction is another subtype. Another variety of subtype is severity. Bipolar disorder can be present as three subtypes called mild, moderate, or severe. Much of the supposed increase in the number of disorders is due to the addition of subtypes and specifiers within disorders. If all these subtypes are counted as separate disorders, then there are seven different disorders, but it is really only one disorder. If one does not count the subtypes, the total number of unique disorders is much lower than the reports in the media.

Of these 468 listings, there are also seventy-three unspecified subtypes. When an individual does not meet all of the criteria for a disorder but is close, this is called an **unspecified subtype**.

Also, there are twelve listings due to medical conditions. For example, generalized anxiety disorder is the name of a common anxiety disorder, but there is an additional listing for generalized anxiety disorder due to another medical condition. Rather than count these as two different disorders, my method counts them as one. When all of the subtypes and medical conditions are ignored, instead of 468 disorders I end up with 177, but there are still more to whittle away.

There are forty different disorders for substance abuse. The reason for so many different substance abuse disorders is that there are so many different substances to abuse, and they all get their separate disorders. For example, alcohol, tobacco, cannabis, and opioids all get their own disorders. If I count these forty disorders as just one substance abuse disorder, then the final total is really only 138 disorders.

The initial *DSM* taxonomy, *DSM-I*, was published in 1952 and contained 102 disorders.[10] This number nearly doubled to 182 disorders with the *DSM-II* in 1968. The number grew again to 265 disorders in *DSM-III* in 1980, and then the numbers from the *DSM-I* nearly tripled to 297 disorders that were published in the *DSM-IV* in 1994.

My personal opinion is that there are not too many diagnoses. In fact, I think there are probably too few disorders in the *DSM-5*. My view is that the current estimate of the number of disorders is probably an underestimate and the current number is probably just a good start.

One of the arguments to support my opinion that there are probably too few diagnoses is that there are dozens of specialized centers in the brain—the amygdala, hippocampus, cingulate cortex, and prefrontal cortex, to name just a few. Each center has regulatory control of one or more aspects of brain function. There are multiple ways the function of each brain center could be abnormal. One way is through malfunction of neurotransmitters within those centers. There are dozens of neurotransmitters, and new ones are being discovered every year.

Neurotransmitters could be imbalanced because of genetic variations that impact their production, abnormalities in enzymes that degrade them in the synapses, abnormalities in receptors within cell membranes, and other conditions. Another way that brain centers could function abnormally is because of altered connections between brain centers. Each center probably has connections for communications with dozens of other brain centers. There are many ways the neural networks that form these communication channels could be disrupted during development.

Using simple principles of mathematic probability, we can see that if one, and only one, of those centers, neurotransmitters, or connections is abnormal, then by simple addition there are actually thousands of ways for things to go wrong. Next, if we allow that there are two ways for each and every entity to malfunction—by being either underactive or overactive—then the number of ways for things to go wrong doubles. To create a disorder, though, probably multiple facets have to go wrong at the same time. The number of unique ways in which multiple abnormalities could occur in combinations to create different outcomes is beyond billions of billions. Whether we use an estimate of three million diagnoses or three billion diagnoses, either estimate is much larger relative to the 138 different disorders in the *DSM-5*.

Critics of the *DSM-5* like to cite the principle of Occam's razor,[11] probably because it sounds like real wisdom and has a cool name. The critics say we ought to have fewer, not more, disorders simply because the principle of Occam's razor decrees that fewer explanations are better than more complicated explanations. What these critics do not understand is that the principle of Occam's razor is not that fewer explanations are better than complicated explanations. Rather, this principle is that the *simplest solution* is usually best. If there are thousands of ways for things to go wrong in the brain, then the simplest solution is probably that there are thousands of different diagnoses. In this case, the simplest solution is also the most complicated explanation. The simplest solution dictates more, not fewer, disorders.

To be clear, I am not saying that I believe there are three million or three billion different psychiatric diagnoses. I am saying the number of ways that things can wrong in the brain are much more complex than most experts seem to appreciate. When we still know so little about the brain, it may be just as crazy for an expert to claim there MUST be fewer than 300 disorders as it would be for someone to claim that there are three million disorders. We are still learning so much about the brain.

Looking at some real data, Ronald Kessler of Harvard University and colleagues published a study in 2008 that estimated that 46 percent of the U.S. population will meet the criteria for at least one *DSM-IV* disorder in their lifetimes.[12] That seems like pretty good data to support the idea that mental problems are pretty common.

3. Do We Need a New Diagnosis to Replace or Complement PTSD?

Much of the momentum for a new diagnosis comes from clinicians who have a special interest in what they call chronic interpersonal trauma. These clinicians apparently feel passionately that they need to advocate for victims of these types of trauma in order to get them special attention.

Judith Herman, MD, a psychiatrist from the Boston, Massachusetts, area who is affiliated with Harvard University, wrote a paper in 1992 that called for adopting a new disorder called complex PTSD.[13] Complex PTSD, according to Herman, applies only to victims who suffered prolonged and repeated trauma, such as concentration camps, prisons, coerced prostitution, or chronic childhood abuse. Herman, summarizing what some other experts believed, wrote that "the diagnostic concepts of the existing psychiatric canon, including simple PTSD, are not designed for survivors of prolonged, repeated trauma, and do not fit them well."[14]

The main justification for this new disorder, Herman stated, was that the current system (i.e., PTSD and comorbid disorders) did not capture the multitude of clinical symptoms in one disorder. Herman wanted to formally recognize a broader number of symptoms beyond what is used in PTSD. She created the myth that these types of patients show a "prodigious array of psychiatric symptoms."[15] Herman also claimed that repeated trauma victims show symptoms of problems in more fundamental and broad personality features. She called it "deformations of personality"[16] that occur by the altering of all "the structures of self—the image of the body, the internalized images of others, and the values and ideals that lend a sense of coherence and purpose."[17] She claimed explicitly that if the complex PTSD diagnosis were used, it would improve recognition and treatment for this group of victims.

Interestingly, Herman's paper provided absolutely no standardized data. It included not a single description of a real patient. Yet this paper has been cited 1,766 times,[18] and complex PTSD has become one of the most influential notions in the field. (Note: Complex PTSD is also called "disorder of extreme stress, not otherwise specified" in other publications.)

At about the same time that Herman's article appeared, changes were being considered for the *DSM-IV*. The planners of the *DSM-IV* decided to test complex PTSD to see if Herman and the others were right, and in 1994 they conducted an experiment. They used standardized interviews on adult survivors of sexual and/or physical abuse.[19] Interestingly, out of 118 adults who qualified for the complex PTSD diagnosis, 113 also qualified for PTSD. Because the PTSD diagnosis captured nearly all of those who would get this new complex PTSD diagnosis, the developers of the *DSM-IV* refused to include complex PTSD. In turned out that in terms of identifying this population with a diagnosis, the *DSM* actually did fit them well, and they were easily recognized.

The mythical new diagnosis of complex PTSD lost traction with the experts who were paying attention after the 1994 study. Herman's complex PTSD had been discussed primarily for adult patients; however, about ten years later a group tried to repackage complex PTSD by restricting it to children and adolescents and renaming it developmental trauma disorder. Bessel van der Kolk, MD, like Herman a psychiatrist from the Boston, Massachusetts, area, had been involved in the earlier attempts to popularize complex PTSD for adults. He wrote a paper in 2005 that called for adopting this so-called new disorder.[20] Recycling many of the same arguments that Herman had used for complex PTSD, van der Kolk claimed that children were being diagnosed with inadequate and misleading diagnoses from the *DSM-IV,* which led to them receiving the wrong treatments. Van der Kolk and colleagues appealed to the developers to include developmental trauma disorder in the *DSM-5.* Failing to provide the basic level of evidence for diagnostic validation such as case reports or standardized group data, developmental trauma disorder met the same fate as complex PTSD. Just as the developers of the *DSM-IV* refused to include complex PTSD as a new disorder, the developers of the *DSM-5* refused to include developmental trauma disorder as a new disorder.

While these proposed disorders have lost traction with many of the experts who pay attention to such things, they have actually gained traction with the majority of clinicians who practice out in the field. Herman, van der Kolk, and other leaders who have battled for a new disorder are heroes to many people in the field. They are viewed as visionary advocates for a disadvantaged and neglected group of patients. The problem, though, is that they approached the issue completely backwards. There may be a subgroup of persons who undergo particular types of traumatic experiences and develop a particularly unique set of symptoms and impairments. The way to demonstrate that, though, is to first publish case studies of individual patients who manifest all of these issues and to clearly demonstrate how they are different from patients who experienced different types of traumas. The next step would be to conduct well-designed group studies using standardized instruments to demonstrate how their traumatic experiences were different, how their symptoms are different, and how they respond to treatments differently. After those things have been shown, and only after those things have been shown, would it be responsible to claim that a new disorder needs to be recognized in the *DSM*. To claim that the disorder should be recognized prior to the collection of adequate data is not science, it is bare-naked, snake oil propaganda.

Another problem I have with Herman, van der Kolk, and the interpersonal trauma believers is that while they are viewed as visionary advocates for a disadvantaged and neglected group of patients, they do a disservice to the victims of all the other types of trauma. They try to elevate victims of interpersonal trauma to a higher platform of suffering, as though the victims of noninterpersonal trauma somehow have it easier. It appears quite patronizing to a victim of a motor vehicle accident who has debilitating PTSD that somehow his or her trauma is less important because it was a not a chronic interpersonal trauma.

The mythical diagnosis idea remains popular. Herman and van der Kolk have been quite successful in drawing attention to their proposed disorders. Despite the nearly complete lack of evidence for the disorders, many clinicians, researchers, and students in the field really like the idea. Indeed, even a respected body such as the National Center for PTSD includes a page on their website for complex PTSD.[21] Consumers who search on the internet for information about trauma reactions are very likely to run across these ideas. And worse, it is likely clinicians are telling patients that they have these nonexistent disorders.

The *DSM* Developers Should Be Saying, "You're Welcome."

Some very influential experts in the mental health field have tried their best to discredit the *DSM-5* diagnostic system, but nobody has been able to knock it off its perch. It is curious that the leaders of previous editions of the *DSM*—Dr. Spitzer, who spearheaded *DSM-III*, and Dr. Frances, who spearheaded *DSM-IV*—became some of the loudest critics. Perhaps they just like change for the sake of change and do not care in which direction it goes.

Nevertheless, lots of smart people have thought hard about classification for a long time, and as of this writing, the only viable classification system we have in the United States is the *DSM-5* (other countries have the *International Classification of Diseases-10*, which is very similar to the *DSM*). No dimensional classification system has been proposed. No neurobiological classification system has been proposed. Besides those facts, the *DSM* categorical system actually has a lot going for it.

One strength of the *DSM* system is that it has fueled an explosive growth in research since the *DSM-III* came out in 1980. Whether or not you like the categorical disorders in the *DSM*, it has created a reliable way to define the categories. This reliability has allowed researchers in different parts of the world to study the same disorders because they have a reliable way to define them. Prior to the *DSM-III* in 1980, there was no reliable system of identification. The *DSM-III* was like giving language to a baby.

Another strength of the *DSM* categorical approach, and the one I think might be the most important, is that it has allowed communication between doctors and patients and among all the people who are interested in the patients' lives, such as family members and teachers. The disorders have intuitive meanings that everyone can understand.

Baseball guru Bill James, the man who influenced the popular book *Moneyball*, which became a popular movie of the same name, realized that communication about complicated topics was hugely dependent on how we choose to package the information. James tried to find new ways to use all of the statistics that are generated from baseball games in order to determine who were really the best players to have on a team.

James realized that many of the statistics were useless for communication because they had no intuitive meaning to people. Some statistics, however, were very useful for communication because they possessed intuitive meanings that everyone could understand. James used the term "imagenumbers." Take, for instance, something as simple as a win/loss record. If a team has a record of twenty wins and zero losses, we know intuitively what that means. That is an awesomely good team. The number "20–0" is a good imagenumber; it conjures an image in our heads that we instantly understand. Next, take a .300 batting average in baseball. It's a bit of an odd metric, but for people who know anything about baseball, a .300 or higher batter is exceptionally good. A .275 batter is average. A .250 batter is on the weak side, and a .200 hitter will not last long in the majors. Those numbers create instant images of specific players in our minds and specific levels of quality and are therefore good imagenumbers.

A psychiatric disorder is like an imagenumber. When someone says that an individual has depression, this creates an instant image in our heads of what that looks like. A disorder, however, is not a number, so it could be called instead an imagename. If we were to adopt a dimensional classification system instead of the categorical *DSM* classification system, we would probably lose much of the intuitive communication we have with the *DSM* system. It is extremely difficult to imagine that dimensional syndromes or neural circuit disorders will be useful imagenames. Can you imagine a picture of a hypoamygdala-hyperprefrontal cortex disorder? Many people do not even know they have an amygdala.

Another strength of the *DSM* categorical approach is that it fits neatly with the way clinicians have to get paid for services by insurance companies. Patients want to be able to use their insurance to pay for their mental health services, so mental health providers need a way to communicate with insurance companies. The *DSM* gives them a common language to use so that fees can be exchanged for specific types of services.

What the *DSM* was intended to do, it has done very well. Criticizing the *DSM* for not being everything to all people is like criticizing a car because it cannot fly. In retrospect, the *DSM* has given us a way to communicate about psychiatric problems like we had never had before. That is no small feat. Thank you, *DSM*.

Recap

- Critics have had many negative things to say about the way we diagnose individuals with the *DSM-5* classification system. Despite the inherent problems of trying to classify something as complex as problems of the human brain, the *DSM* system actually does well on a number of fronts and has been quite productive for research, clinical practice, and communication. Further, no competing classification system exists as a viable alternative.

For Parents to Do

- The *DSM-5* is not well suited for every purpose that every critic would like, but it is the best we have, and it actually has pretty good strengths going for it. Someday the dream for a different classification system may be a reality, but I wouldn't bet on it, and I'm not sure I would want it to replace the *DSM*. If you are dissatisfied with the way psychiatric diagnoses have been given to your children, this knowledge may give you some peace of mind to recalibrate your expectations. The current categorical system has weaknesses of an inability to explain the reasons for comorbidity and taking no consideration of underlying neural circuits. But it has strengths of providing labels for clear and reliable communication, a system for insurance reimbursement, and a basis for systematic research.

Chapter Nine
Blame the Mother

If you are parents with children who are suffering from traumatic experiences, you will likely be blamed for your children's problems. Indeed, you will likely blame yourselves. There is a long and wretched history of it.

Wanda and the Unabomber

From 1978 to 1995, a person known as the Unabomber placed a series of homemade bombs in a random pattern around the United States. Sixteen booby-trapped bombs killed three people and wounded twenty-three others. These events became even more infamous because the Unabomber mailed lengthy manifesto letters to newspapers. Was the Unabomber an intelligent and crafty modern terrorist who was part of a secret organization with bigger plans? Or was the bomber a lone psychopath who just wanted to see the world burn?

In 1996, after one of the most famous manhunts in history, police captured a dirty, unkempt, strange, and lonely man in the woods outside Lincoln, Montana. Theodore Kaczynski, the Unabomber, was fifty-three years old. He was living in a crude log cabin in the remote wilds with no running water and no electricity. Who was this monster, and how had he been created?

Having few other causes to blame, some of those in the media speculated about what they thought they knew best. A prominent theory was that he must have had bad parenting. A 1996 *Newsweek* magazine cover story recreated "how a troubled boy turned into a dangerous man."[1] The "first clue" occurred when Kaczynski was only six months old. Reportedly, Kaczynski was hospitalized for an allergic reaction to a medicine he was taking. Because he had to be isolated in a hospital room, he was denied the comfort of his parents for several weeks. It was reported that the baby's personality instantly changed. This incident was also noted in the court-ordered psychiatric examination from 1998. "Information provided by Wanda Kaczynski [his mother], however, indicates her perception that his hospitalization was a significant and traumatic event for her son, in that he experienced a separation from his mother (due to routine hospital practices). She describes him as having changed after the hospitalization in that he was withdrawn, less responsive, and more fearful of separation from her after that point in time."

The second "blow," according to the *Newsweek* article, occurred when he was seven years old and his younger brother, David, was born. An aunt told a newspaper that young Ted became less snuggly, perhaps because the adults paid too much attention to the new baby. This sibling rivalry soon "would become a curse." The psychiatric examination that was conducted after he was caught, however, revealed little evidence of a bitter sibling rivalry.

The third damning event allegedly was his mother's parenting. "The Kaczynskis, particularly Wanda, demanded academic excellence. While other children played around the neighborhood, Wanda sat with Teddy on the porch reading *Scientific American*. She also kept a meticulous journal of his development." While he excelled academically in high school classes that were too easy for him, "his social skills lagged behind." That was the extent of the evidence against Wanda Kaczynski—she sat on the porch with her son and read *Scientific American*.

At age thirty-five, Kaczynski got a job in a plant where his father and brother worked, but it didn't last long. He was fired by his supervisor, who happened to be his younger brother. It was around this time, as the court-ordered psychiatric examination reported, that Kaczynski realized he was willing to kill to provide relief from his own despair and suicidal thoughts. Having never been in trouble with the law except for one traffic ticket, he began making and delivering bombs. The *Newsweek* article had a clear theory. His mother seemed partly to blame. The theory was that his demanding, cold, insensitive mother helped to create this dysfunctional, despairing, and suicidal killer.

However, there was a spectacular problem of logic about that theory. The problem was that he had a younger brother who had been raised by the same mother and who was quite normal. This brother was well-adjusted, was married, and eventually became a social worker. This brother was in fact the one who had turned Ted in to the FBI.

Psychiatric Disorders

One of the dark sides of the history of psychiatry is that parents have been blamed for their children's problems since psychiatry has existed as a profession. Leo Kanner, MD, widely considered to be the first physician in the world to be called a child psychiatrist, was a giant in the new field of child psychiatry in the early twentieth century. He founded the first child psychiatry department at Johns Hopkins University in 1930 and published the first English-language textbook on child psychiatry in 1935. He is best known for his paper that was credited with being the first description of autism in 1943.[2]

Kanner's commentary in that famous 1943 paper speculated that the cause of autism was a mix of parenting and genetics, but he did not dwell at that time on the subject of what caused autism. By 1949, however, Kanner felt confident enough to have a stronger opinion about parenting. He wrote a follow-up paper in which he suggested that autism was due to a lack of maternal warmth. He observed that children were exposed from "the beginning to parental coldness, obsessiveness, and a mechanical type of attention to material needs only . . . They were left neatly in refrigerators which did not defrost. Their withdrawal seems to be an act of turning away from such a situation to seek comfort in solitude."[3]

Recently, others have come to Kanner's defense to explain that Kanner never meant to blame parents for autism and that Kanner went out of his way later in life to not blame parents.[4] Perhaps, but in 1949 Kanner wrote clearly enough that he does indeed need defending.

Kanner was known for coining the famous phrase "refrigerator mother," but it was Bruno Bettelheim who did the most to make it popular. Bettelheim, a self-taught psychologist at the University of Chicago, also made contributions to the early growth of child psychiatry. For many years, Bettelheim was well regarded, known perhaps mostly for his writings that interpreted children's fairy tales in terms of Freudian concepts. Bettelheim seemed to acknowledge that there was a genetic component to autism, but strongly believed autism was largely caused when mothers withheld affection from their children. In his 1967 book *The Empty Fortress*, highly regarded at the time, Bettelheim expressed his opinion that autism was not simply present at birth when he wrote, "My own belief, as presented throughout this book, is that autism has essentially to do with everything that happens from birth on."[5] He directly attributed those events "from birth on" to poorly responsive mothers: "If things go wrong because such anticipatory behavior is not met by an appropriate response in the mother, the relation of the infant to his environment may become deviant from the very beginning of life."[6]

Bettelheim was widely discredited after his death, but not because of his promotion of mother blaming. He was accused of misrepresenting his credentials,[7] plagiarizing material for his book,[8] and reportedly beating his former child patients.[9]

Theories about blaming mothers did not stay confined to autism. Schizophrenia is one of the most debilitating illnesses of the brain. Patients with schizophrenia are often paranoid, see strange and terrifying hallucinations, and hear voices that are often threatening and violent. Patients with schizophrenia also usually have profound impairments to smooth personal interaction with other humans. They frequently end up unable to hold jobs, and require assistance and supervision with living.

Unable to understand what caused schizophrenia, early theories blamed the parents. A prominent advocate of environmental causes of schizophrenia was Theodore Lidz, MD. Dr. Lidz did his residency training at the Johns Hopkins department that was founded by Leo Kanner, and then took a job on the faculty of Yale University. Dr. Lidz summarized his beliefs in his 1965 book titled *Schizophrenia and the Family*. In that book, Lidz and his two coauthors frequently referred to the concept of "schizophrenogenic mothers" as "seriously disturbed and strange women" who caused schizophrenia in their children.[10]

One subtype of the schizophrenogenic mother in Lidz and colleagues' book allegedly worked out her own psychological problems from her frustrated life by treating "the child as an extension of herself, intruding but impervious to the child's needs and wishes as a separate individual." Another subtype "fitted the category of the 'rejecting' mother who did not and could not 'cathect' the child, a factor which has been described as causative of schizophrenia."[11] The term *cathect*, now rarely used in psychological writings, meant to show emotional responsiveness, warmth, or bonding.

These theories that severe mental disorders were the product of mothers who were cold and rejecting, resulting in a failure to bond with their children, were widely believed through the 1950s and 1960s. The theories that mothers caused autism and schizophrenia have since been discredited as we have learned more about genetic contributions to mental problems and the resilience of children who experience insensitive parenting. But the blame-the-mother theory keeps finding new homes.

As the examples of the Unabomber, autism, and schizophrenia show, there are spectacular problems of logic in blaming mothers. Spectacular problems of logic do not, however, carry much weight against strongly held beliefs. The theory that cold parents cause autism and schizophrenia may have lost its sizzle, but the blame-the-mother theory has moved on to other disorders and lives on as strong as ever.

Posttraumatic Stress Disorder

The blame-the-mother theory has also found a comfortable home with researchers who study PTSD. I read lots of papers and review lots of research grant proposals on PTSD by the best researchers in the world who apply for funding from government agencies. It is easy to find examples of mother blaming. To pick just one example from 2013, the author of a grant proposal stated, "[P]arental PTSD has been found to substantially contribute to the development and maintenance of trauma symptoms in children." If the author had said "associate with" instead of "contribute," it would have been right. By using "contribute," the author clearly meant to say that parents *cause* problems in their children, but there are actually very few data to support that belief, as I will describe later.

What Is It Like to Feel Blamed for Your Children's Problems?

If parents exhibit any features that could lead clinicians to perceive them as lacking warmth or sensitivity (as the clinicians define it), these parents have a big red bull's-eye on their backs and they do not even know it.

I will get to the data on parenting shortly, but it is important first to understand the problem from the family's point of view. It is one thing to sift through research papers and conclude that there is a big problem with blaming the parents for children's PTSD symptoms. It is another thing to try to stand in the shoes of those parents, usually mothers, who have sat in the chairs in the offices of clinicians and been blamed and feel the nauseating horror they must feel about being blamed.

Raising a child is the most special and transformative event in people's lives. If you cannot understand that notion, it is probably because you have not raised your own child, and you really have no idea what it is like to be a parent. Nothing makes parents happier than to see their children happy. Nothing makes parents more frustrated than to see their children struggling. Parents sacrifice constantly for the safety of their children. Parents would sacrifice their lives to protect their children. Imagine, then, seeking help from mental health experts who suggest that parents caused their children's psychiatric problems.

Case in point: Cheryl had to convince her husband over a period of three years that they needed to take their daughter to see a clinician. Their daughter, Catherine, was thirteen years old, and had PTSD caused by a dog attack. Three years earlier, the family had visited the mother's sister. During a visit to a nearby park, the aunt's large dog, without warning, pounced on Catherine and latched its jaws around her skull. The adults eventually overpowered the dog and forced it to remove its grip. Catherine required many stitches and one plastic surgery to graft skin. She immediately developed PTSD. In addition, as is common with children, she developed separation anxiety. She followed her parents around the house, and one of her parents had to sleep next to her through the night.

After the father finally agreed to take Catherine to a therapist, they met with the therapist for an evaluation session before starting the counseling sessions. During the evaluation, the therapist interviewed the parents without Catherine in the room. The therapist gave the parents the impression that she believed the parents were coddling Catherine. The therapist asked about their practice of sleeping with Catherine. As the mother was the parent who usually slept with Catherine, the therapist pointed this question directly at Cheryl. The therapist did not ask Cheryl how this sleeping arrangement helped reduce Catherine's feelings of terror and helped the parents feel rested enough to function during the days. Instead, the therapist asked Cheryl, with a disapproving attitude, what her plan was for how Catherine was going to learn to sleep on her own someday.

The therapist asked the parents if they had tried to take Catherine around dogs after the attack to try to desensitize her. The way the therapist phrased the question struck both parents as odd. The question was not asking if the parents had taken Catherine around dogs to see whether she was still scared of dogs or not. The question was phrased to imply that the parents had failed to do something that might have helped Catherine. It felt quite clearly to the parents that the therapist believed the parents were feeding into Catherine's fears and making them worse.

Once therapy started, the therapist took Catherine alone with her into the therapy room. At most sessions she did not meet with the parents before or after. Periodically, she would talk to the parents briefly at the end of sessions to ask them why they hadn't tried this or that. The lack of involvement and the blaming attitude from the therapist made Cheryl feel like she was treated as the problem instead of part of the solution.

The mother already felt guilty because she had not protected her daughter from the dog. Cheryl had had misgivings about going to the park with the aunt's large dog, but she had not said anything because she did not want to offend her sister. Now, as the therapist implied that Cheryl's parenting had failed, it was like pouring salt into a wound.

I saw Cheryl and her daughter after they left that therapist, and I asked Cheryl what their experience had been like with the therapist and why they left. In addition to Catherine not getting any better, Cheryl said that the therapist failed to include her and her husband in the treatment, and when she did include them in the therapy sessions it seemed only to be to tell the parents what they were doing wrong.

I asked, "Did you feel like you were being blamed?"

"Yes, I did. But I didn't want to say anything because I thought she was doing some good things with Catherine and I didn't want to, you know, sour that relationship. I just kind of didn't tell her those things anymore."

I replied, "You didn't feel like you could trust her, huh?"

"Yes, exactly. Catherine liked her, and so I just kind of went along. Plus, you know, I was worried that if she already held those kinds of opinions, if I argued with her about it, she might get defensive and think even more negatively about me, and I didn't want her taking that attitude back in her sessions alone with Catherine. I mean, who knew what she was telling Catherine about me and her father? I don't have any evidence that she did, but naturally, you know, that's the sort of thing you worry about after she already made it clear she thought I was part of the problem."

As Cheryl's comments indicated, the resentment parents feel due to being blamed is not just from the things that are said and done to them, it is also from the things that are hinted at and implied. Parents are not idiots. When they are treated in a patronizing fashion and with a disapproving tone, they get the message loud and clear.

I can easily imagine that when mothers feel blamed by clinicians for their children's problems, they feel stabbed in the back. This would put a chill on their relationship with the clinicians, and they would feel like removing their children from these clinicians and moving to new clinicians. The mothers are likely to keep bringing their children to these clinicians, however, because it would be difficult and more expensive to start over with new clinicians.

Even if the mothers wanted to leave and find new clinicians, where would they go? It is likely that the next clinician holds the same misconceptions about parents as the first clinician. In many parts of the country, it might be difficult to even find other clinicians. No, the mothers will rarely leave these clinicians. The mothers keep coming back to these clinicians because they have neither choices nor ways to find better clinicians. But the mothers would likely begin to withhold from the clinicians details that they think the clinicians might use against them. They would likely paint the accounts of how things happened at home in more positive ways in order to keep the clinicians off their backs. The mothers would be correctly wondering, *What else are those clinicians saying to my children when I am not in the room?* They would also correctly wonder, *What treatment techniques are those clinicians not pursuing that could help the children because they are too focused on blaming me?* The clinicians appear to resemble the classic case of a homicide detective who has made up his mind on who he thinks is the killer and spends all his time building a case on the suspected killer, and never spends time pursuing leads on other potential killers. At best, even if their children improve with the treatment, the mothers are left with a negative impression of our profession.

Blame-the-Mother Theories

What exactly is the blame-the-mother theory? The blame-the-mother theory for PTSD has two main forms depending on where the mothers supposedly act on their children's symptoms. The first form of the theory states that insensitive parenting acts at the very onset of children's symptoms and thereby directly causes their PTSD symptoms. That is, children would not develop certain PTSD symptoms, or wouldn't develop them as severely, were it not for insensitive parenting.

The second form of the blame-the-mother theory says that insensitive parenting acts later in the process and prevents children's symptoms from getting better. The first form says that parents cause symptoms, whereas the second form says the symptoms were caused by other factors but parents prevent the symptoms from getting better.

How do mothers allegedly cause problems in their children? The theory is that mothers who are insensitive and lack warmth cause problems in their children's capacities for emotion regulation, which then leads to psychiatric disorders in the children. The following are two examples of how mothers supposedly wield their tremendous power.

Yvonne: A Therapist Encounters a Mother Who Is Mad

Yvonne and her mother are one case in point. Yvonne had been raped by her father, the mother's husband. She had severe PTSD, and on top of that argued with her mother and often refused to listen to her. It drove her mother crazy that Yvonne refused to keep her room clean. Yvonne, thirteen years old when she began CBT treatment in one of my research studies at Tulane, refused to make the slightest attempt to clean her room or do other chores. Yvonne's mother seemed more concerned about these chores than about the bigger picture that Yvonne was emotionally distressed and had intrusive memories about being raped. The mother was determined "not to lose her to this event." She wanted her child to overcome what happened to her by acting as though everything were normal.

From the very first assessment session, the therapist wondered to herself, *How could the mother not have known that Yvonne was being molested by the father?* The mother had been suspicious from the start because she had told Yvonne to make sure she wore pajamas when she slept at her father's house. During visits, the mother knew the father made Yvonne sleep in his bed with him. Yvonne had complained about a burning feeling in her pelvic area for months, but the mom's first thought was a bladder problem. Yvonne had not told her mother about the rapes because, as usual, the man threatened to kill the girl and her mother if she told.

Once the rapes were discovered, her mother's first reaction was to be mad at her daughter for not protecting herself. She was mad at her daughter for still being upset about it. She was mad that this made her job as a mother more difficult. She was mad because her own father had molested her. She was mad at herself for letting her father molest her as a child. She was also probably mad at herself for not handling all of the above very well. Not able to be more flexible with her daughter, she was impatient. This made her appear insensitive, but did that make Yvonne's PTSD symptoms worse?

To figure out whether her mother's insensitivity made Yvonne's PTSD symptoms worse is a bit of a chicken-or-egg problem. My research team was not involved with Yvonne either before the rapes or during the early days when symptoms were developing, so I do not have the data to tell me whether Yvonne's symptoms developed first or her mother acted insensitively first.

The idea that Yvonne's mother made Yvonne's PTSD symptoms worse is only one of several possible theories. It is also possible that Yvonne's PTSD symptoms made her mother distressed and more insensitive. It is also possible that Yvonne's PTSD symptoms developed because of genetic reasons and the symptoms would have developed no matter how her mother acted. Yet, like the homicide detective who focuses his investigation on only one suspected killer, clinicians tend to think only of the blame-the-mother theory.

Lena: A Mother Afraid of Losing

The following case describes a mother who has trouble protecting herself and her daughter from abusive men. Lena witnessed domestic violence by her father against her mother. Lena, eight years old at the time, was seen in one of our studies at Tulane University. She was terrified of her father, and she had made it clear that she never wanted to speak to or see her father again. Lena's mother honored Lena's wish temporarily. Lena was treated with CBT in our study. By the fifth session of CBT therapy, it was very close to Father's Day. Lena's mother insisted that because Lena's PTSD symptoms had been improving, she had to visit her father on Father's Day.

Lena's mother said, "It would hurt his feelings more if she didn't see him."

When asked by the therapist if she thought this would hurt Lena's feelings, the mother said, "I don't think it would bother her."

Perhaps in recognition of how little sense this made, the mother went on to explain her real reason: "If she's allowed to not visit her father, what about Mother's Day and she doesn't want to see me?"

After the Father's Day visit with her father, Lena's PTSD symptoms became more severe. Listening to Lena talk about her distress and listening to the mother's neediness made the therapist's blood boil. It is in the bones of therapists to want to do something to help. There must be a reason that Lena was not getting better. There must be something to do. There must be someone to blame. Perhaps that reason was Lena's mother. The mother seemed more concerned about her own feelings than the child's feelings.

In our supervision and team meetings, the therapist made it clear that she believed the mother caused Lena's symptoms and that the mother was preventing Lena's symptoms from getting better. When I asked the therapist how she could be so certain to blame the mother, the therapist said her intuition told her so, replying, "Isn't it obvious?"

The Research Data: The Correlation

Is it really that obvious? In 2001, I wrote a review paper with my coauthor in which we were the first ones to summarize all of the studies that had assessed traumatized children and their parents. We found a total of seventeen studies. We learned that in sixteen out of the seventeen studies, researchers had discovered that the children who had the most severe symptoms had parents and families with more severe problems.[12]

We had expected to find such a pattern, but we did not expect it to be that consistent. In the complex world of psychiatry, finding the same correlation in sixteen out of seventeen studies is like a horse winning the Triple Crown. It happens, but not very often. Thus, the correlation between children having lots of PTSD symptoms and their parents having lots of their own problems is one of the most predictable findings in all of child psychiatry.

The types of problems parents possessed included their own PTSD symptoms, depression, and high levels of marital conflict. This makes it pretty clear that the best predictor of which children will have the most severe problems is the correlated finding of parents with more severe problems of their own. This would seem to be the research data needed to support the blame-the-mother theory. Most mental health professionals, if not nearly all, would look at that consistent pattern of findings and conclude that those distressed parents must be causing their children's problems, or at the very least, making their children's problems worse.

But, as the famous saying goes, "Correlation is not causation." Just because children with problems have parents with problems does not mean that parents caused the children's problems. There are two major flaws with all seventeen of those studies. One major flaw is that both children and parents were assessed at just one point in time, well after everybody's problems had developed. These are what we call **cross-sectional studies**. Because cross-sectional studies cannot tell us what the children or parents were like before the children's problems developed, these studies simply cannot explain *how* the children's problems developed. We have a chicken-or- egg problem.

The second major flaw of those seventeen studies is that none of them actually measured any type of parenting behaviors. The researchers in those studies never asked the parents or children and never observed the parents with their children to see if the parents were cold and insensitive. Those parents with PTSD and depression symptoms and marital problems could have been warm, sensitive parents.

In our 2001 paper, we offered several theories that could explain this correlation. One of the theories was the traditional blame-the-mother theory: Children initially develop PTSD symptoms because of the traumatic events, but parenting that is cold and insensitive makes the symptoms worse.

A second theory we offered to explain the correlation was that children could develop PTSD without ever having experienced or witnessed actual traumatic events, but they learned about them vicariously through family stories. For example, we cited a case that was published by Lenore Terr about a younger sister who believed that she had seen her older sister injured in a swimming pool accident when in fact she had never seen it.[13] The younger sister had only heard about the accident from family conversations within the home. In this theory, though, we expanded a bit from Terr to suggest that the parents were traumatized by their own traumas, which somehow affected their parenting, which somehow caused the children to feel that they had also been traumatized, which caused the children to develop PTSD symptoms. So this, too, was a version of a blame-the-mother theory, and we called this the **vicarious traumatization effect**.

A third theory we offered was a combination of the blame-the-mother theory and the vicarious traumatization effect. That is, the children experienced their own traumas and the parents experienced their own, separate traumas. The direct exposure to trauma, hearing about family stories of trauma, and insensitive parenting all combined to cause the children's PTSD symptoms.

We also added a fourth theory to explain the correlation. To take a direct quote from our paper, "Lastly, genetic factors cannot be ruled out yet as explanatory factors for the association between parental and child symptoms. The fact that children and parents in the same families show elevated post-traumatic symptoms may be due to a shared genetic vulnerability rather than parent-child dynamics."[14]

As a young, naïve investigator at the time, I added this fourth genetic theory almost as an afterthought. Whenever other researchers cite my paper, they never mention this theory. I now believe the genetic theory is the one that seems to be supported the best by the data, and if I were to write that paper again today, I would give the genetic theory much more attention.

The first three theories were the theories that were emphasized in our article, and they were all variations of blame-the-mother theories. I believe those blame-the-mother theories now to be almost entirely wrong. In my own defense, we had made it clear back then that these were just theories. We proposed these theories for the purpose of "generating testable research hypotheses."[15] I am somewhat comforted when I reread that paper now to see that we were careful to state that "the identification of an association between parent and child outcomes is not sufficient to proclaim a causal association between parent and child."[16]

The "Imply-Suggest-and-Hint" Problem

I say, however, that we were only somewhat careful. We knew those seventeen studies could not prove a causal association with parenting because they were cross-sectional designs and they did not assess actual parenting behaviors, but we did not put a lot of effort into persuading the readers of this. While we did include one single, clear sentence stating that the correlation "is not sufficient to proclaim a causal association between parent and child," we included only that one lonely sentence. In contrast, more sentences were devoted to implying, suggesting, and hinting that there probably was a causal association with parenting. This is an important point worth emphasizing for parents who try to sift through the scientific literature on their own. Scientific articles can be truthful in the technical presentation of facts but can be extremely biased at the same time in how those facts are discussed.

A typical mental health research article is about 5,000 words. Of those 5,000 words, about 1,500 have to be allocated to cut-and-dried descriptions of the research methods and the results, and the other 3,500 can be allocated to background information and discussion of the results wherein the authors have discretion to convey their personal biases. Within those 3,500 words, authors can write balanced arguments that describe the pros and cons of both sides of the argument. Instead, what happens probably 99 percent of the time is that authors use that space to repeatedly imply, suggest, and hint that one attention-getting interpretation of the facts is the one they want us to believe.

Here is an example. A group of investigators at Kent State University published a review article in 2012 that was very similar to the review article I published in 2001. That is, they summarized the published studies that had examined the relationship between children's PTSD symptoms and parental PTSD or depression symptoms.[17] The Kent State group conducted a more rigorous test than I did; they conducted a statistical meta-analysis. They also had more studies to review because they conducted their review eleven years after mine. From their examination of thirty-five studies, they found, as expected, a strong correlation between parents' post-traumatic symptoms and children's post-traumatic symptoms.

On the one hand, the Kent State article is an excellent example of careful and systematic techniques to analyze data. In the first paragraph of the discussion section, they adopted a fairly balanced interpretation with only a trace of bias toward blaming parents:

> Several mechanisms may explain the association between parent post-traumatic distress and child PTSS including the following: a shared genetic diathesis . . . modeling and reinforcement of anxious or avoidant behaviors by parents . . . and decreased positive parent-child interactions.[18]

That sentence, sadly, was the last mention of any possible genetic explanation. The authors used many more sentences to imply, suggest, and hint that parents caused their children's PTSD symptoms. In the final paragraph of the paper, for example, which is where many readers often skip to to get the gist of the article, the authors concluded:

> Despite these limitations, the current findings highlight a need to expand current assessment models of child PTSS to include the influence of parent post-traumatic distress and depression. Clinically, these results suggest a family-focused approach to the treatment of child PTSS after a trauma. Failure to address parental, primarily maternal, post-traumatic stress may hinder PTSD treatment in child trauma victims.[19]

The statistical correlation between parent and child symptoms had magically become a causation of children's PTSD symptoms. The authors wrote unambiguously that there was an "influence" from the parents toward the children. Even worse, while the meta-analysis had nothing whatsoever to do with analyzing treatment studies, the authors felt compelled to conclude that treatment for children needed to focus on the parents! And if you dare to ignore this advice to focus on the parents, your ignorance "may hinder" the treatment of these unfortunate child victims. With that type of not-so-subtle shift of language and unchallenged leaps from assessment to treatment, we get a dramatic blame-the-mother finale. In other words, "Hey, pay attention to this!" By the sheer weight of these repetitive hints and suggestions that parenting has a causal effect on children's PTSD symptoms, the article conveys the overall impression that the results must support a model in which parenting causes children's problems.

There is a saying about those who spread propaganda: If you repeat a lie enough, people think it's true. Also, there is the maxim of the news business: "If it bleeds, it leads," meaning if you make it sound scary enough, people will pay attention. But these sayings describe only what some researchers are doing; they do not quite explain why the researchers want the theory to be true or why they want people to pay attention.

Why Do They Do This?

Consumers who are outside the mental health industry might be wondering, "Why do researchers write articles that are so biased?" We can understand the "if it bleeds, it leads" business mentality of publishers and editors who have to sell their journals, but I think the researchers really believe what they write.

The answers go deep into the problems of intuition, bias, and why people want to believe certain things about the world. Most people hold personal beliefs that parenting can permanently shape and mold the development of children. These beliefs lead them to pay attention to only the data that confirm their personal beliefs and to ignore any data that might disconfirm their beliefs. Psychologists have coined a term for this, and it is called **confirmation bias**.

One of my goals in writing this book is to help consumers understand that confirmation bias is happening everywhere, all the time, even with caring clinicians who believe in their hearts that they are objectively trying to help children. The root of the confirmation bias for blaming mothers comes directly from our beliefs about normal child development.

Normal Child Development

Normal child development is the natural biological, psychological, and emotional changes that occur in stages throughout childhood. These changes occur on a predictable schedule, so predictable that pediatricians can track whether children reach developmental milestones on schedule by following a development chart. The major domains of development are generally agreed to be physical (learning to sit and to walk, and eye-hand coordination), cognitive (understanding language, speaking language, and overall intellectual function), and psychosocial (ability to interact and get along with others, and learning to express and manage different emotions).

Nearly everyone, it seems, believes that parents can have a major influence on how children develop normally—at least, nearly everyone I have known and whose works I have read, which admittedly is limited to North American and European countries. We, as a species, seem to want to believe that our experiences can make us who we are, and that for children, the experience of being parented is one of those major influences.

This belief is widespread in all walks of life, and it is easy to find. It can be found in biographies of famous people in which profound personality patterns are attributed to seminal childhood events. For example, in the brief biography of actor Kevin Costner on the Internet Movie Database, it was said of him: "His father's job required him to move regularly, which caused Kevin to feel like an Army kid, always the new kid at school, which led to him being a daydreamer."[20] Note the explicit attributions in that sentence that his father's parenting "caused" a feeling in Mr. Costner, which then "led" to a permanent personality characteristic.

Famous people even make the attributions themselves. The American president Abraham Lincoln was quoted as saying, "All that I am or ever hope to be, I owe to my angel mother." I think it is safe to assume that Mr.

Lincoln meant it was not his mother's genetic material that she passed on to him in her reproductive egg, but it was his mother's parenting behaviors to which he owed everything. That would be amazing if we were to take it literally.

Psychologists who specialize in normal child development share this belief, too. A typical illustration of this belief comes from a college textbook titled *Child Psychology: A Handbook of Contemporary Issues*:

> Overall, research on how families influence children's social development has shown that the quality of relationships within the system is of critical importance. Parents (i.e., primarily mothers) characterized as low in responsivity and sensitivity and high in control, intrusiveness, and harshness have children who are less socially competent.[21]

The general beliefs about the importance of parenting are clearly enormously strong. Talking about parenting is like talking about one of the "big beliefs" of human societies—race, religion, politics, or sex. Everyone, no matter their training or station in life, holds their own deep-rooted beliefs. The prevailing belief among both experts and parents is that parents have a powerful influence on their children's normal development and future personalities. The belief is so strong within most people that to claim otherwise amounts to radical heresy.

Because experts and parents believe parenting has powerful impacts on normal development and personality, it is natural that they also believe parenting causes psychiatric problems in children. The logic is straightforward: Good parenting causes good kids; bad parenting causes psychological problems.

Among the various constructs of social-emotional development, emotion regulation has been considered the keystone development in the early years of life, and maternal sensitivity in parent-child interactions has been viewed as the essential driver for the development of good emotion regulation in children. The natural extension of this belief is that poor emotion regulation caused by lack of parental sensitivity leads to psychiatric disorders in children. According to this lockstep chain of reasoning based on experts' beliefs about parenting, everything essentially boils down to the impact of parental warmth and sensitivity on children's emotional regulation skills.

In the Shoes of Therapists

When clinicians and researchers turn their attention from normal child development to children who are being treated by mental health professionals, it is an easy step to move from believing that parents shape normal development to believing that parents cause psychological problems in their children. Turning blame onto parents is attractive to clinicians because parent-child relationships are things that therapists know how to explore. Parent-child relationship problems are problems therapists think they can do something about; these problems have behaviors and feelings attached to them and those are things clinicians know how to talk about. Those problems are something that can make therapists feel like they are doing *something*.

Therapists want to be helpful, and it makes therapists feel better about themselves if they can do something *now* rather than wait. When they want to be helpful, they listen for things that could be causing the patients' distress. When they listen to stories of parents who are insensitive or too sensitive, their clinical intuition tells them that bad parenting must be a problem they can help with. When their clinical intuition tells them that parenting must be a cause of the children's symptoms, they sometimes tell parents to change their behaviors. The parents feel blamed because, well, they *are* being blamed.

The biggest reason I believe therapists blame mothers is what I call the "maximized benefits" problem, which is a constant problem in any type of business that involves repairs or renovation. Let's start with a hypothetical situation in which the owner of a car hears a noise coming from the front right side of the car that occurs only when stopping. At the first repair shop, a mechanic says he cannot find anything wrong with any of the parts, but he can replace the brakes for $500 and that might fix the noise. So the owner takes the car to a second mechanic at another repair shop. The second mechanic says he also cannot find anything wrong with any of the parts, and he suggests doing nothing and just monitoring the noise for a while. The second mechanic understands that the services he has to offer cannot properly address the problem he has been presented with. His inspection of the car's parts maximizes the benefits that he has to offer. To offer any further services beyond the inspection is probably charging the owner for inappropriate services.

When children are not getting better in therapy and the services that therapists have to offer are not helping, therapists have two choices. Like the first mechanic, they can say that they can try different things and charge you for it. Or, like the second mechanic, they can say that maybe there is no fix for the problem right now and the children have maximized the benefits from psychotherapy with this particular therapist.

It is extremely difficult for therapists to tell families there is no fix for the problem right now and that children may have maximized their benefits from psychotherapy. Therapists are at an extreme disadvantage in this situation because the fields of psychiatry and psychology tend to have a severe case of the Rodney Dangerfield syndrome. Rodney Dangerfied was a legendary comedian whose most famous line was "I don't get no respect." Because of the highly interpersonal nature of the business of therapists, that is, the constant face-to-face interaction with patients, therapists very much want the respect of patients in order to do their job. Yet, for a variety of reasons, psychiatrists and psychologists are not as well respected as professionals in other medical specialties such as surgeons and cancer specialists. Due to these types of factors, it can be quite difficult for therapists to tell patients they have maximized the benefits of psychotherapy, and their symptoms may not improve much more, which is essentially telling patients that there is nothing they can do to help them.

Because of widespread, strong beliefs that good parenting influences normal development and bad parenting causes psychiatric problems, and because of the reluctance to acknowledge when maximum benefits have been reached, perhaps nothing creates more controversy in our field than the topic of parenting. The next chapter is devoted to sifting through the data on this topic, which will show that these traditional beliefs are most likely wrong. Indeed, a full and unbiased view of the data suggests that there is a fundamental flaw underlying our tendency to blame parents for their children's PTSD problems.

Chapter Ten

The Facts on Parents: Do They Help, Hurt, or Make No Difference?

Judith Rich Harris was dismissed from the psychology doctoral program as a student at Harvard University in 1960 because the quality of her work supposedly was not up to Harvard's standards. Unable to complete her doctoral degree, she subsequently spent her career writing psychology textbooks. As she reviewed hundreds of studies to provide the content for the textbooks, she became increasingly concerned that the conclusions in those studies about parenting were all wrong. She noted that the discussion sections of research articles made speculations about causation of parenting when the studies only had the ability to show correlations, and the researchers' speculations about causation seemed to be pointed in the wrong direction.

In 1998, Harris, with few journal articles to her name and never having received funding for a research study, had the audacity to publish her first book at the age of sixty.[1] Her book, *The Nurture Assumption*, challenged the theory that parents determined how children turned out. She challenged the notion that one's personality was determined by how one was raised by one's parents. She reviewed numerous studies to support her controversial contention. She showed how studies that credited parents with the ability to mold children's personalities had failed to consider genetic influences. She also cited studies that suggested that peer groups, rather than parents, may be important for shaping one's character.

For her efforts, Judith Rich Harris was promptly crucified by the so-called experts. In one review of her book the year it came out, Jerome Kagan, PhD, a psychologist at Harvard University and one of the most respected voices in child development, reportedly stated, "I am embarrassed for psychology."[2] Another expert, Frank Farley, PhD, a psychologist at Temple University and past president of the American Psychological Association, reportedly said, "She's all wrong . . . Her thesis is absurd on its face, but consider what might happen if parents believe this stuff! Will it free some to mistreat their kids since 'it doesn't matter'?"[3] Wendy Williams, PhD, a psychologist and later the founder and director of the Cornell Institute for Women in Science, said, "By taking such an extreme position, Harris does a tremendous disservice."[4]

Kagan, Temple, Williams, and other experts were willing to write melodramatic propaganda to try to scare readers and persuade them that Harris got it very, very wrong. After reading the published personal diatribes like these from the experts, parents should understand that, in the eyes of most mental health professionals, they have big, red bull's-eyes painted on their backs as the people to blame for their children's problems.

The blame game, however, is in no way limited to normal development or to psychiatric problems. The blame game seems to be a way that humans react after nearly any misfortune. The universality of the blame game was illustrated well in Russell Banks's novel *The Sweet Hereafter*, which was made into a movie of the same name.[5] The novel was based on a true incident in Alston, Texas, in which a school bus crashed into a body of water and twenty-one children drowned. In the novel, an attorney seeks to file a class-action lawsuit, but first he must find someone to sue. Some company or some person must be to blame. Ignoring the evidence that it was just an unfortunate incident due to bad luck and poor judgment by the driver, the attorney keeps searching for someone to blame. As a character says in the novel, "People have got to have somebody to blame."

Problems with the Data about Blaming Mothers

I believe Judith Rich Harris got it right, that is, that parents do not possess the extraordinary ability to mold their children's personalities. She did not, however, write about psychiatric problems in general or trauma-related problems specifically. So, let's look at some of the important findings from the research on trauma and see if there are data to support one position or the other about parenting.

In the previous chapter, I introduced the paper I published in which my colleagues and I reviewed all seventeen of the studies that had assessed children's problems following trauma and that had also assessed parental problems.[6] In sixteen out of the seventeen studies, researchers had discovered that the children who had the most severe symptoms had parents and families with more severe problems. There was a strong correlation between children's problems and parents' problems.

Now we can spend some time looking at the flaws of those studies, and there were two very big ones. The two very big flaws with those seventeen studies were that (1) those studies had not measured actual parenting behaviors, and (2) those studies had not measured changes over time.

Regarding the first flaw, none of the studies had employed observational measures of actual parenting. The researchers of those seventeen studies had measured symptoms of the parents or problems of family discord, but did not observe how parents actually interacted with their children.

As scientists, it is not sufficient to assume that parental factors, such as parental PTSD symptoms, translate directly into insensitive parenting behaviors. As scientists, we must observe and measure the actual parenting behaviors before we can make reliable conclusions. Because none of those studies had employed observational measures of parenting, those studies could not make any valid conclusions about whether parenting practices cause children's symptoms.

The Results when Parenting Is Actually Measured

When **measures of parenting** have been used in later studies, the results have mostly not supported a blame-the-mother model. For example, Alytia Levendosky, PhD, a psychologist at Michigan State University, assessed 103 mothers and their preschool-age children, many of whom had experienced domestic violence.[7] They attempted to measure parenting in three different ways. First, they used a self-report questionnaire, called the Parenting Style Survey, which focused on their perceptions of how effective they believed their parenting skills were. Second, they observed parents playing with their children. From these videotaped observations, parents were rated on a scale called **authoritative parenting**. Third, using videotaped observations again of mothers playing with their children, mothers were rated on a scale called **negative parenting**.

They did not measure the children's PTSD symptoms because not all of the children had experienced traumas. Instead, they measured children's problems on two more general scales, called **internalizing problems** and **externalizing problems**. Levendosky found at least two interesting things. First, regarding children's internalizing of problems, there were no associations among any of the three parenting scores. Second, regarding children's externalizing of problems, the measure of parenting from the mothers' self-reports was found to be a mediator, but the two observed measures of parenting had no relation.

In summary, neither of the two observed parenting measures was associated with either children's internalizing or externalizing of problems. The mother's self-report of parenting was associated with externalizing but not internalizing of problems. Overall, there was much more evidence against the blame-the-mother model than for it.

The Results when Symptoms Are Tracked over Time

The second big flaw of those seventeen studies was that they had not measured changes over time. Instead, they had assessed children and parents at just one single point in time. Studies that assess participants at just one point in time are called **cross-sectional studies**. Cross-sectional studies are weak types of studies because they cannot report how things or people change over time.

Imagine you have a loaf of bread that is sliced into twenty slices. Each slice is a cross-sectional slice of the loaf. When you examine only one slice of bread, you can understand only that one slice. One slice can tell you what the beginning of the loaf looked like or what the end of the loaf looked like, but one slice cannot tell you how the beginning of the loaf influenced the end of the loaf. With only one slice of bread, you cannot see the whole loaf, and you are left with the chicken-or-egg problem of not knowing whether children's symptoms or parenting behaviors came first, or even whether either one came before the other. What cross-sectional designs can tell us is extremely limited because there is no way to sort out the direction of effects and no way to observe changes in outcomes over time.

A much stronger design for assessing parents and children over time is called a **prospective longitudinal design**. In a prospective longitudinal design, the parents and children are assessed at two different points in time at a minimum. Prospective longitudinal studies are more powerful because they provide much more reliable information about how things change over time. If we could examine the loaf of bread by looking at the first slice, then a slice in the middle, and then another slice at the end, that obviously would provide much more information than just one slice in the middle. Because of the requirement to gather data over time, prospective longitudinal studies are more difficult to conduct than cross-sectional studies, and that is the primary reason that there are roughly 100 times more cross-sectional studies than there are prospective longitudinal studies.

One example of a prospective longitudinal study was conducted by Harold Koplewicz and colleagues at New York University. Koplewicz followed a group of second-, third-, and fifth-grade children (approximately seven through eleven years old) following the first World Trade Center bombing in 1993. The second graders were on the observation deck, while the third and fifth graders were trapped in elevators when the explosion occurred. The researchers showed that parental PTSD symptoms were not correlated with children's PTSD symptoms three months after the event, but elevated parental PTSD symptoms correlated with elevated children's PTSD symptoms nine months after the event.[8] That is, relatively soon after the event, there was no relationship between parental symptoms and children's symptoms of PTSD. But as time went on, a relationship between parents' symptoms and children's symptoms seemed to develop.

Koplewicz reasoned that it did not seem likely the children were being affected by parents because the parent and child symptoms were not correlated at the three-month time point. Instead, Koplewicz reasoned, as the children's symptoms persisted out to the nine-month mark, parents became more and more affected by their children because they were empathic and caring parents and were sensitive to their children's persisting distress, and the parental PTSD symptoms became correlated with the children's symptoms by the nine-month time point. The researchers speculated that parents were affected by children, not vice versa. The Koplewicz study did not, however, measure actual parenting behaviors.

To try to address this issue, I conducted my own study, which is the only study so far that includes both measures of actual parenting and a long-term prospective longitudinal design that follows changes in children's PTSD symptoms. When I started this study, I thought this would be, as they say in basketball, a slam dunk, meaning that I thought I knew exactly what I would find ahead of time and the findings would be obvious. By using better research methods than the previous studies, I predicted I would be able to demonstrate that children with more PTSD symptoms had mothers with worse maternal sensitivity in real-time observations of them interacting with their children. It would help to solidify the notion that parents have an important and clear contribution to their children's symptoms. My research colleagues and I were extremely thorough. We didn't measure maternal sensitivity just one way. We measured sensitivity seven different ways, and we followed the children for nearly two years.

However, I did not get a slam dunk. In fact, I got my shot blocked in my face. I found rather surprising results that came out exactly the opposite of what I had predicted. The children with the most PTSD symptoms had mothers with the best sensitivity to their children.[9] This is worth repeating for emphasis. *The children with the most PTSD symptoms had the mothers who appeared the most sensitive toward their children when they were measured on how they actually interacted with their children.* This was true both at the beginning and at the end of the study.

At the beginning of the study, the children with the most PTSD symptoms had mothers with the most PTSD symptoms and the most depression symptoms, just as in all of the previous studies, but when I took the additional step that most of the other studies did not take and measured the actual parenting behaviors, it turned out that these highly symptomatic mothers had the best sensitivity toward their children, not the worst sensitivity.

After two years of our following these children in a prospective longitudinal design, the results did not change. Mothers with more emotional sensitivity associated with more children's PTSD symptoms over time, contrary to our initial expectations.[10] Contrary to the popular blame-the-mother wisdom, poor emotional sensitivity of mothers did not seem to cause or worsen their children's symptoms.

Treatment: The Mother Does Not Have to Get Better

It appears the blame-the-mother theory was wrong, or at least overly simplistic, about another thing. In the conclusion of my paper that reviewed those seventeen studies, I had written with unwarranted faith, which I regret to this day, that the "implications for evaluation and treatment are clear,"[11] the implications being that "it is important to attend first to the caregiver's symptomatology and only then to the child's symptoms." This advice was based on the assumption that parents had a causative impact on children's symptoms, which I now believe to be wrong, and I helped to prove it wrong in a subsequent study that I just described.

From 2004 to 2008, I conducted a treatment study in New Orleans for three- to six-year-old children with PTSD.[12] The treatment was a twelve-session CBT protocol that was developmentally adapted for young children. In addition to tracking the change in children's symptoms, my colleagues and I tracked the changes in mothers' symptoms, and we found something curious.

The children's PTSD symptoms improved dramatically during the treatment, but the mothers' PTSD symptoms, which were extremely high in this group, did not improve at all.[13] So, in contrast to my erroneous advice from an earlier paper "to attend first to the caregiver's symptomatology," we did not need to attend to the caregivers' symptoms at all in this treatment study. As long as mothers brought their children for psychotherapy, the children got better without the parents' PTSD having to get better first.

The mothers' PTSD symptoms did not improve, but the mothers did report that they felt less distressed as the therapy progressed. That is, as the children got better during the study, we found that the mothers felt less distressed even though the mothers' PTSD symptoms were not improving. This gave me the idea to ask mothers directly for their opinion on whether they thought their children got better after they felt better or they felt better after the children got better. So, near the end of therapy, the therapists asked the mothers directly who they thought improved first, the children or the parents. The majority of mothers responded quite clearly that their children improved first. A typical comment from mothers was "When I saw my child get better, then I relaxed." This directly contradicts what I wrote in my earlier review paper that it was important to attend first to the caregivers' symptomatology and only then to the child's symptoms. These results are likely to be surprising to a lot of mental health clinicians. The following case nicely illustrates these points.

Chris: Unusual Homework in the Attic

Chris was a three-year-old African-American male I have described before in a case report that was published in the *Journal of Traumatic Stress* in 2007.[14] The purpose of that article was to demonstrate the feasibility of doing CBT for PTSD with preschool children. What was not emphasized in that report was the role of Chris's parents.

Chris and his family lived in New Orleans. As Hurricane Katrina bore down on the city in late August of 2005, his parents had decided not to leave the city. When the water surged through the floodwalls, their house was quickly flooded. Chris, his mother and father, his mother's parents, and their dog all scrambled into the attic. They lived in the attic in the sweltering, humid August heat for two days and nights. They eventually escaped in a small boat, but then they wandered on foot and slept on a highway. They found their way to the convention center, where they spent two days surrounded by more than 19,000 desperate people without food, electricity, or bathrooms.

Chris and his family moved back to a new home in New Orleans seven months later, and then his mother saw our advertisement in the newspaper for our treatment study for preschool children. Chris had six symptoms of PTSD. More importantly for this story, his mother had eight symptoms of PTSD herself, plus three symptoms of major depression.

One of the key aspects of CBT therapy, especially with very young children, is homework assignments. CBT homework assignments for treating PTSD work by having children re-expose themselves to real-life reminders in their communities that stir up their anxiety related to their traumas. As children re-expose themselves in this controlled, step-by-step fashion, they use their new relaxation skills to master the anxiety that is associated with the memories. Young children cannot do these types of homework assignments on their own, however, and they need their parents to do it with them.

Through the first nine sessions of CBT, Chris was making some progress but he had not really turned the corner to make significant improvement. It was decided then that they would need to do the next homework assignment at the old house that had flooded and climb up into the attic where they had spent two horrible nights during the flood.

Their old house had been stripped down to the studs. Parts of the ceiling were missing. The attic floor still had holes scattered throughout. When they climbed into the attic, Chris's mom found a patch of the floor that looked safe and they sat down. Chris crawled into her lap. At first, he did not seem too anxious. She, however, was very scared. The memories came crashing back to her—the flood, the dark nights in the attic, the dead bodies floating in the water, and more death and despair at the convention center. But she knew she had to stick with the exercise to help Chris.

Chris's father was standing down below and they could see him through a hole in the attic floor. She called down to him to close the stairs to make it dark. She could feel Chris stiffen and then start to tremble in her lap, so she told him to start doing his breathing. After about one minute, she called to her husband to pull down the stairs, and they ended the exercise. After that homework, Chris dramatically improved from six to two symptoms of PTSD, but his mother still had six symptoms of PTSD.

I have seen hundreds of children with PTSD, but something about this case strikes me. It is the image of the mother, doing what she knows she has to do to help her child even though she is frightened. The image of those two sitting alone together in the dark is for me the archetypal image of the importance of parents. She is the image of the miraculous mother goddess. As long as she brought him to therapy and helped him through his homework, Chris got better. She did not cause Chris's PTSD. She did not make Chris's PTSD worse. But she could help him get better. She did not even have to get better herself.

Treatment: Parents Can Help Children Get Better

The two lessons learned from the case of Chris were that parents do not have to get better first, contrary to the traditional wisdom from experts; and that parents can play a key role in children getting better.

Parents can help their children; that's not news. What makes it worth emphasizing again and again, though, is that it is a very different kind of message from the traditional focus of experts on their preoccupation with the notion that insensitive parents are harmful to their children. When researchers and clinicians are focused on how parents may be harmful to their children, they cannot be fully focused on paying attention to the ways that parents can be helpful to their children.

The case of Chris illustrated quite well how a mother can help a very young child, who is relatively more dependent on a parent than an older child. But how can mothers help older children?

Alex: A Father's Tough Love

Alex had been anxious all of his life. For example, from the age of three years he would not be alone in any room in their house. When doing his homework, he spent unnecessary hours erasing and rewriting to get the letters and numbers just perfect.

Alex came by his anxiety honestly, as they say. He was just like his mother. She had had almost the exact same type of pervasive anxiety since she was a child. Alex got his mother's genes for anxiety. I know his anxiety was caused by genes and not by his mother's parenting, because Alex had a brother who was not anxious at all. The brother was just like his dad.

Alex was an excellent soccer player, just like his father was. During one soccer game when Alex was ten years old, he and a boy from the other team raced toward a free ball that took a high bounce. Both boys arrived and tried to kick it at the same time. The other boy missed the ball and Alex's lower leg took the full force of the boy's kick. Alex's lower leg snapped so loudly that the parents could hear it on the sideline. Both bones broke clean through. Before Alex hit the ground, everyone could see the bottom half of his lower leg bent at a grotesque angle from the upper half. The boy who kicked Alex's leg took one look at Alex's leg and fainted on the field.

His leg made a full recovery, but he immediately developed the full diagnosis of PTSD. Alex gradually rejoined the team, but he was never quite the same player. He backed away from contact and flopped to the ground whenever it couldn't be avoided.

His father had been an excellent soccer player, and it was important to him that Alex be successful at soccer, too. He felt Alex should be able to get over the incident, so his version of trying to be helpful was to make Alex go out to the practice field where he would kick balls forcefully at Alex, many times aiming for his leg. Needless to say, this did not make the PTSD symptoms go away.

Alex kept playing soccer, though, partly because his anxiety-driven perfectionism drove him to keep striving and partly because he still loved soccer. He played through almost every game with racing heart rate, sweaty palms, and shaking knees. Before many of the games, he vomited due to his anxiety.

After two years of trying, plus a few fanatical pep talks from guest coaches who fancied themselves amateur sports psychologists, his mother finally enrolled him in treatment with us for PTSD. By the end of CBT, Alex's PTSD symptoms had reduced by more than 65 percent and he no longer qualified for the PTSD diagnosis. He never did get back to the level of aggressiveness and confidence he had before the injury, but he was able to play without shaking or vomiting.

Alex's mom was critical to Alex's improvement in several ways. First, she brought him to treatment, over the objections of her husband. This may sound overly simplistic, but if parents do not bring children, then the children obviously never receive treatment.

Second, by watching the therapy sessions on a TV monitor in an adjacent office, Alex's mother learned that Alex believed she thought he was a failure because he could not shake the PTSD symptoms and vomited before games. She was able to talk about this with Alex, and shared with him that she had felt the same way when she was a little girl.

Third, she learned about triggers for Alex's anxiety that she had not known about. Alex was able to tell the therapist that his dad watching soccer on TV was a trigger. They developed a plan to do some other activity when his dad was watching soccer.

Clinical Intuition Is Notoriously Wrong

Five hundred years ago, most, if not all, people believed the sun revolved around Earth. To the naked eye, the sun does indeed appear to move around our sky. There were always other observations available to suggest that Earth revolved around the sun, but given the strength of what the naked eye could see most obviously, their intuition was that the sun revolved around Earth. That should have been one strong history lesson that intuition should almost never be trusted.

Formal definitions of intuition include the elements of rapid insight, immediate apprehension, conviction, and the absence of rational thought and inference—in other words, gut intuition without thinking much. It is interesting that the definition of intuition includes the idea that it is lacking in evident rational thought, yet intuition has been considered one of the human species' greatest gifts. Albert Einstein himself highly valued intuition when he said, "The only real valuable thing is intuition." Intuition is perhaps one of the things that sets us apart from other animals. Intuition somehow embodies the superior cognitive abilities of humans that make us unique as a species.

Clinicians value their intuition, too. They even give it a special name—clinical intuition. Clinical intuition is a highly prized characteristic among clinicians. Most clinicians believe they have a talent to read other people that nonclinicians do not have. Clinicians decided early in their lives to become clinicians because they have this intuition, whereas others decided to go into other fields of business because they lacked this intuition. To be clear, this intuition is not wisdom that has accumulated from years of experiences in the field. This intuition is something many clinicians feel they are born with. Clinicians are a self-selected group of people who have convinced themselves they have superior intuition to understand other people.

Unfortunately, clinical intuition is notoriously wrong. Leo Kanner and Bruno Bettelheim were wrong when they speculated that parenting causes autism. Theodore Lidz, was wrong when he speculated the same thing about schizophrenia. It seems that it is extremely easy for clinicians to be fooled by their clinical intuition.

According to Richard Feynman, PhD, "The first principle is that you must not fool yourself and you are the easiest person to fool."

Even if I am right—that faulty intuition is largely to blame for why people hold mistaken beliefs about parenting—it still does not explain why people have faulty intuition. Why would humans have such a powerful tool as intuition, yet it can do more harm than good? Ultimately, I do not know why intuition is so faulty, but I have my suspicions.

I suspect that the reason clinicians and most people in general are tricked by their intuitions into believing that experience makes us who we are is because humans have a strong instinct to believe that the wrong experiences can make us something we do not want to become. Humans are highly social creatures because they are wired to belong to their family, tribe, clan, state, country, or whatever social unit provides them protection and comfort. It makes sense that the need to belong to a clan for safety, protection, and survival is an instinct that is hard-wired into the genes.

Because most people instinctually, almost desperately, fear anything that would make them different from their family or social unit, they avoid those experiences they fear will make them different. If they believe they need to avoid the wrong experiences so that they do not become what they do not want to become, it is not a big leap to believe the related idea that any experience, including the experience of being parented, can shape them to be different in many other ways, both good and bad. This belief may be true for such things as cultural norms that can be learned and unlearned. It is quite another thing to believe it for fundamental, inherent, hard-wired traits of development and personality.

Whatever the reasons for why people turn out the way they do, to blame parents is a strong assertion. We ought not blame parents until we have more than clinical intuition. That's why we do research, and why we ought to pay some attention to research results, whether or not we like the answers, because sometimes, perhaps most of the time, there is nobody to blame.

Recap

- Most everyone, laypeople and professionals alike, believes he or she is an expert on parenting.
- It is a widespread belief that parents have a profound influence on the fundamental domains of normal child development and the abnormal development of psychiatric disorders through their parental capacities to be warm and sensitive and to modulate the self-regulation skills of their children. There is, however, little to no well-controlled, causal scientific evidence to support this belief.
- One of the most consistent findings in research on children with PTSD is that children with more severe PTSD symptoms have parents with more severe problems of their own. This is a correlation, but it does not show causation.
- There are at least several different possible models that could explain this correlation. The blame-the-mother theory, which is by far the most popularly held, is only one of the possible models.
- Most of the research that has been conducted on this topic has suffered from two major limitations—the investigators did not assess actual parenting behaviors and they did not assess changes over time.
- The model that children affect their parents actually has more research support than the model that parents affect their children.

- The correlation that children and parents both show high levels of the same types of psychiatric symptoms is probably best explained by the shared genetics model.
- Clinical intuition is notoriously wrong. Historically, parents have been blamed by so-called experts for autism, schizophrenia, and other problems; those experts have been wrong.
- There is absolutely no solid evidence that parents cause their children's PTSD symptoms.
- While the notion that insensitive parents cause or worsen their children's symptoms is wrong most of the time, like everything else, there are always exceptions. But if you are reading this book, you are unlikely to be one of those exceptions.
- Parents are important, but not in the way that old theories blame problems on insensitive parenting. Parents can probably be the most helpful and have the greatest impact by helping their children during psychotherapy. Parents are important in the ways that Chris's mother and Alex's mother helped their children recover from PTSD.

For Parents to Do

- Given that the role of parenting is highly controversial, it is unlikely there will be a consensus about the influence of parenting anytime soon. Hence, parents need to be aware there is this trend to blame parents for their children's symptoms, and it is largely based on speculation and notoriously wrong clinical intuition. Many clinicians believe in the power of parenting either to harm or to cure their children. When counseling isn't working, clinicians almost inevitably try to blame parents. If that shoe seems to fit for you, then fine. But be skeptical. The truth is probably much more complicated.

- The trend of blaming parents knows no professional boundaries. If your child has PTSD, you will probably blame yourself at some point. That probably means you are a good parent because you care about your child. Rather than blame yourself, however, you probably ought to blame your genes that you passed on to your children.

- The best way parents can be involved is by finding the right kind of therapy for their children, bringing their children to the therapy, and being supportive throughout the process.

- It is important that parents be sensitive to help their children cope. There are many things parents can do that are likely to help their children. The Appendix includes a list of tips based on my years of experience with those things that seemed helpful.

Chapter Eleven

The Decision to Get Help: If You Build It, They Won't Come

In the movie *Field of Dreams*, farmer Ray Kinsella is minding his own business on his farm when he hears a mysterious voice say, "If you build it, they will come." After much initial reluctance and repeated visits from the mysterious voice, Ray figures out that he is being told to build a baseball field on his farm. He builds the baseball field, and indeed they come. Long-dead baseball players walk out of the cornfield and, in the rapturous joy of childhood games, get to play baseball once again.

What does this have to do with trauma and PTSD? The world has recognized that trauma can have powerful psychological effects on people and frequently leads to the development of PTSD. Mental health professionals have heard the call, so to speak, and built treatment programs that work. But will the clients come? Will the longtime sufferers of PTSD come out of their homes and into the clinics to get these treatments? The following story about a natural disaster in Queensland, Australia, provides a surprising answer.

The Queensland Floods Story

In December of 2010, the heaviest rainfall in the history of the state of Queensland, Australia, fell over a series of days. Queensland, occupying the northeast region of Australia, is the second-largest state in the country, nearly three times the size of Texas and larger than France and Germany combined. Some flooding began in December, and as the rainfall picked up again in January of 2011, flooding became widespread, sudden, and extremely dangerous. Nearly three-quarters of the state was eventually declared a disaster zone. Over thirty-five people were killed, at least eighty-six towns were affected, and 20,000 homes were flooded.

The extent of this disaster was not really the remarkable part. Disasters have always occurred that were huge and shocking, and disasters occur quite regularly. The remarkable part was the psychological treatment for trauma that was made available afterward to the survivors of the Queensland floods. The Australian and Queensland governments allocated over $37 million to hire over 130 full-time mental health specialists. These specialists formed ten Recovery and Resilience Teams around the state. They created fact sheets, websites, podcasts, and YouTube videos to reach out to the survivors. Approximately 300 parents attended seminars.

Schools were targeted to reach youths. Teachers were trained to identify trauma reactions. A teacher manual and tip sheets were distributed and explained in small groups. Over 250 workers were trained to deliver the program. They developed an organized procedure to screen youths with simple, easy-to-use measures. Those who screened above a certain threshold were given a more in-depth interview assessment, and those who qualified were offered CBT treatment for trauma symptoms.

Despite these enormous outreach efforts, they treated only around fifty children and adolescents.[1] The Queensland program was probably the most well-organized, high-quality psychological trauma relief program ever organized in the world, and it treated a grand total of around fifty youths. In an enormous state of over 4.5 million people, in which there were approximately half a million people with treatable symptoms of PTSD, a relatively tiny number of people took advantage of this program to get help. There appeared to be an enormous failure of engagement between the providers and the potential consumers. What went wrong?

Disasters in New York, Florida, and New Orleans
The Australian program was not the first failure of engagement. Following the World Trade Center attack in 2001, the United States Federal Emergency Management Agency (FEMA) provided $3 million

to the Child and Adolescent Trauma Treatments and Services (CATS) Consortium of providers in the New York City area to provide free treatment.[2] It was estimated that 520,000 developed PTSD, including more than 100,000 children and adolescents.[3] CATS was a group of nine agencies with eighty-one clinicians primarily delivering the therapy at forty-five clinic sites. Yet, in the published report of their project, a mere 385 children had received at least one therapy session.

Following the 2004 Florida hurricanes, in which four major hurricanes struck the state, FEMA allocated over a million dollars to Florida so that officials could provide direct and free treatment. Using an intervention called Adolescent and Child Component Therapy for Trauma,[4] Florida officials created the first-ever federally funded psychological trauma program following a natural disaster. As of this writing, more than thirteen years after the disaster, there has never been a public report on how many youths were treated.

Following the Hurricane Katrina disaster, the Fleur-de-Lis school-based program was created with funding from the Sisters of Mercy of New Orleans. Out of 609 fourth- to eighth-grade students with whom consent forms were sent home from three schools, seventy-one students began an intervention and only sixty-two completed treatment.[5]

In the movie *Field of Dreams*, Ray Kinsella built the baseball field and the people came. The people came and worked out some of their unresolved issues with the help of divine intervention. Queensland, New York, and New Orleans could have used some of that divine intervention.

Lest one think these failures of engagement are unique to large disasters, the same failures occur for all types of individual traumas. In Chapter Four I presented the case of Jade, who had developed PTSD from being raped but did not reach out for help for two years. I also presented the case of Enrique, who had witnessed years of domestic violence before seeking help. In Chapter Ten I presented the case of Alex, who had PTSD from a soccer injury and waited two years before getting professional help.

Even when families do come for treatment of trauma, they do not always remain in treatment. From 2004 through 2008, we conducted a clinical trial for three- to six-year-old children with PTSD symptoms in

New Orleans. The treatment was twelve sessions of cognitive behavioral therapy. Of sixty-one families that were eligible for treatment after the evaluation and were offered to begin treatment, 25 percent never returned for any therapy sessions and an additional 25 percent dropped out before completing the majority of the twelve treatment sessions.

From 2010 through 2012, we conducted a clinical trial for seven- to eighteen-year-olds with PTSD symptoms. The treatment was again twelve sessions of CBT, but this time patients also took either the medication D-cycloserine (an antibiotic for tuberculosis discovered by accident to help with anxiety) or a placebo pill one hour before each session. Of ninety-eight families who were eligible for treatment after the evaluation and were offered to begin treatment, 29 percent never returned for any therapy sessions and an additional 14 percent dropped out before completing the majority of the twelve treatment sessions. This level of retention is typical of treatment studies for PTSD.

Why Don't They Come?

This failure of engagement between providers and consumers reminds me of the saying "You can lead a horse to water, but you can't make it drink," except in this case we often are not even getting the horse to the water.

It is largely a mystery as to why people do not use mental health treatment for certain types of problems. It is difficult to find research data on the topic, and it is difficult to find the people to ask because they do not come to clinics where we can ask them.

In the absence of data, we are left to make guesses based on anecdotal information. One guess that almost everybody would think of is the stigma associated with mental illness. All of us probably are familiar with friends or relatives who need mental health treatment but refuse to go while claiming, "I'm not crazy!" Going to a mental health provider is like admitting failure and, like a bird trying to build a nest in a windstorm, many people will never admit failure. Psychologist Vanessa Cobham, PhD, one of the architects of the Queensland program, gave me a somewhat novel guess that the more stoic and/or altruistic individuals would not reach out for help following the Queensland floods because they did not want to use up resources that could have been better used on others who were worse off. Still others probably refuse to go to mental health providers because they are very private or have introverted personalities and feel the treatment of talking to someone about their personal issues would be more painful than having the PTSD symptoms.

In thinking about the unique situation of children, perhaps many parents view children as marshmallows. You can press lightly on the sides of a marshmallow and temporarily distort the shape, but as soon as you release the pressure the marshmallow pops back to its original shape. Therefore, if children show symptoms of PTSD, it is no big deal because the symptoms will go away after the trauma has passed.

Problems of access are probably additional barriers to many people. Mental health providers are mostly solo or small group practices. There are no chain-store monopolies that make access easy. There is no obvious "front door" to our industry. In the New Orleans region alone, there are over 400 providers for children and adolescents. It is a confusing and intimidating task to find a good provider.

Stigma, stoicism, privacy, marshmallow children, and problems of access with the lack of a "front door" are all good guesses, but they do not quite add up in my mind. All of those guesses seem to have an underlying assumption that people want mental health. Through many of my interactions with patients and potential patients over the years, I have wondered if that assumption is just plain wrong. *What if people are not that interested in mental health?* While thinking about many of these issues one day, I saw an advertisement for a show to be performed by a famous comedian. The event was labeled as a "mental health awareness" event. It struck me that the person who wrote the ad assumed learning more about "mental health awareness" would automatically be attractive. Who wouldn't want more awareness about better mental health? But I was also struck by how unattractive the advertisement seemed.

If people truly are not too interested in better mental health, then it will never matter how much we reduce stigma or make access easier. There may be a fundamental issue that the process of asking for help is worse than living with psychiatric problems. There are lots of individuals who seek out and benefit from mental health services, but it seems that many, if not most, trauma victims just don't want the services badly enough to put up with our business model, or they just don't want the services at all. Maybe we are trying to engage people the wrong way.

The Marketing of Mental Health

How would a genius marketing expert approach this problem from a purely business perspective? Imagine that mental health treatment is a product like any other product that can be purchased off the shelves in grocery stores. This product languishes on the shelves and few people buy it. From a business perspective, consumer demand is low. Apparently, consumers do not believe treatment will have substantial and meaningful benefits in their lives or do not believe the cost is worth the benefits, or both. Consumers need their laundry detergent, toothpaste, and peanut butter, but most consumers do not see the need for mental health treatment.

In this new perspective, fault does not lie with consumers. Consumers are not the problem. The fault lies squarely with the mental health profession. It is our job, as mental health professionals, to make and market a product that sells. We have done the first part in that we have made a product that works well. We have not done the second part of marketing our product.

How does one market mental health treatment? Isn't it obvious that mental health treatment makes people feel better? We make problems go away like detergent removes stains on one's laundry. How can people not want our wonderful product?

I am no marketing genius, but I think I understand that there are three basic things that need to happen. First, trying to make stigma go away is a losing battle. I am afraid the abolition of stigma about mental health, along with world peace, will not be achieved in my lifetime, and perhaps not ever. Humans have unique and exceptionally intimate relationships with their minds, and they do not want others knowing they need mental health treatment. Every patient needs to be treated with the privacy of a VIP. More private waiting areas in clinics and greater use of telemedicine to reach patients in their homes could go a long way to providing greater privacy.

Second, consumers need to know that our product works. In Chapter Thirteen I will discuss how effective treatments have become for PTSD, but getting the word out could involve so much more. If we thought of mental health treatment as a new type of toothpaste, our marketing genius would create advertisements for magazines and television, put our product in attractive packaging, and hire a celebrity spokesperson. In 1971, McDonald's nailed it with the famous slogan "You deserve a break today." Why don't we have a slogan?

Third, consumers need to know the right time to get help. Research has repeatedly shown that nearly all individuals who experience life-threatening traumatic events show some symptoms within the first month. For about 70 percent of individuals, those symptoms will disappear by the end of the first month. About 30 percent of individuals will have enduring symptoms of PTSD, and we can tell who they are by the end of the first month.[6] Watchful waiting during the first month is the official recommendation of experts.[7] One may, of course, make exceptions to this rule and begin treatment within the first month for those with severe symptoms.

There is no reason to wait longer than one month to seek treatment for PTSD. If the PTSD symptoms are still present after one month, the symptoms will be chronic and will likely only go away with treatment.

In a large study with 808 Australian children exposed to a bushfire, it was observed that their PTSD symptoms did not decrease more than two years after the fire.[8] In a study of thirty children following Hurricane Andrew, it was observed that 70 percent of them still were in the moderate-to-severe category of post-traumatic stress symptoms nearly two years later.[9] And in my study of sixty-two one- to six-year-old children who had experienced a wide range of different types of traumatic experiences, we observed that their PTSD symptoms did not decrease after two years.[10]

The research is consistent and clear. *After one month, if PTSD symptoms are still present, the PTSD symptoms are chronic and need treatment.* Finding the right kind of treatment is another adventure and the subject of the next chapter.

Chapter Twelve
How to Find Good Treatment

When it comes time to find clinicians and make appointments to start treatment, it is illuminating to compare that to another type of shopping experience. For instance, shingles for the roofs of houses provide an interesting comparison, because like treatment for children, shingles are necessary and important, but for different reasons.

Consumer Reports magazine, famous for protecting consumers from unsafe products by testing everything from toasters to cars, publishes extensive data on roof shingles to help consumers shop for the right product. The magazine regularly provides transparent test results on price, weight, strength, wind resistance, weathering, impact, and duration of warranty for shingles. Another product safety organization, Underwriters Laboratories, provides ongoing testing of shingles for fire safety classifications in their independent lab.

No ratings of any type exist for providers of mental health treatment; you must rely on word of mouth and a whole lot of luck. Few therapists list what kinds of services they offer on their websites. Most therapists don't let parents watch therapy sessions, so parents don't know firsthand what goes on inside the therapy rooms. Even if the therapists claim to provide certain techniques, it is nearly impossible for consumers to conclude whether those techniques were actually delivered and whether or not the consumers were ripped off.

It is incredibly alarming to note that you are better off shopping for shingles for your roof than you are for mental health providers for your children. You want to find the best treatment possible for children, but you face one exceptionally huge problem when trying to find high-quality mental health treatment: You have no systematic data to know who is good and who is bad.

All is not lost, though. There are good treatments available, and there are good therapists out there (usually). Finding them, however, is likely to take some trial and error.

Evidence-Based Treatment

One way to shop for good treatment is to look for evidence-based treatments (EBT). Before the coveted honor of being called an evidence-based treatment can be bestowed, there must be at least one published research study on the therapy that showed that it actually worked in a randomized clinical trial. Ideally, there should be more than one randomized clinical trial by different groups of researchers.

In a randomized clinical trial, half of the participants are randomly assigned to receive the EBT and the other half are assigned a different type of treatment (or to a wait-list period during which they do not receive any treatment). It is important to randomly assign participants to the different treatments in order to avoid the researchers' stacking the deck in favor of one of the treatments with all of the patients who are easier to treat.

Before starting therapy, parents ought to feel comfortable enough to ask therapists for the name of the therapy they propose to use and whether or not the therapy is an EBT, that is, whether any randomized clinical trials have been conducted with this therapy for PTSD in youths. If therapists cannot provide that information, it should serve as a red flag that perhaps their treatment plans are not appropriate for the children.

CBT Has Won the Horse Race So Far

John March, MD, MPH, a child psychiatrist at Duke University, is one of the most prolific researchers in the business, with nearly 200 publications. He has developed and tested psychotherapy treatments for PTSD and obsessive-compulsive disorder and has been involved in some of the biggest multisite randomized treatment trials for children and adolescents in the world. March is what one would call a straight shooter. He does not say something unless he has the data to back it up, and then he says it bluntly.

In 2009, March published a scientific paper that reviewed psychotherapy treatments typical of his no-frills practice titled "The future of psychotherapy for mentally ill children and adolescents." One of the section headings in the paper was the immodest phrase, "The psychotherapy horse race is over: cognitive-behavior therapy wins."[1] While he was speaking about psychotherapy for all types of disorders, the statement was applicable to PTSD.

March was spot-on. CBT is by far the most well-studied treatment for PTSD. The best-known version of CBT for youths, called **trauma-focused cognitive-behavioral therapy** (TF-CBT) has been shown to be highly effective in multiple randomized clinical trials. There are other versions of CBT, including my own version.

What Is Cognitive Behavioral Therapy?

CBT for PTSD usually is conducted in forty-five- to sixty-minute weekly sessions over twelve to fifteen weeks. There are several methods to practice CBT that have been written up as how-to manuals. These manuals include instructions for clinicians to follow. Several of these methods can be purchased as books, and other methods are available only from their developers who are usually willing to share them. The methods differ from each other in the amount of detailed step-by-step instructions, the rigidness that is needed to follow steps in a certain order, the degree of emphasis on relaxation skills, the methods used to tell the trauma stories (such as talking versus drawing, imagining, or writing), the importance that is placed on doing homework between weekly sessions, and the amount of time spent to explore psychodynamic meanings that might be connected to the patients' thoughts and behaviors.

The name of the method that has been both researched the most and spread the most widely around the world is called trauma-focused CBT (TF-CBT). The creators of TF-CBT are psychiatrist Judith Cohen, MD, and psychologist Anthony Mannarino, PhD, based at Allegheny General Hospital in Pittsburgh, and psychologist Esther Deblinger, PhD, based at the University of Medicine and Dentistry of New Jersey. Their method is described in a book written for therapists.[2]

I have developed my own method, called Youth PTSD Treatment (YPT), which has many similarities to TF-CBT but differs from TF-CBT in being more structured and emphasizing parental involvement more. A session-by-session outline of YPT is in the Appendix.

There are several main elements of YPT that are conducted in a stepwise program. The first four weeks are spent getting ready for the more difficult work that lies ahead. In session one, therapists educate patients about the symptoms of PTSD and begin to develop a common language of how to talk about these symptoms. In session two, the focus is on oppositional and defiant behaviors, and therapists develop simple behavior-management plans with the youths and parents. In session three, youths learn how to develop greater awareness of their feelings. In session four, therapists teach the youths new relaxation skills to deal with their worries.

The next six weeks are spent with the clients telling the story of their traumatic events. This is done repeatedly during sessions five through ten, with a little bit more detail presented each time. During these repeated "tellings" of the stories, therapists help patients learn how to master their distressing feelings and identify their negative thoughts about shame and guilt. It takes much practice and skill to learn new ways to reframe those thoughts.

Next, one session is devoted to anticipating what will happen in the future. In session eleven, the therapists help youths imagine situations in the future in which their memories might get retriggered. Getting retriggered in the future happens to everybody, and this session helps to normalize it and take the shock out of it when it actually happens.

Lastly, therapists and youths have to review the work they have done together. All of the worksheets that were completed during earlier sessions have been kept in a binder, which makes it easy to flip through these worksheets one at a time. This grand review is conducted in several steps over sessions ten through twelve, and helps the youths feel a sense of mastery for conquering their fears, almost like a graduation from school.

YPT was effective in greatly reducing the symptoms of PTSD in a study we conducted with fifty-seven youths who were seven to eighteen years old. My YPT method is currently available for free on my Scheeringa Lab website.[3] The YPT method is also available in a developmentally modified version for three- to six-year-old children, called Preschool PTSD Treatment (PPT). PPT is available in a book I wrote that was published in 2016[4] titled *Treating PTSD in Preschoolers*.

Chris

In Chapter Ten I introduced you to Chris, who was three years old when he and his family barely survived the Hurricane Katrina disaster. I used Chris as an example to show how parents can be helpful to their children during treatment. I described how his mother bravely tolerated her own fears in order to do the homework exercises by returning with Chris to the tattered attic of their ravaged home. Their task during the homework exercises was to physically visit the place where the traumatic events occurred in order to make Chris anxious on purpose so that he could use his new relaxation skills to master his fears.

Chris had actually already imagined doing something similar during the CBT sessions with his therapist in the therapist's office. Before Chris and his mother returned to the real attic, the therapist taught Chris how to draw nearly exactly the same scene on a sheet of paper in the office. Chris had already visited the attic in his mind before doing it in real life.

The whole process in the therapist's office took about ten minutes during each weekly session. First, the therapist explained to Chris that they were going to draw the scary scene from the hurricane on paper so he could "make the scary thoughts go away." As Chris drew the house surrounded by floodwater, the therapist made comments on the drawing to try to add more detail and draw his mind back to the event. The goal of the drawing was to make Chris a little bit anxious. After a couple of minutes of this, the therapist asked Chris to rate how worried he felt on a three-point rating scale, and then did relaxation exercises with him. After a couple of minutes of relaxation exercises, they went back to the drawing to add more detail.

This process of exposing Chris to memories of his trauma through drawing and talking, and then doing relaxation, was repeated many times during sessions five through ten. By the end of therapy, the process of reengaging with his memories while being able to control his worries had become routine.

The Angry Play Therapist

It is unfortunate that most therapists refuse to use CBT to treat PTSD. Therapists diagnose what they know and can treat, and often refuse to see what they don't know and can't treat. Most therapists are either not trained in CBT or they simply don't like using CBT because they like doing different types of therapy. "If you have a hammer, everything looks like a nail" is an apropos saying in this situation. Because most therapists have only their one favorite hammer, which is usually not CBT, they try to use their favorite therapy on everything that comes through their doors. The tragedy for consumers is that the therapists get away with it every day because there are not enough therapists to handle all of the families that need help.

In my experience, many therapists are not very open-minded about using different therapy techniques. Let me give you a personal example that I believe is fairly typical of most therapists. Some years ago I presented the findings of my randomized study that used my CBT method for young children, Preschool PTSD Treatment, to treat PTSD in three- to six-year-old children at the annual meeting of the International Society for Traumatic Stress Studies, which is the major gathering of trauma experts every year. During the question-and-answer period at the end, a woman stood up in the back of the room to express how I had offended her.

With intense earnestness, she defended play therapy as a useful technique for traumatized preschool children. She described her years of experience of using play therapy for young children and felt it was the only thing that could have helped them. She felt that many young children were too young and too traumatized to be forced so quickly into the exposure exercises of CBT. She was not only offended, she said that she was disturbed and angry to hear me talk about CBT for young children with PTSD. She didn't think children that young could even understand CBT techniques, and she thought the children I had treated were not really doing CBT. She stated that she was offended because she thought I did not understand play therapy. She went on to tell me how she felt researchers like me, who were partial only to CBT, always disrespected play therapy.

I tried to explain to her that I was indeed familiar with play therapy, which is what I had tried to use to treat young children and found that it rarely worked, and that is why I moved on to developing CBT for this age group. I acknowledged that play therapy could have a useful place with some children.

I asked her if she was trained in CBT and whether she had ever tried to use it with this population. She replied that she was not trained in CBT and had never used it.

What Makes a Good Treatment for PTSD?

This example of the angry play therapist raises the question, What makes a good treatment for PTSD? CBT is good, but maybe there are other methods that are equally good. A group of researchers reviewed all of the studies that have been shown to be effective to treat PTSD.[5] They distilled the essence of the successful therapies into three components: (1) emotional engagement with the trauma memory; (2) organization and articulation of a trauma narrative; and (3) modification of basic core beliefs about the world and about oneself. The following case is an excellent illustration both of the frustrating process that consumers go through to find mental health treatment and the advantages of CBT.

Tammy and an Ice Cream Truck

Tammy, four years old, and her mother had waved down an ice cream truck to stop in front of their house. The truck stopped on the other side of the street, so they had to cross. Her mother purchased the ice cream that Tammy wanted, and they began to cross the street again to return home. Because the ice cream truck was blocking their view, they did not see the car that was speeding down the street. The car knocked Tammy down and she was dragged underneath the car for about thirty feet. Her mother had been a step behind and she was not struck.

By an enormous amount of luck, no bones were broken. Tammy suffered bruises, cuts, and scrapes over much of her body, but there were no major injuries. She was going to make a full physical recovery. However, her mother was concerned that Tammy was fearful about crossing the street. Her pediatrician told her not to worry, but Tammy's mother knew something was wrong psychologically.

Her mother waited six months, but Tammy's fears did not go away. She then took Tammy to a counselor for children. The counselor declared that children this young could not get PTSD; nevertheless, she would be happy to do some play therapy with Tammy to help her express her feelings about the accident. The play therapy did not focus on the traumatic car accident, and Tammy's symptoms did not improve. After two months of weekly sessions, Tammy's mother stopped taking her and looked for another therapist.

This is about the time they came to my clinic. Following an assessment that included standardized questionnaires, we discovered that Tammy met the full criteria for the diagnosis of PTSD. We began CBT with my Preschool PTSD Treatment protocol, and her symptoms drastically improved over the next two to three months.

The difficulty Tammy's mother faced to find appropriate treatment and the "doctor shopping" she had to go through is unfortunately typical. Many therapists still do not know how to conduct an adequate assessment for PTSD. Even when therapists do make an accurate diagnosis of PTSD, they use outdated and ineffective psychotherapy methods.

The first component, emotional engagement with the trauma memory, means that the patients have to spend some time during therapy sessions thinking and talking about their memories of the traumatic events. Patients usually will not do this on their own initiative because avoidance of the trauma memory is part of the diagnosis of PTSD. Left to themselves, people who suffer from PTSD will not spontaneously talk about their traumas with other individuals.

When Tammy was seeing the play therapist, she avoided talking about the car accident, and the therapist, using the play therapy technique of "follow the patient's lead," did not try to coax her to talk about the accident. The CBT therapist, in contrast, following the CBT technique of gentle exposure to reminders of the events, taught Tammy to draw specific scenes from the traumatic event. They would then use the drawings to talk about Tammy's feelings and thoughts related to the accident.

The second component, organization and articulation of a trauma narrative, is a fancy way of saying that individuals need to be able to tell the stories of their traumatic events from start to finish. Individuals with PTSD often get stuck on the most distressing moments of their events, where they shut down and refuse to talk about them. Patients do not have to recount every single detail, but they need to be able to talk through a fairly complete narrative of their story from beginning to end. This also implies that they have learned to regulate their distressing feelings and negative thoughts sufficiently to talk through the story.

In Tammy's case with the play therapist, there were probably times that she wanted to talk more about her accident, but she did not know where to start and it was overwhelming to be flooded by distressing feelings, so she shut down. CBT anticipates that this will happen and teaches patients new skills to handle the frightening memories in a step-by-step fashion. Tammy's CBT therapist spent the first four sessions teaching Tammy how to identify and talk about her feelings, how to rate the strength of her feelings, and several new relaxation skills to cope with the strong feelings. Only after Tammy had these new skills did the CBT therapist start teaching Tammy to draw and talk about small pieces of her accident one step at a time.

The third component, modification of basic core beliefs about the world and about oneself, addresses the aftereffects of trauma for individuals to question their basic safety in the world. The magnitude of life-threatening events seems to arouse an instinct in individuals to wonder what they are supposed to learn from these events for their future safety and survival. Trauma victims tend to question their place in the world and often wonder to themselves, *Why did this happen to me?* Some trauma victims blame themselves for what happened even though it was not their fault. Others believe that bad things will always happen to them.

Tammy, being only four years old, did not yet have the ability to think abstractly about her place in the world, but her mind was capable of developing an irrational fear of all streets. The play therapist could never address this irrational fear because, first, this therapist did not believe Tammy had PTSD, and second, the technique of play therapy allowed Tammy to avoid the topic. The CBT therapist, on the other hand, directly addressed Tammy's fear of streets. Homework was assigned after several sessions that required Tammy and her mother to practice crossing streets around their home while using relaxation techniques they had learned during the therapy sessions. If Tammy had been older, the CBT therapist could have systematically examined her thinking patterns and helped her replace any negative beliefs with more realistic and positive beliefs.

Myths of CBT

I think consumers need to know that many, if not most, therapists not only do not know how to do CBT, but they, like the angry play therapist, are actively against CBT. Using the analogy of the car and the mechanics I used in Chapter Nine (In the Shoes of Therapists), suppose the car owner agrees to let the first mechanic replace the brakes for $500. The mechanic tells the car owner that he will install ceramic brake pads. He does not discuss with the car owner the different types of brake pads or the pros and cons of different brake pads. He purposely fails to mention that the evidence is clear that semi-metallic brake pads are better. He fails to mention this because he knows that semi-metallic brake pads are more difficult to install and therefore he simply prefers to install ceramic brake pads. The mechanic actively dislikes semi-metallic brake pads and therefore he does not provide these as an option to the car owner.

The situation above is nearly identical in the treatment of PTSD. Therapists simply do not offer CBT as a treatment option to consumers, because many actively dislike it. Further, in order to bolster their preferred type of therapy and to try to discredit CBT, therapists have created a number of myths about CBT. Whether you are adults seeking treatment for your own childhood traumas, parents seeking help for your children, or teenagers seeking help for yourselves, I think you need to be forewarned about the tall tales you are likely to hear. The following are the main myths I have heard about CBT.

(1) **CBT only addresses thoughts, not emotions.** When I was in my early training, I attended a bit of an unorthodox conference in California, called "The Evolution of Psychotherapy." One of the main events was a face-off between Aaron Beck, MD, widely considered to be the founder of CBT, and one of the leading disciples of another type of psychotherapy called Ericksonian therapy. The big accusation against CBT, which was totally false, was that patients were not allowed to talk about their feelings. So Beck made a point of showing a video clip of a real patient's therapy session that involved a fairly in-depth discussion of feelings and the interpretation and meaning of those feelings in his life. Beck felt that he had to make the point to the audience, "See? CBT therapists talk about feelings." That is very true about CBT. The way we conduct CBT, and the way I believe all therapists conduct CBT, is to include a tremendous amount of discussion about feelings.

(2) **In CBT, the therapeutic relationship is not important.** Nothing could be further from the truth. To cooperate in psychotherapy, which requires allowing oneself to be vulnerable and talk about traumatic experiences, one has to feel safe and comfortable with a therapist. To cooperate with the exposure and relaxation exercises, one has to work together with a therapist. The therapist has to be empathic, gentle, tolerant, and likeable. While the unconscious feelings toward therapists are not a focus of treatment, as they could be in psychodynamic therapy, the patients' feelings of trust toward therapists are frequently discussed in CBT.

(3) **CBT is too mechanical.** CBT is by nature repetitive. In order to truly conduct CBT therapy, therapists have to follow a structured protocol that involves basically the same steps for every patient. Structure and repetition for therapists, who feel empathic toward pain and like listening to human stories, can be boring. People don't want to go to work to do boring jobs. It is just so much more fun to listen to people's stories and talk about feelings in psychodynamic therapy.

What most therapists don't understand, or perhaps choose to conveniently ignore, is that CBT does not prohibit them from using their psychodynamic skills. They can still use these skills in well-chosen spots, and listen to the stories and talk about feelings. In fact, to be a really good CBT therapist, you have to mix in a good deal of psychodynamic skill to help patients process their thoughts and feelings and help them make meaning out of their experiences.

(4) **CBT only treats symptoms, not the whole person.** When I hear this criticism, I understand the sentiment behind it, but the statement itself is a large heap of psychobabble nonsense. It has been fashionable for some time now to criticize modern medicine for treating patients like numbers and not treating the whole person. The mantra of treating the whole person is a bit of a transient fad, which seems to reflect more of a feeling against medicine than a real description of an alternative strategy. On the one hand, there is no treatment method that is guaranteed to treat the whole person, whatever that psychobabble means. How a person feels treated in any type of encounter with health professionals depends more on whether the patient feels understood by the clinician than what treatment techniques are used.

(5) **CBT requires patients to be super-motivated.** There is absolutely no evidence that CBT requires more motivation than any other type of therapy. All forms of psychotherapy require voluntary motivation to want to change.

(6) **CBT only helps superficially.** As briefly mentioned in the previous chapter, I recently completed a randomized trial to test whether the addition of the drug D-cycloserine would make CBT work faster or better to treat PTSD. The addition of D-cycloserine to CBT did not help, but that is not the point. The point is that everybody in that study received my CBT protocol, called Youth PTSD Treatment, so we were able to lump every participant together to look at how they improved with CBT. We looked at a broad range of disorders

so we could see whether CBT helped only superficially by working only for PTSD, or CBT helped more comprehensively by working for multiple disorders. As one can see in Figure 12.1, the group significantly improved on PTSD symptoms; they improved from an average of eight symptoms to an average of four symptoms. Figure 12.1 also shows that the group improved on depression, anxiety, oppositional defiant disorder, and the inattention and hyperactivity problems seen in attention-deficit/hyperactivity disorder (ADHD).[6]

Figure 12.1. Changes in PTSD and Comorbid Syndromes in 7–18 Youth (N=62) Treated with Cognitive Behavioral Therapy Focused on Trauma and PTSD (Scheeringa, unpublished).

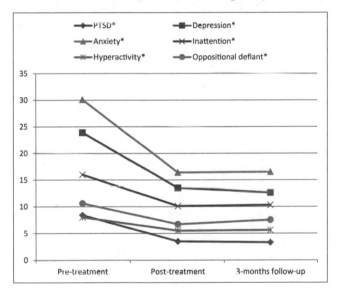

We also have shown similar results with very young children. We completed the only randomized trial to treat PTSD symptoms in young children who had experienced any type of trauma.[7] Twenty-five three- to six-year-old children completed my twelve-session Preschool PTSD Treatment, a manualized protocol of CBT. As Figure 12.2 shows, they not only improved on PTSD symptoms, but they also significantly improved on depression, separation anxiety, and oppositional defiance. They improved on ADHD symptoms immediately after treatment, but this improvement had disappeared by the six-month follow-up.

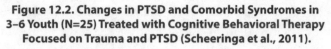

Figure 12.2. Changes in PTSD and Comorbid Syndromes in 3–6 Youth (N=25) Treated with Cognitive Behavioral Therapy Focused on Trauma and PTSD (Scheeringa et al., 2011).

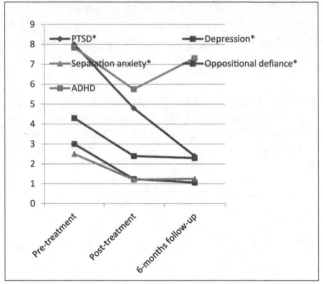

*Change from pretreatment levels was significant, p<.05. All syndromes were measured as the number of *DSM-IV* symptoms with a structured interview of caregivers.

Luke was introduced in Chapter Five as a young boy whose PTSD had been mistaken for ADHD. Luke was a four-year-old who was in his grandmother's legal custody because Luke's mother lost custody due to her drug abuse and neglect. His preschool teacher had told his grandmother that she ought to get him evaluated for ADHD. I mentioned Luke again in Chapter Seven as an example of a complicated case with more types of symptoms above and beyond PTSD symptoms.

Throughout the first eight treatment sessions with CBT, Luke was very oppositional and distractible with the therapist. These types of behaviors made it extremely difficult to perform the CBT techniques with him in the psychotherapy sessions. During the weekly meetings of the research team, we discussed whether to stop the CBT protocol and switch to giving him medication for ADHD. Our reasoning was that he might not be benefiting from the CBT sessions because he was too distracted and the CBT might actually work better once his ADHD was under control. However, we decided not to switch to ADHD medication because there were enough moments when he seemed focused in between the distractible moments, so much so that we gambled on our belief that it was not true ADHD.

It was fortunate that we plowed ahead and stuck to the CBT protocol. After the eighth session, the exposure exercises finally seemed to be working. At the beginning of the ninth session, Luke's grandmother reported that he had behaved much better and was much happier during the previous week. During the therapy session, his behavior while alone with the therapist was drastically different, too. He was cooperative, focused, and pleasant. This was such a radical turnaround in his behavior that the therapist double-checked with the grandmother later to make sure he had not started taking a new medication that she forgot to tell us about.

This was a dramatic case of symptoms that were not true ADHD symptoms drastically improving with CBT focused on PTSD symptoms. Luke and his grandmother completed all twelve sessions of the CBT protocol. By the end of the protocol, his PTSD symptoms had decreased from thirteen to one; ADHD symptoms had decreased from seventeen to two; ODD symptoms had decreased from eight to two; depression symptoms had decreased from six to zero; and separation anxiety symptoms had decreased from five to zero.

(7) **CBT is just about positive thinking.** It is true that one of the CBT techniques is to reframe negative thoughts into more positive thoughts, but that does not mean the negative thoughts are ignored. Good CBT therapists actually spend a lot of time discussing the value of the negative thoughts and how those have been helpful ways for patients to cope.

Also, therapists and patients talk about a lot more than thinking in CBT. A common technique we use during CBT is called the **cognitive triad.** We teach patients that thoughts, feelings, and behaviors are interconnected. Thoughts can drive feelings and behaviors and vice versa, and all three components are important.

(8) **CBT only works for "simple" problems.** This is the most common criticism I hear from skeptics when I give presentations. It is usually phrased as "You don't see the patients I see," implying that clinicians in the community see more complicated and more severe patients than I see in my research studies.

Community clinicians try to support their claim by noting that research studies have exclusion criteria that limit who can be in the research studies. So, let us look at who gets excluded in research studies. In our published clinical trial in which we treated seven- through eighteen-year-old children and adolescents, out of 142 youths assessed, a grand total of nine were excluded.[8] That is, only 6 percent of the youths were excluded from the study. The youths who were excluded were one person with autism, one person with intellectual disability, one teenager who had to be hospitalized halfway through the treatment due to suicidal ideas, one child with a history of seizures (because he might be randomized to receive the medication D-cycloserine), and five youths with psychotic symptoms.

Except for the child with a history of seizures whom we had to exclude due to the experimental medication, the excluded children were not able to meaningfully participate in psychotherapy because of their cognitive disabilities. If community clinicians are attempting to treat PTSD in children with the disabilities we excluded, then they are probably attempting inappropriate treatments.

The sample in our research study was 42 percent Black/African American and 82 percent from divorced or single-parent families, and had experienced an average of three different types of traumas. These characteristics seem to match pretty well with the types of patients seen in community clinics. But it is hard to tell. Community clinicians who claim "You don't see the patients I see" have never supported their claims with their own data about the patients they see. It is difficult to verify their claims unless they present their own data.

What's Wrong with the Mental Health Business?

If CBT is so darn effective and therapists are truly good-hearted people who want to help children, why don't therapists use CBT? That is one of the great questions about the whole psychotherapy business.

In the well-known fairy tale about the three little pigs, the first little pig built a house of straw, but the big bad wolf blew it down and ate the pig. The second little pig built a house of sticks, but the wolf blew it down and ate that pig, too. Every pig would know that it would be much safer to build a house of brick, so one has to wonder, what were those first two pigs thinking? Therapists seem to be like the first two little pigs who knew it wasn't too smart to build houses of straw or sticks, but they did it anyway. The third little pig is like the uncommon therapist with good sense who uses CBT.

There is a strangely hostile feeling within many therapists' communities toward structured protocols like CBT that is hard to capture and describe to someone outside the profession. These hostile critics of CBT give many reasons for why they believe it does not work (see the above myths), but I think these are mostly a smoke screen for something bigger.

That something bigger is that many therapists are worried their clients will not like them. Therapists are people who by their very nature tend to be concerned about their personal-relationship status with others; that is part of what makes them good therapists. Their strength in excess, however, is often their weakness. When children put up resistance in therapy sessions to following directions from therapists (and talking about their traumatic events), the children look distressed and resistant. When the children look distressed and resistant, the therapists often become worried that the children will not like them. To prevent being disliked, the therapists backpedal by trying to empathize and negotiate with the children. This negotiation almost inevitably takes them out of the structure of the CBT protocol.

If you are or have been a parent, you know this feeling. I am sure you can remember the first times your children were unhappy with you because you told them they could not do something or could not have something they wanted. Your heart starts to break a little because you love your children. But, as parents, you either know intuitively or you learn the hard way that you have to say no to your children many times for their own good, sometimes for their own safety and survival. If you backpedal now, you will be in bigger trouble later. Therapists who do not have children of their own are not at their full potential as therapists because they have not yet really learned that hard lesson of parenting. Sometimes you have to be unpopular for your child's own good.

One huge attraction of psychodynamic therapy and play therapy for therapists is that they almost never have to say no to clients. If clients put up resistance to talking about a topic, the technique of psychodynamic therapy is to "follow the patient" and ask, "How does that make you feel?" Psychodynamic therapists always get to be the good parents. For children who have had little experience with empathic, warm, sensitive parents, play therapy does have benefits for them. It does not work very well for PTSD, though. That third little pig may have had to work harder to build a house of bricks, or he may have been teased for being overly cautious, but he lived.

Recap

- If your children have had symptoms for more than one month, it is time to get treatment. There is no useful purpose in waiting any longer.
- For a therapy to earn the label of evidence-based treatment, there must be at least one published randomized clinical trial showing that the therapy actually worked.
- CBT is the best evidence-based treatment for PTSD.
- Play therapy is usually not a good treatment for PTSD because it is not structured and directive enough to push patients to confront their memories and triggers of traumatic events.
- There are strong forces that compel therapists to use play therapy instead of CBT. These forces benefit the therapists, but not the consumers.

For Parents to Do

- Search for therapists in your communities who specialize in treating PTSD.

- Continue to learn. The more you become educated about PTSD, the better you will be able to help your children. Explore websites and skim through books to find the kind of information that is best suited for you. Many websites, blogs, and books are dominated by sexual abuse, which may or may not be applicable to you. Much of the information on the internet is first-person experiences, which may be dramatic but not terribly generalizable to other people. Much of the information on websites of national organizations and in textbooks is generic and vague and not always very practical. If you cannot find the information you want, start your own discussion thread or website and create your own social network of people with similar needs.

- Your main job is to find good solutions to all three of these challenges: (1) your children get good assessments to find the right diagnoses; (2) your children get the right treatments; and (3) you get therapists whom your children like. If you find all three of these things in your shopping, you should feel enormously lucky.

- If you are using insurance to pay for treatment, first go to the provider directory on your insurance website or call the company and get a list of the providers who take your insurance.

- Next, ask friends, neighbors, and coworkers for their recommendations about the doctors and therapists on your list. Also, fax or email the list to your pediatrician. Ask your primary care doctor for recommendations, because they refer their patients to therapists every day. Word of mouth is often the best way to find good clinicians. You may also want to search on the internet for the terms trauma, PTSD, evidence-based, and cognitive behavioral therapy.

- If the providers on your list have websites, go to the sites and look for information on what they specialize in. Do they list experience with trauma? Do they mention evidence-based treatments and CBT?

- If a clear winner does not emerge from your inquiries, call the providers and screen them over the phone. Yes, you can do that, and the good therapists love it when you do that because they know that means you will be an informed and involved patient. Do they have experience with trauma? Do they know and value evidence-based treatments and CBT? It may be difficult to get straight and clear answers to these questions, so try to gauge whether they seem relieved or defensive that you ask those questions.

- Think of doctors and therapists as trying out for a part in a play when you visit them for the first time. If you and your child don't like what you see or hear, try someone else. There is no penalty for doctor shopping except the cost of your copay.

- You do not have to see only the providers who are on your insurance list. You can always see anyone you want who is out of your network. It will cost you more up front, but you can usually get some portion reimbursed to you from your insurance company

- Insist on regular meetings with your children's therapists so you can learn the things that children will not spontaneously tell you.

- During therapy, use Elements of Cognitive Behavior Therapy for PTSD in the Appendix as a springboard to discuss with your therapist whether or not the therapy truly appears to be CBT.

Chapter Thirteen
Treatment for Complicated Cases

Liam: PTSD Diagnosis Missed for Years

In Chapter Seven I introduced you to Liam as an example of a complicated case with multiple diagnoses who was misdiagnosed for years. Liam was a fourteen-year-old who was being seen by a psychologist for attention problems, oppositional behavior, depression, and failing grades at school. The real problem for Liam, and his family, was that the psychologist had completely missed the diagnosis of PTSD and decided to focus first on treatment for his depression. After treatment for depression did not work, the psychologist decided to focus instead on ADHD and referred him to a psychiatrist for an evaluation for medication. His case would be astonishing if it were not so common.

Luckily, this psychiatrist finally conducted a screen for trauma events and PTSD symptoms and discovered that Liam had full-blown PTSD brought about by the experiences of many frightening events with his drug-addicted mother. Liam had suffered for years unnecessarily because he had been misdiagnosed and given the wrong treatments.

At the end of his successful treatment with us for PTSD, his caregiver wrote a note to the therapist to thank her for helping Liam. She recognized that our focus on the past traumas and the way we refocused his treatment on PTSD had been, as she phrased it, "the turning point" for his recovery.

It Is Always Complicated, but There Are Two Issues More Troubling than Most

I also discussed in Chapter Seven that there are many ways PTSD can be complicated. It is impossible in the space of this book to discuss all of the possible ways PTSD can be complicated. There are, however, two challenging issues that cause the most problems for successful treatment of PTSD in youths. When I am supervising therapists or running a research study on CBT, the two most common complications that we run into are co-occurring disorders and family problems.

1. PTSD Does Not Like Being Alone: Two Types of Co-occurring Disorders

It is still a mystery why PTSD almost never exists alone. Nearly all individuals with PTSD also have a second psychiatric diagnosis, and many have several other psychiatric disorders. With different disorders present at the same time, it can get confusing to know where to start treatment. Liam was a perfect example of that.

We can take some of the mystery out of it, though, by recognizing that there are two main types of co-occurring disorders based on when they started. The first type involves co-occurring disorders that followed the traumatic events. These disorders, like PTSD, are caused by the traumatic experience. The second type involves co-occurring disorders that existed prior to the traumatic events. These disorders have absolutely nothing to do with the traumatic experiences. We have substantial research that shows both types are common. The first type, where co-occurring disorders followed the traumatic events, is relatively easy to deal with.

First Type: Co-occurring Disorders Follow Traumatic Events

When co-occurring disorders like depression, anxiety, and oppositional behavior develop following traumatic events, they usually improve quite nicely with CBT for PTSD. In the previous chapter, I presented the evidence from research studies that when CBT for PTSD is used on children and adolescents, these co-occurring disorders improve at the same time the PTSD improves. This makes good sense because the disorders were all caused by traumatic events, so addressing the traumatic events should help all of the disorders.

But how do you know whether the co-occurring disorders started before or after the traumatic events? Well, it is one of those things that is amazingly simple but apparently difficult to do for many therapists: You ask when they started.

There has been a lot of unnecessary confusion in our field because researchers have had a difficult time recognizing that this is an important issue. Consequently, they simply have not asked when co-occurring disorders started in their research studies.

Curtis McMillen, PhD, a social worker, recognized how absurd this was. He, along with trauma researcher Carol North, MD, conducted a study of trauma survivors that addressed this shortcoming of previous studies. When he worked at the George Warren Brown School of Social Work at Washington University in St. Louis, he and Dr. North published a study that was titled, appropriately, "Untangling the psychiatric comorbidity of posttraumatic stress disorder in a sample of flood survivors."[1] They assessed 162 adult victims of the 1993 Great Midwest Floods. They assessed five other disorders in addition to PTSD and carefully tracked the number of symptoms in each disorder and the onset of the symptoms.

Interestingly, they found that 100 percent of the victims who developed one or more of the five other disorders also had a striking number of PTSD symptoms following the floods. They concluded that "no evidence was found to suggest that comorbid disorders develop independently of PTSD following trauma or that comorbidity was due to symptom overlap among disorders."[2] In other words, if individuals developed new non-PTSD disorders after the flood, they also developed significant PTSD symptoms. New non-PTSD disorders do not develop after traumas in isolation from PTSD symptoms, and this indicates how central PTSD is to post-trauma reactions, which again explains why co-occurring disorders so often improve along with PTSD when CBT is used.

In 2008 we replicated McMillen's findings in our study of survivors of Hurricane Katrina in New Orleans.[3] In a sample of seventy three- to six-year-old children, we also found that 100 percent of those who developed one or more of four other disorders also had new PTSD symptoms. In addition, in the mothers of those children, we found that only two of them developed a non-PTSD disorder in the absence of new PTSD symptoms.

McMillen's study should have had a major impact on the thinking in our field about how to consider co-occurring disorders with PTSD. If not putting some controversies to rest, it should have at least stimulated similar studies to replicate the findings. It should have been widely cited in subsequent papers on this topic. Instead, after fifteen years it has been cited in only about fifteen papers outside of McMillen's colleagues' or my own papers.

It should have influenced experts to realize that PTSD is the core psychological injury that ought to be the primary focus of treatment following trauma. Instead, the common way of planning interventions for trauma survivors is still to focus on depression or anxiety separately without a central focus on PTSD. After Hurricane Katrina, a high-ranking administrator in Louisiana state government who was involved in Louisiana's mental health response testified in front of a legislative committee that because there would be a lot of depression following the disaster, the state needed to fund programs to treat depression, without ever mentioning PTSD.

And in 2012, I was part of a group of nine states that was funded to address the trauma-related needs of children in child welfare. The commissioner of the federal agency in charge of the grants stood in front of the grantees in a large hotel ballroom and presented the well-known data that traumatized children show multiple co-occurring disorders in addition to PTSD. The response to this by most of the states was to mistakenly plan to implement five or six different interventions instead of focusing on PTSD.

Second Type: Co-occurring Disorders
Existed Before Traumatic Events

The second type involves co-occurring disorders that existed prior to the traumatic events and have absolutely nothing to do with the traumatic experiences. This type can be much trickier to deal with than the first type. The reason for this is that therapists fail to recognize that the co-occurring disorders were present before the traumatic events. The therapists never bothered to ask the question that Curtis McMillen asked about when each disorder started. That alone would not be so bad except that they nearly always assume the co-occurring problems were caused by the traumatic events. That's all interesting stuff to researchers, but how does it impact consumers?

It impacts consumers because there has been a trend to think about traumatic experiences as being of two main types—interpersonal and non-interpersonal. **Interpersonal trauma** is any type of trauma between two persons. This would include sexual abuse, physical abuse, and witnessing of domestic violence. **Non-interpersonal trauma** is everything else—automobile accidents, natural disasters, injuries, and so forth. Many therapists, and perhaps nearly all of them, are blindly in love with the theory that interpersonal traumas cause more severe and more complex types of PTSD because the interpersonal nature of the trauma impacts individuals' shame, sense of self, and capacity for trust, among other things. Those who believe in this theory believe all problems stem from the interpersonal trauma because it fits nicely with their belief that personal relations are the most important of all things in life. That is, they cannot seem to see that maybe some of the non-PTSD issues existed before the traumatic events. These therapists believe CBT is not adequate because it focuses narrowly on trauma and not on all of the other issues. Therefore, youths with interpersonal trauma often do not get offered CBT.

Suppose you go to the dentist because you have pain and temperature sensitivity in a tooth. The dentist takes an x-ray of the tooth, which suggests there may be nerve damage, but there also may not be damage. This dentist has a personal belief that a root canal is needed to fix the problem because he heard of this somewhere or was taught this while in dental school. So he is persuasive at scaring you that your tooth is going to die and you are going to be in a world of hurt, and you spend $1,000 to replace a perfectly good tooth when all you really needed was for the dentist to shave down a point on the upper tooth that was making hard contact with the lower tooth, and to use toothpaste for temperature-sensitive teeth and practice a little patience.

Therapists who love the theory that interpersonal traumas cause more severe and more complex types of PTSD are like the dentist who replaces a perfectly good tooth. There are absolutely no good facts indicating that interpersonal trauma causes more severe or more complex types of PTSD than other types of traumatic experiences. Children who have PTSD following interpersonal trauma deserve to receive CBT just like children who have PTSD from all other types of traumas.

The Narrative Fallacy of Complex PTSD

Why do therapists want to believe so badly in the myth that interpersonal trauma causes more complex PTSD? I think a good part of the answer is that the myth makes for a nice and tidy explanation for everything. The notion that a nice and tidy explanation creates a streamlined and simple story is called the **narrative fallacy**. This is a term that was coined to describe the human need to have an explanation for a set of facts, even when no such explanation is true. Humans probably resort to the narrative fallacy even more strongly when the facts are more and more complicated.

In the book *The Everything Store: Jeff Bezos and the Age of Amazon*,[4] author Brad Stone describes a meeting with Jeff Bezos, the founder of Amazon, in which he asked for Bezos's cooperation in writing the book. Bezos asked the author how he was going to handle the narrative fallacy problem. Bezos knew the story of the creation and growth of amazon.com was a complicated one without simple explanations or linear storylines. There were no simple heroes and villains. But Bezos was anticipating that Stone was going to feel tempted to downplay the complexity of the story and create one-dimensional characters in order to create a simpler, more dramatic, best-selling story.

I think this anecdote about the story of amazon.com is a perfect analogy for the interpersonal trauma problem. The real explanation for how and why youths have the problems they have is complicated. A much simpler explanation to comprehend is the fallacy that all of their problems stem from their interpersonal trauma rather than from a mixture of genetics and trauma.

It is curious that such confusion reigns around PTSD and co-occurring disorders. Co-occurring disorders are actually common throughout psychiatry. For example, people with schizophrenia have another psychiatric disorder about 50 percent of the time.[5] Yet there does not seem to be quite the same amount of controversy and clinical mismanagement as there is with PTSD. I believe the reason for the mismanagement of PTSD treatment is the unique under-recognition of PTSD, which I covered in Chapter Five. Every doctor can identify a patient who has full-blown schizophrenia, but not everyone knows what transient, triggered fear reactions to a reminder of a traumatic event from the past look like.

Ella: Preexisting Personality Disorder and Drug Abuse

Ella was a seventeen-year-old white female who had been sexually molested by her father at age twelve. She was also raped by an acquaintance at age fourteen. The rapist was arrested and sentenced to prison. She had been in counseling for two years at the local community mental health center, but she was not showing any improvement. Neither Ella nor her mother could describe what type of psychotherapy she had been receiving at the community mental health center or exactly what problems they were working on.

Based on the intake assessment at our clinic, we diagnosed Ella with PTSD, major depressive disorder, and some moderate problems with anxiety. Her symptoms overall appeared fairly severe. Her mother described her as a "shell of a child." Ella had been harassed and bullied at school by friends of the rapist, so she had dropped out of school.

We began to treat Ella by focusing on the trauma and PTSD symptoms because we felt these were likely to be underlying her other behaviors, and it appeared that her PTSD had not been addressed at the community mental health clinic. After eight CBT sessions, however, Ella revealed to the therapist for the first time that she was using drugs and that she was cutting her skin to relieve her pain. With further questioning, Ella revealed that she had been using marijuana and cutting herself since she was eleven years old. We had asked her about those issues earlier, but Ella admitted she had lied during our intake assessment.

Several days later Ella was hospitalized. She had been walking down the highway near her home in a methamphetamine-induced stupor. When her brother tried to pick her up in his car, she attacked the car and he had to call the police. The police arrested her and took her to a hospital from where she was transferred to a psychiatric hospital. This incident led to the discovery that she had been prostituting herself to get drugs for months, perhaps years, and had a serious methamphetamine addiction.

In this case it took some time to figure out, but it eventually became clear that Ella had problems with a personality disorder, drug abuse, cutting, and depression before she had experienced any of her traumatic events. This explained why she did not improve with CBT focused on PTSD.

2. Family Problems

The second complication we commonly run into is family problems, and these have hundreds of variations. Examples of family problems include a father who is overwhelmed with being a single parent because the mother died of cancer; a parent stressed out by the demands of work; a child dealing with a father's alcoholism; a divorced couple who argue over visitation schedules and custody; a child with one or both parents in jail; or a child moved frequently to different foster homes.

Therapists believe family problems need to be resolved first, and they put off treatment for PTSD for several reasons. First, many therapists believe stability is needed in the home before patients will feel safe enough to talk about their traumas. Second, these family problems tend to cause logistical problems in simply bringing the patients to therapy appointments consistently. If the children cannot attend therapy appointments regularly, it is difficult to make steady progress. Third, the family problems tend to create new and urgent problems each day and these can sidetrack youths from being able to focus on their past traumas. Each of these reasons by itself can appear daunting, but at the same time all of them can feel overwhelming to therapists.

There are two rather huge flaws, though, with this family-first strategy of putting off treatment for PTSD in favor of dealing with family problems. One huge flaw of the family-first strategy is that many of these family problems can never be resolved. Because the therapists struggle with these problems with no end in sight, they never get to the treatment of PTSD. These youths are then faced with the prospect that they will not be offered appropriate, evidence-based treatment for their PTSD. The second huge flaw of the family-first strategy is that there is no evidence that these family problems prevent youths from being able to focus on their PTSD problems.

I once helped to treat a five-year-old boy who had witnessed repeated episodes of domestic violence. In the final episode of violence, the father shot the mother in front of the children. She survived. He went to jail. Many months later, we started CBT to treat the boy's PTSD. In the middle of the CBT work, the father was released from jail and, to the amazement of all of us on the team, the mother allowed the father to rejoin the family.

There ensued a vigorous debate within our team about whether or not it was wise to continue with the CBT. One part of the team took the family-first approach and advocated that we needed to pause the CBT and help the boy deal with his feelings about his father and monitor the situation for a while. The other part of the team noted that there was absolutely no good evidence in the research literature that the boy would be unable to do CBT in the midst of such family problems, and if we did not stick to our guns and complete the CBT protocol, then it was likely the boy would never receive good treatment for his PTSD for the rest of his life. We stuck to our guns and plowed ahead with the CBT and, as I completely expected, he made fantastic improvements in his PTSD symptoms.

The Constant Gardener

It is easy to say "stick to your guns," or to say the research evidence shows this or shows that, but it is enormously difficult to actually stick to your guns in the heat of the moment. In the novel by John le Carré titled *The Constant Gardener*, which was made into a popular movie, the reference to gardening in the title seems to apply to the constant digging and burying of things. The wife in the story was constantly digging into an international conspiracy of profiteering by a pharmaceutical company, for which she was murdered. The husband in the story constantly investigates, or digs, into her murder to find out why she was murdered.

I think of constant gardening as an excellent analogy for treatment of complicated cases of PTSD, but I think of it in terms of constant planning and arranging a complicated garden. Shade versus sun is one complication. Some areas of the garden are in shade because there are trees or buildings that block the sun. Other areas of the garden receive harsh sun most of the day. Other areas are part shade and part sun. Because some plants thrive in sun and some thrive in shade, it requires careful forethought about which plants to place where. Moisture is another complication. Some areas are raised and stay dry while other areas are low-lying and stay wet. You put a plant in a spot with the wrong amount of sun or moisture and it will die. In addition, a gardener wants plants blooming all year round, so one needs a mixture of plants that bloom at different times of the year. Also, plants must be arranged by height so that shorter plants are not blocked from view by taller plants. And sometimes the expert advice about plants is not quite accurate for your climate and soil conditions, so trial and error are sometimes needed to discover where some plants will thrive the best.

Bringing to bear all those pieces of information is a constant and complicated task, but gardeners love the challenge to their creativity. No single strategy works for every part of the garden. A stepwise, multifaceted plan is needed to deal with the different levels of shade, moisture, time of year, and plant height.

In a stepwise, systematic plan to treat complicated cases of PTSD, the therapists and patients are in a similar constant struggle. They must first realize what problems can change and what problems cannot change. Personality traits, such as narcissism (being overly self-centered), self-defeatism, anger regulation, shyness, and extroversion (being extremely outgoing and talkative), cannot change much, if at all. Because patients cannot change these traits very much, therapists must adapt the treatment strategies around these traits. Having this understanding up front helps tremendously with appropriate expectations for treatment.

Other problems, such as drug use, can change but often take a long time and are lifelong challenges. Many of the common psychiatric disorders, such as PTSD, anxiety, and depression, can change relatively rapidly, within one to four months.

A stepwise, systematic plan can be as simple as making a list of each problem, the expectation of how much each can change (none, a little, or a lot), how rapidly each can likely change (never, slowly, or rapidly), the treatment strategy for each, and the order in which to tackle the problems. A stepwise plan is only a good starting place. A plan must be constantly reevaluated and adjusted during the course of treatment as situations and symptoms change.

The presence of multiple disorders can make it confusing to clinicians about which disorder to treat following traumatic events. The treatments for PTSD, depression, anxiety, defiance, and other problems are all vastly different. As we saw with the case of Ella, treating the wrong disorder as the primary problem led to a waste of time and money, and she had to be hospitalized due to her drug addiction. The problem with Ella was that she withheld information from us about her drug use. In the unique world of PTSD, treatment can be complicated by another type of problem, memory, which is the topic of the next chapter.

Recap

- Following trauma, PTSD is the core psychological response that requires attention. Research has shown that non-PTSD disorders almost always arise in conjunction with PTSD.
- The research findings chart a clear course for treatment. PTSD is the core psychological injury following trauma. Treatment ought to focus on PTSD. Other comorbid disorders also improve as PTSD is treated.

For Parents to Do

- Carefully consider whether focusing treatment on PTSD might be the most efficient and rational treatment that would also help with the comorbid disorders.

Chapter Fourteen

Memory: The Unwelcome Guest and the Girl Who Forgot She Was Abused

Memory is crucial for PTSD. By definition, PTSD cannot develop unless there are memories of traumatic events. Among the more than 100 disorders in the *DSM-5*, PTSD is one of the few that require memory of an event as part of the diagnostic criteria.

Yet memory is a tricky thing. Super memory power is one of the traits that most separates humans from other species, but our memory is far from perfect. Researchers have shown that we can be tricked into believing we remember things that did not happen. We can also remember real things in the wrong order and with the wrong details. And in PTSD, survivors would rather forget than remember.

Dr. Judith Herman wrote, "The conflict between the will to deny horrible events and the will to proclaim them aloud is the central dialectic of psychological trauma."[1] Her statement is not 100 percent correct, but, as usual, she makes a dramatic point that to deny or proclaim the existence of traumatic events tends to be important for the recovery of trauma survivors. This could be interpreted as the capacity to forget or remember traumatic events, but it is much trickier than that.

Memory is a particularly challenging issue for researchers to study because it has features of what psychiatrists and psychologists call a **latent construct**. We cannot see a memory. We cannot touch a memory. In these ways, memories are hidden and concealed, that is, they are latent. We can only ask patients to tell us what they remember, and they may opt to not tell us some things they do remember, or they may not

185

be able to easily retrieve some memories because they are old or painful. In contrast to a latent construct, a **manifest construct** is something such as blood pressure that can be measured or hyperactivity that is difficult to conceal.

PTSD Symptoms That Require Memory

Of the twenty symptoms in the *DSM-5* diagnostic criteria, at least seven of them require some form of autobiographical memory of past events.

- **Recurrent, intrusive, distressing recollections of the event.** Memories of traumatic events pop into patients' minds when they are unwanted.
- **Distressing dreams of the event.** While the contents of dreams are usually, or perhaps always, a disguise to hide the true content underlying the dream material, there nonetheless needs to be memory of events to serve as the raw material. For example, a child who has PTSD from witnessing domestic violence may have a frightening nightmare about the boogeyman under his bed. The dream is not about the boogeyman. The dream is about the man who beat his mother, but the nature of dreaming disguises him as the boogeyman.
- **Psychological distress from reminders.** For example, a girl who was sexually abused by her father is now distressed whenever any male enters her home.
- **Physiological distress from reminders.** An example includes a boy who was involved in a motor vehicle accident. Now, every time he has to ride in a car, his brain remembers the accident and his heart beats fast, his palms sweat, and his hands tremble.
- **Avoid activities, places, or physical reminders.** A girl who has PTSD from a variety of invasive and painful medical procedures that were needed for her cancer treatment may become resistant and distressed every time she has to return to the hospital unit because it triggers bad memories.
- **Avoid people, conversations, or interpersonal situations that are reminders.** A boy developed PTSD after Hurricane Katrina partly from living for two days under a highway overpass with hundreds

of other victims. There was no food, shelter, or toilets. He was in fear for his life the whole time as men walked around openly with guns and fights broke out. Now he refuses to go anywhere where there are crowds.

- **Dissociative reactions** (e.g., flashbacks) are a seventh possible symptom that requires memory. Some dissociative episodes can be triggered by events that resemble the traumas. Other types of dissociative experiences appear to develop when patients have no or little conscious recollection of their traumas.

Because so many symptoms depend on memory, PTSD is to a large degree a disorder of memory. Memories of traumatic experiences are intense and inappropriately connected to emotions of fear. Fearful memories are inappropriately triggered by cues in the environment that are not truly threatening situations. Memories of traumatic events in PTSD are unwelcome guests.

Limitations of Research

Besides the challenges of memories being latent constructs that are difficult to measure accurately, an additional problem with studying memory is that everyone's traumatic experiences are different. Hence, everyone's memories of their traumatic events are different. Even for two individuals who were involved in exactly the same traumatic event, there are differences in the types of threats they experienced, the number of threats, other people involved, injuries, physical sensations, and so forth. Research thrives on being able to standardize assessments so that the same things are being measured in the same way on all subjects. This standardization of assessments is what allows one person to be compared to another person in a reliable fashion. Memories have so many differences between people that it is not easy to compare them. As a consequence, the published literature on memory and trauma has been dominated by speculation, debate, and individual case studies. Research studies are critical but have limited capacities to teach us about memory and trauma.

Remembering Too Much May Be a Problem

On May 20, 1988, a mentally deranged woman went on a daylong terror spree in an affluent suburb about twenty miles north of Chicago. In the middle of her spree, she entered an elementary school in Winnetka, Illinois. She shot one boy in a bathroom and then wandered into a second-grade classroom and shot five children, one of whom died.

After the event, researchers assessed those present at the attack for symptoms of PTSD and asked questions about their whereabouts and sensory experiences during the attack.[2] The sensory experiences included how distressed they felt at the time, how much they feared for their lives or the lives of loved ones, and what they saw of the shooting scene. Twenty-four school personnel completed the measures five months after the attack, and thirteen of them repeated the measures seventeen months after the attack. Twenty-five percent of the subjects changed their answers of where they were when the shooting happened; all of them moved themselves closer to the shooting than they actually were.

More interesting, the school personnel who believed they saw more details at the scene seventeen months after the attack compared to what they reported five months after the attack had more symptoms of PTSD than those who did not remember more. That is, those who developed more severe symptoms of PTSD also changed their memories to believe they saw details of the shootings. It was not clear whether they really saw more details but would not or could not recall them at the five-month assessment, or they did not really see those details but their memories tricked them into believing they did over time.

This study not only provided some of the earliest systematic data on how memories change after traumatic events, but it documented that remembering more may be a problem. At least, believing that one saw more may be a problem. The authors speculated that the process of subjects believing they saw more of the trauma scene than they actually saw was a "malignant memory process" that was counterproductive to recovery.

Another study confirmed that this memory process is common. Researchers gathered detailed eyewitness memories from fifty-nine veterans from Operation Desert Storm in Kuwait and Iraq one month after the war and repeated this process two years later. Seventy percent of the subjects appeared to remember more events as time went on, in that they reported traumatic events two years after the war that they had not reported one month after the war.[3] Just as in the school shooting study, those who appeared to remember that they had seen more traumatic events as time passed had more symptoms of PTSD. Interestingly, 46 percent of the subjects appeared to forget events, as they reported traumatic events at one month that they did not report at two years. Because 46 percent and 70 percent add up to more than 100 percent, it appeared that some subjects both forgot about some events and newly remembered other events.

The Illinois school shooting study and the Desert Storm study converged in a similar pattern. Those who believed they had seen more traumatic events as time passed had more severe PTSD. One must be careful, however, of the chicken-or-egg phenomenon in relation to these types of data. It is tempting initially to believe the malignant memory came first and PTSD came second. That is, the faulty memory of some individuals led them to believe they witnessed more traumas than they actually did witness, and this stimulated more PTSD symptoms. However, it is equally plausible, and probably more likely, that those individuals who were vulnerable to developing PTSD had their affective, arousal, and cognitive fear reactions cued more frequently by their PTSD symptoms, which in turn heightened their memory functions to falsely remember things they may have never witnessed.

What about children? Robyn Fivush, PhD, a psychologist at Emory University in Atlanta, has managed to perform some remarkable work on early memory capacities by studying young children. Fivush was part of a group of researchers who were the first to classify the quality of children's trauma memories and to examine whether these predicted the severity of their PTSD symptoms.[4] They interviewed a group of three- and four-year-old children several months following their exposure to Hurricane Andrew and asked them how much they remembered of the events. The children who remembered less had more symptoms of PTSD, suggesting that those who could not recall their experiences or were simply less willing to talk about them fared worse.

Six years later, when the children were nine and ten years old, they interviewed them again with the same question and found that the same relationship held up. Those who continued to recall fewer details were the ones with more symptoms of PTSD, and vice versa; those who could recall more, or were more willing to talk about their experiences, had fewer symptoms of PTSD.

Richard Meiser-Stedman, PhD, a psychologist at the Brain Cognitions Unit in Cambridge, England, is another expert in studying the memory of children who have lived through traumas. Meiser-Stedman was interested not so much in how much detail children could recall about their past events but in how intense the memories were inside their brains. Part of the reasoning was that maybe it didn't matter how much they remembered. Even if they remembered very little, if those few memories were particularly intense, then that would be more important.

To investigate this idea, Meiser-Stedman created a measure called the Trauma Memory Quality Questionnaire.[5] The questionnaire, consisting of fourteen "questions," include such questions as "When I remember the frightening event I feel like it is happening right now," and "My memories of the frightening event are like a film that plays over and over." In a study of over 300 youths eleven to eighteen years old, those who scored higher on the questionnaire, indicating that their trauma memories were relatively more intense, had more symptoms of PTSD.

Putting the findings of Fivush and Meiser-Stedman together, an interesting picture comes together of how memory is related to PTSD. Fivush and her team had found that those who recalled less, or at least were less willing to talk about their events, had more symptoms of PTSD. Meiser-Stedman found that those who had more intense memories had more symptoms of PTSD. One interpretation is that when memories of traumatic experiences are intense and overwhelming to individuals, this causes them to remember less or be less willing to talk about them.

Memory is one of the traits that most separates the higher mammals from other species. But like any strength, in excess it is a weakness. The study by Meiser-Stedman seemed to bear that out again. In essence, remembering things too well and too vividly—or at least remembering the memories with all of the negative emotions still connected to them—is a fundamental part of the problem with PTSD. It would seem that those who can forget more easily would be luckier.

As usual, things are never that simple. It appears there are degrees of being able to forget. For some other individuals, the entire traumatic episode is sort of screened off from their awareness. If they were asked whether the event happened to them, they would say yes, and they would be able to pull up details about the events. But in day-to-day living the memory exists behind a frosted glass. The person knows it's back there but doesn't have to see any details clearly. It is as though memories of events can be held in the brain but can be blocked from conscious awareness until the person wants to go looking for them.

Remembering Things That Never Happened May Be a Problem

In the studies just described, researchers did not attempt to untangle whether participants had really seen the traumatic events. For a subject who, for example, denied seeing a disfigured body one month after Operation Desert Storm but endorsed seeing a disfigured body two years later, we do not know which one of those memories was true. We cannot be sure whether the problem lies with "forgetting" events they really saw or believing they saw events they never saw.

We are all familiar in our everyday lives with the phenomenon of forgetting events we really saw, so it seems plausible that research participants could have truly seen some traumatic events but "forgot" to report them to investigators on one or more occasions. We know a few of the symptoms of PTSD involve avoidance of cued reminders of traumatic events. Thus, it makes even more sense that participants possessed internal motivation to avoid and "forget." But is it possible to believe that we remembered events we never really saw?

Psychologist Stephen Ceci, PhD, at Cornell University has conducted some remarkable experiments with very young children that help to answer that question. Forty children, three through six years of age, were interviewed repeatedly and led to believe some events had happened to them that really never happened.[6] One of these false incidents was the rather bizarre fabrication that they had gotten their hand stuck in a mousetrap and had to go to the hospital to get it removed. Remarkably, 34 percent agreed that this false event had really happened. Planted memories from artificial laboratory situations may be one thing, but can this happen in real life in relation to traumatic events?

Vicarious Memories from Family Stories

In Chapter Nine I introduced Lenore Terr's case of a young girl whom she evaluated several years after a horrible accident.[7] The family told a story that when this girl was two years old, her older sister was severely injured in a swimming pool accident. The older sister had accidently been caught by the suction of a drain in the bottom of a swimming pool. The suction was so strong that her intestines were pulled outside of her rectum. The younger sister was present at the time of the accident, but was in a different part of the pool area and never saw her sister's physical injuries.

Fast-forward from the swimming pool accident to several years later. The younger sister began to claim that she actually saw her sister's accident. If we trust the parental recollections, we know for certain that the younger sister could not have seen the accident. Terr speculated that the young girl had heard the family talk about the event often enough to know the story and some of the details. Over time, the girl, for whatever psychological reasons, developed a vicarious memory of the event from the family conversations.

Inflated Allegations Due to Pressure from Interrogations

Perhaps the most common real-life situation in which children and adolescents are under pressure to remember truthfully is during legal investigations about child abuse. When children report allegations of sexual or physical abuse, they are typically questioned by law enforcement investigators to gather evidence. Diane Schetky, MD, a child psychiatrist in Maine who writes frequently about legal issues involving children for the American Academy of Child and Adolescent Psychiatry, described a case of a fifteen-year-old girl who was questioned by police investigators about an alleged sex ring. Schetky wrote that the girl was made to feel like part of the investigative team in order to help other children. Investigators used leading questions about the girl's participation in the alleged sex ring, to which the girl initially agreed. The girl later retracted her unusual claims and admitted that she was trying to please the investigators.[8]

Dr. Schetky described another legal case in which multiple children were questioned by investigators about alleged abuse by their teacher at a New Jersey day care. The teacher was initially convicted and sent to prison based on the testimony of the children and on the testimony of expert witnesses who stated the children showed signs of sexual abuse. After the teacher had spent five years in prison, the conviction was overturned because the interviews with the children were improper and had involved coercive and suggestive techniques.[9]

False Beliefs of Abuse Due to Other Problems

Not everyone who is questioned or interrogated will remember events falsely or exaggerate their "memories" to please others. In the studies that have been discussed previously, the proportion of participants who changed their stories or endorsed false memories was always less than 100 percent, and sometimes far less than 100 percent. Who, then, is prone to have faulty memory? I discussed one possibility briefly before, that is, those who were vulnerable to developing PTSD had their affective, arousal, and cognitive fear reactions cued more frequently by their PTSD symptoms, which in turn heightened their memory functions to falsely remember things they never witnessed.

Other possibilities have been suggested from in-depth, long-term psychotherapy with adult patients. Cases have been described in which adult patients have come to therapy seeking explanations for their problems and suspecting that the explanation was that they had been sexually molested when they were children. The suspicions turned out to be not true, and the conclusion of the therapist for some patients was that patients were driven by their excessive narcissism to these speculations.[10] In another case, it was apparently preferable to the patient to believe she had been sexually traumatized as a child rather than to accept that she was a lesbian.[11]

*"The charm, one might say the genius, of memory is that
it is choosy, chancy, and temperamental: it rejects the
edifying cathedral and indelibly photographs the small
boy outside, chewing a hunk of melon in the dust."*

Elizabeth Bowen

Not Remembering May Be Protective

The marvel of memory gets even more complicated. Consider the flip side of those who remember too intensely or remember things that never happened. What happens to those who are good at forgetting bad things that really happened? If PTSD is in part a disorder of memory, that is, the unwelcome guest in the form of memory that is too intense, then it would make sense that the ability to keep the unwelcome guest out of one's head would be protective. Alexander McFarlane, MD, a psychiatrist in Australia who has conducted a long list of groundbreaking studies in relation to PTSD, provided some of the surprisingly rare data that exist on this topic. McFarlane studied 469 firefighters who were exposed to a bushfire disaster. He asked the firefighters about the extent of their personal injuries from the bushfire four months after the fire and repeated the questions eleven months after the fire. For those with chronic PTSD, their memories of personal injuries did not change over time. But for those who did not have PTSD, 57 percent reported injuries at four months but did not report those injuries at eleven months. In other words, the majority of those without PTSD seemed to have "forgotten" that they had been injured.[12]

Intuitively, this makes a lot of sense. Intuition suggests that forgetting should be good; remembering too intensely should be bad. The human brain seems designed to be able to downgrade the intensity of unpleasant memories. One causes a sibling to be injured due to carelessness, but is able to "forget" about it as an adult lest one be wracked with guilt every day. One gives an embarrassing public speech but is able to "forget" about it, or at least remember it with less emotional distress as time passes. The details can be kept behind the frosted glass.

Enrique: Memories Remembered but Locked Away

Enrique, introduced in Chapter Four, was a child who had witnessed severe domestic violence for years. He admitted that he never really thought about the domestic violence for all those years because he was able to push the memories to the back of his mind. The frosted glass kept him safe. Then, something changed when he turned twelve years old. Enrique didn't know what triggered it, but all of a sudden he started remembering the events of domestic violence in great and distressing detail. After being kept behind the frosted glass for many years, suddenly this protection fell away. After holding it all together for years, the memories about his mother being threatened and terrorized now intruded into his thoughts constantly. During psychotherapy sessions, Enrique finally poured out all of his memories—everything that had been stored behind the frosted glass for so long.

Is Remembering Nothing Possible?

Lenore Terr, the pioneer researcher in San Francisco who wrote about children following traumatic experiences, described at length the case of an eight-year-old girl, Eileen Franklin, who reportedly witnessed her father rape her playmate in the back of a van and then smash her skull with a rock.[13] The scenes of those events were allegedly blocked from her ability to recall them for the next twenty years. She literally did not recall the rape and the murder. As this girl grew up, she wondered occasionally what had happened to her playmate and blithely shrugged it off, believing that her friend must have moved. Then one day, when she was twenty-eight years old, something triggered Eileen to suddenly start remembering. She had her own daughter now, who was five years old and close to the age Eileen was when she had witnessed the rape and the murder. Terr speculated that perhaps it was the way her daughter looked up at her for help on a certain day when the sunlight caught her hair in the same way she had seen her friend. Over the next several months, bit by bit, the twenty-eight-year-old woman seemed to be slowly recalling details of events from twenty years ago.

Many articles have been written about the prosecution of the father that followed, and much doubt has been cast on Eileen's recall about this and other violent incidents that she recalled.[14] The father was convicted of murder, partly based on the expert testimony of Dr. Terr. He spent five years in prison until his conviction was overturned based in part on growing skepticism about recovered memories and in part on new DNA evidence in other cases in which Eileen had implicated him.[15]

The Girl Who Forgot She Was Abused

Far and away, the majority of cases of lost and then regained memories in scientific literature have been about sexual abuse. Recovered memory, still controversial but decidedly less heated these days, has been mainly about what adults remember. Probably the most often-cited case of a blocked and then recovered memory of trauma was described by David Corwin, MD, a child psychiatrist who was one of the founding members and is currently the board chair of the Academy on Violence & Abuse. This case is unusual because of the presence of videotape of the girl's accusations when she was six years old and videotape of the girl discussing the accusations eleven years later.[16]

Corwin had interviewed the six-year-old girl on tape in 1984 in his role as an evaluator during a child-custody case. During this interview, the young girl stated that her mother had rubbed her fingers in the girl's vagina and had burned her feet on a stove. Based on this and other information, the mother lost custody and visitation rights. Corwin contacted the girl eleven years later to get her permission to use the videotape for teaching purposes and to find out what she remembered. The girl, seventeen years old at the second meeting, agreed to let Corwin interview her on tape again. The girl initially claimed not to remember the details of the sexual abuse, but then did remember some of it. She then watched the videotape of herself as a six-year-old talking about the abuse.

The details of the interviews have been published, and nonbelievers have thoroughly dissected the case. One group even interviewed family members to collect new information and further investigate the claim that the girl had recovered repressed memories of abuse.[17] Proponents of repressed memories believe that this is a locked-down, solid case of recovered memories. Skeptics of repressed memories believe equally strongly that there are tremendous holes in the story.

At this point, it does not seem useful to inflame the debate and take a position either way. The usefulness of the discussion would seem to be to expand one's mental horizons in both directions. The point of noting these issues here is not to score a touchdown for either side and claim victory. When trying to understand your child, when trying to treat an individual case, when trying to do what is helpful to an individual in distress, it seems wise to keep an open mind and consider all the options.

For those on the extreme opposite ends of the recovered memory debate, there seems to be little common ground. Finding the common ground for the rest of us is a frustrating task. It is difficult to determine how often repressed or recovered memories truly occur. If one wanted to design a problem that was close to impossible to study, this would seem to be it. How does a doctor ask someone whether the person forgot something he or she can't remember? The answer would always have to be no. A patient could only answer yes if he or she had already recalled the event after the period in which he or she had forgotten it. How does a researcher confirm that a supposedly new memory is truly a new memory and not simply a vaguely known memory that had been lurking behind the mind's frosted glass? A research subject could say he or she does not remember the event previously and we would have to take that person's word for it. Even if there is videotape footage of subjects, such as children saying that they could not recall abusive events, we would still have to take the words of the children.

From where I sit, as someone concerned about children and adolescents, the bigger problem historically has been that professionals and other adults involved with youth have ignored the issues of trauma. Doctors and other professionals have refused to ask children about traumatic experiences. Far too many children with trauma and PTSD have been missed and have never received the treatment that could have helped them. The big problem is not that therapists are trying to plant false memories of abuse in the minds of pediatric patients. The much more common problem is that there are lots of children with emotional and behavioral problems that are the result of traumas being missed in doctors' offices because the doctors don't ask about trauma and PTSD symptoms. Those children remember everything; they just aren't being asked the right questions.

Does Memory Predict Who Will Get Better with Treatment?

All of the previous discussions have been about the existence of memory for traumatic events and how that memory might influence the development of PTSD. These are indeed important considerations, but another concern should also be about how memory is important during treatment—where it matters perhaps the most. There has been relatively much less research on how the quality of memory can influence treatment outcomes.

I recently published the first study of its kind to describe the different ways that youths recall their traumatic experiences during psychotherapy sessions.[18] My team videotaped the psychotherapy sessions of forty-seven youths, seven to eighteen years of age, all of whom received the same highly structured CBT. Research assistants transcribed every word of the sessions onto paper. Then two raters read every transcript to try finding any patterns in how the youths recalled their traumatic experiences.

The two raters found four types of recall styles. The first type we called the **expressive type**. Youths with the expressive type included all of the attributes that might be considered the "ideal" narrative for which we historically have believed psychotherapy is supposed to work; these youths recalled lots of details about their trauma events, expressed their emotion during the retellings, and increased how much they recalled and expressed as they progressed further along in treatment.

The second type we called the **avoidant type**. These youths seemed to avoid giving details about their traumatic event(s). It was like pulling teeth to get any specifics out of them. They rarely seemed to connect feelings to their past memories, and they added only a few details of what they recalled as they progressed further along in treatment.

The third type we called the **undemonstrative type**. Youths of the undemonstrative type rarely, if ever, talked about negative feelings. They were often able to provide new details of their traumatic experiences as they progressed along in treatment, but they would not, or could not, connect and talk about their feelings related to those memories.

The fourth type we called the **fabricated type**. These youths recalled events to their therapists that had never happened. They did not make up entirely new events. They recalled events that had never happened that were pieces of the larger traumatic event that really did happen. For example, a boy who witnessed domestic violence against his mother told his therapist that he joined a SWAT team that arrived on the scene and handled their tracking dog that led them to the perpetrator. These were not small errors of details, such as remembering that a car was blue when it was really red. These were whole scenes that had never happened, such as recalling a car that was never there.

We didn't stop there. Next, we asked the question of whether these different recall types led to better or worse treatment outcomes. Somewhat to our surprise, there were no differences in improvements in their PTSD symptoms among the four types. Whereas most people would have thought the expressive type would do better in treatment, this turned out to be not true at all. If anything, the data seemed to point out that the avoidant, undemonstrative, and fabricated types reduced their PTSD symptoms more than the expressive type. Yet another example of what happens when we stop to carefully collect data is that we find our intuition that we cherish so much is completely wrong.

This study was the first of its kind to describe the details of how youths remember their traumatic events in the course of psychotherapy sessions. Other researchers need to repeat our study and see if they come up with similar or different findings. In general, the field needs much more research in this area to try to find better ways to understand patients and help them recall their trauma memories.

Rose: Too Hot and Too Cold

It seems repetitive at this point to say that memory is complicated, but, well, it can get even more complicated. Rose, the teenage patient I discussed in Chapter Five, remembered her trauma well. What bothered her the most was that she remembered the details all too well. She remembered the trauma when she didn't want to remember it. She could not block it out of her mind. Rose had the PTSD symptom of intrusive and spontaneous recollections of the trauma that would pop into her mind uninvited. The event would play like a movie in her mind over and over. She also had the PTSD symptoms of being psychologically distressed and physiologically aroused when she was confronted with reminders of her trauma, such as a parking lot.

Rose wanted to get better, and she wanted to remember more. In our study on narratives, she was classified in the expressive group because she was able to recall her traumas in detail, talk about additional details as time went on, and talk about her distressing feelings, as painful as that was. Despite that, she had considerable difficulty remembering details of her rape. She seemed to have the dual problems of remembering too intensely and not remembering everything. We recorded her therapy sessions as part of our research study. The following piece of one of her therapy sessions is a good illustration of the struggle to remember versus not being able to remember.

Therapist. What are some thoughts that go through your head?

Rose. One thing is just frustrated 'cause I can't remember. Like I've tried. I'll sit there for hours just trying to remember things and I can't.

Therapist. So for you that's frustrating. [Teen nods.] Okay. Some people might say thank God I don't remember it, you know. Well, what's frustrating about that?

Rose. It's just like. It's like I want to know, I don't want to know what happened, but I want to know what happened to me. Like, it's something like, it's almost like you know it. Like, for example, like you know something that happened, and you want to know the details of what happened. But then you don't 'cause it's going to hurt you. But it happened to you and like you just want to know what happened to you. You don't want to look back. And it's just like this big, black cloud.

Therapist. Right.

Rose. And you can't, you don't know. You just know something happened but you don't know what happened.

Conclusion: It's Impossible to Forget a Truly Traumatic Event

Even in the dramatic cases of truly recovered memories of childhood sexual abuse, the memories were eventually recovered. They were never completely forgotten. As I hope this chapter has made clear, memory is complex, and many strange things are possible. The consensus among experts is that it is entirely possible to completely block recall of traumatic experiences and then remember them at a later time. This temporary blocking may be partial or complete. This forgetting may be largely conscious as a more or less voluntary way to cope and move on, or it may be largely unconscious as an involuntary defense mechanism. At the same time, some supposedly recovered memories have been found to be false and developed as a way to try to explain other problems, created by overly suggestive investigators or due to other reasons. The point is that people can remember or forget a lot of things a lot of different ways.

> *"Human memory is an extremely complex phenomenon."*
> Richard Kluft[19]

I have seen children refuse to admit to their misbehaviors. I have seen children deny they had experienced a variety of traumatic experiences, only to admit to the experiences after my telling them I already knew about them from their mothers. I have seen mothers explain that they had no idea their daughters were being molested by their husbands, but at the same time say they had their suspicions for very specific reasons. I have seen a woman claim that she had no knowledge of being stabbed, even though I had the copies of her treatment in an emergency room and showed them to her. After years of practice and hundreds of patients, I cannot tell whether a patient is lying to me or not. And I cannot tell whether patients believe that they do not remember something when in fact they have faint memories they would prefer to keep faint.

Recap

- Memory is indeed a tricky thing.

For Parents to Do

- If children make allegations that they were sexually or physically abused, they should be believed unless there is some clear evidence that they made up false allegations. These allegations should be reported immediately to child protection services or the police. Abuse from first-degree family (parents and siblings) is generally handled by child abuse investigators; abuse from all other individuals is generally handled by the police.

- Don't be alarmed if their recall seems imperfect or evolves with time.

- While you would like to understand what your children recall, remember that your children are struggling too with their memories. They are probably trying to figure out what happened to them while at the same time wanting to forget what happened to them.

- Most trauma survivors are not eager to tell their stories to anyone, especially their parents. It is recommended to make several gentle and patient attempts to let them know you are available to listen. If children do not want to tell you what happened to them, it may be best left for them to do that with a trained therapist.

- Feel confident that talking about it is almost always better than not talking about it. If your child is willing to talk with you or a therapist, that ought to be encouraged.

Chapter Fifteen

Neurobiology: Does Traumatic Stress Damage the Brain?

Symptoms of trauma-related problems such as in PTSD have always been described as thoughts, feelings, and behaviors because those are what we can see and observe. These thoughts, feelings, and behaviors are what we can see on the surface as the end products of the underlying neurobiology that is far more difficult to see and observe. The underlying neurobiology consists of the electrical impulses and neurotransmitters of neurons in the brain, and the interconnected regulatory relationships among the specialized brain centers. So, if we want to truly understand a psychiatric disorder, we must understand the underlying neurobiology of the brain.

The neurobiology of the human brain is enormously complex—much more complex than scientists have been able to understand so far. And because the brain is so difficult to study directly, it is likely even more complicated than what we can currently imagine. More than 100 neurotransmitter chemicals have been discovered along with over 200 specialized brain areas. There are over eighty billion nerve cells, or neurons, that compose and connect these brain areas. Each brain center has interconnecting neural pathways to other brain centers, so there is rarely, if ever, a simple one-to-one path of communication between two brain areas. Each brain area is therefore influenced and regulated by more than one other brain area, either directly or indirectly through other connecting brain areas. The number of possible pathways to influence and modify the end products of thoughts, feelings, and behaviors is incredibly large and variable.

There are nevertheless two main stress-response systems that have been fairly well described—the **autonomic nervous system** (ANS) and the **hypothalamic-pituitary-adrenal** (HPA) **axis**, which have been the focus of the majority of the research related to trauma.

Autonomic Nervous System

The ANS functions mostly unconsciously and regulates basic body functions such as heart rate, blood pressure, respiration, sweating, and other functions. The ANS consists of two branches: the sympathetic nervous system and the parasympathetic nervous system. For many organ systems, the two branches have opposite functions to each other; one branch activates a response and the other inhibits the response in a seesaw type of balancing act.

The sympathetic branch has also been called the "fight or flight" system because it activates the body for physical action. The end products of the sympathetic branch include diversion of blood away from the digestive tract, inhibition of intestinal contractions, increased blood flow to the muscles and the heart, dilation of airways in the lungs, dilation of pupils, and increased heart rate.

The parasympathetic branch has been called the "rest and digest" system. The end products of the parasympathetic branch are often the opposite of the sympathetic branch, and these include increased blood flow to the digestive tract, promotion of intestinal contractions, stimulation of salivary glands, constriction of airways in the lungs, stimulation of sexual arousal, constriction of pupils, and decreased heart rate.

Further complicating the picture is that there are two main states of interest for the ANS system. The first is when organisms are at rest. This is usually called the **resting baseline**. If organisms have been profoundly affected by stressful life experiences, it is thought that their baseline states may shift from normal such that they are in never-ending, constant states of arousal.

The second state of interest is when organisms have to react to stimuli. This is usually called **reactivity** or **responsivity**. If organisms have been affected by their life experiences, they may overreact or underreact compared to how they reacted prior to these experiences.

In the largest study ever conducted on heart rate in PTSD, Terrence Keane, PhD, a psychologist at the National Center for PTSD and the Veterans Affairs Medical Center in Boston, and his colleagues measured the heart rate reactions of 1,210 participants.[1] They recruited exclusively adult male veterans who had served in the Vietnam War. Nearly 60 percent of them currently had PTSD; about 10 percent had had PTSD in the past but not currently; and about 30 percent of them had never had PTSD. Before their heart rates were measured, research assistants interviewed the veterans to gather details about their most stressful combat experiences.

At resting baseline, when sitting quietly and not being stimulated, the group with current PTSD had heart rates that were on average more than three beats per minute higher than the group that had had PTSD in the past and the group that had never had PTSD. Next, when it was time to measure their heart rate reactivity, the veterans listened for thirty seconds as research assistants read prepared descriptions of their personal combat experiences. The veterans were told to sit quietly and imagine those experiences in their minds for another thirty seconds.

The veterans with current PTSD reacted by increasing their heart rates by over three beats per minute. The veterans with lifetime-but-not-current PTSD increased their heart rates by two and a half beats per minute. There was not a statistically significant difference between the current and lifetime PTSD groups. The group that had never had PTSD, however, increased their heart rates by only about two beats per minute, which was statistically significantly lower than the two PTSD groups. Overall, the group with current PTSD seemed to be in a never-ending state of heightened stress at resting baseline and, on top of that, they reacted more strongly when triggered by reminders of their traumatic events.

Hypothalamic-Pituitary-Adrenal Axis and Cortisol

The second major stress response system is a complex set of direct influences and feedback regulation among the hypothalamus, pituitary gland, and adrenal glands, called the HPA axis. The hypothalamus secretes vasopressin and corticotropin-releasing hormone, which regulate the pituitary gland. The pituitary gland secretes adrenocorticotropic hormone, which regulates the adrenal glands. The adrenal cortex secretes glucocorticoids, mainly cortisol, which acts on the hypothalamus and pituitary gland in a negative feedback cycle. The HPA axis plays an enormous role in regulating homeostatic functions that are necessary for survival, such as the immune, cardiovascular, metabolic, and reproductive systems.

Cortisol is the major stress hormone and has many effects throughout the body. Cortisol is released by the adrenal glands in response to stress and in response to low blood glucose levels. Once released, cortisol acts on many systems to produce many different effects, including increased blood glucose levels and suppressed immune system functions. Cortisol also appears to impact the central nervous system through enhanced memory formation and concentration. The absence of a cortisol response in times of stress, therefore, would have a wide range of implications on multiple major organ systems.

An excessive cortisol response may be even worse, though. Cushing's syndrome, for example, is a severe disease that is caused by prolonged and excessive production of cortisol. The signs of Cushing's syndrome include high blood pressure, abdominal obesity coupled with thin arms and legs, weak bones, weak muscles, fragile skin, changes in mood, headaches, and tiredness. Cushing's syndrome is caused either by prolonged use of a medication like prednisone or by a tumor that causes the adrenal glands to produce too much cortisol. There are no known cases of Cushing's syndrome caused by PTSD. This is an extreme example to illustrate the powerful effects of cortisol and the concern that scientists would naturally have about any dysregulation of the HPA axis and cortisol system.

Over 1,000 studies have been conducted to measure cortisol in patients who have PTSD or who have been exposed to trauma, and most of them have been conducted with adults. There was early excitement about cortisol studies because it was relatively easy to study and cortisol has well-known effects on the body. The pattern of results unfortunately turned out to be inconsistent and confusing, as some studies suggested that PTSD was associated with lower cortisol[2] while other studies suggested that PTSD was associated with higher cortisol.[3]

In the latest meta-analysis of all of the studies on this topic, the results are that there is no clear association between trauma or PTSD and cortisol.[4] While it appears there is no consistent pattern of cortisol that fits everybody with PTSD, there are many studies that have discovered abnormalities in cortisol, which most likely means there are different ways to be abnormal for different individuals. In other words, some individuals with PTSD probably have low cortisol and others probably have high cortisol, while still others have normal cortisol, and there is no single pattern that fits everybody with PTSD.

Researchers have also conducted hundreds of studies to scan brains and measure the sizes and activities of brain centers. There are over 200 specialized brain centers, but researchers tend to focus on four main centers of the brain: the hippocampus, the amygdala, the cingulate cortex, and the prefrontal cortex. These four centers appear to be most critical for memory formation and emotion regulation. The **hippocampus** is believed to play critical roles in the consolidation of short-term memories into long-term memories. The **amygdala** plays a role early in the chain of events of interpretation of emotional events and formation of related memories. The **cingulate cortex** sits in the middle of the pathway for processing of emotions, learning, and memory. The **prefrontal cortex** is thought to sit at the end of the pathway for processing of emotional events and makes high-level associations to interpret the information and decide how to respond; these are also called executive functions. The leading theories based on these brain scan studies are that the hippocampus is smaller and functions abnormally,[5] the amygdala is smaller and overactive, and the cingulate cortex and prefrontal cortex are underactive in individuals with PTSD.[6]

How Did the Neurobiology Get There?

Researchers have been intrigued by the search for these neurobiological differences, but they have also been vexed in terms of understanding how the neurobiological differences came into being. Did the neurobiological differences exist before individuals were exposed to trauma and served as risk factors for the development of PTSD? Or did the neurobiological differences come into being as consequences that were caused by traumatic events?

To try to explain how these abnormalities got there, two main theories have been put forth that are the extreme opposites of each other. On one hand is the theory that the brain abnormalities existed prior to the stressful experiences; this is called the **diathesis-stress theory**. Diathesis is a fancy word for predisposed. The diathesis-stress model means that certain individuals possess preexisting conditions that make them vulnerable to the effects of stress. In this case, the diathesis is the brain abnormalities. To prove this theory, we do not have to know why the abnormalities existed prior to the stressful experiences or how they got there; we just have to satisfy the condition that they existed prior to the stress. In other words, the stress did not cause the neurobiological abnormalities to exist.

On the other hand is the **stress-damages-the-brain theory**. This theory states that these brain abnormalities were not present before stressful experiences occurred, and that the stressful experiences caused the neurobiological abnormalities to exist.

In the minds of most researchers, the stress-damages-the-brain theory is the reigning champion, the one nearly everyone believes. Nearly all experts in our field believe that severe stress causes changes in the biology of the brain and the body, which translate into functional changes. To cite just several of thousands of possible examples, Douglas Bremner, MD, a psychiatrist at Emory University in Atlanta who has conducted perhaps more brain imaging studies on adults with PTSD than anybody in the world, wrote a paper published in 2001 that focused on the hippocampus, stating that "the evidence collected to date is consistent with the idea that stress can damage the brain in some individuals."[7]

In 1999, I was in the audience at the American Psychiatric Association for a presentation by another well-known researcher who had published many, if not the most of anyone, neurobiological studies on trauma in adults. After presenting his group's findings on brain scans that showed the hippocampus and amygdala were smaller in individuals with PTSD, he stated unequivocally, "There's no doubt in my mind that early trauma causes the kinds of brain changes I've shown you today." I was so struck by how forcefully he stated it that I wrote it down immediately.

Bessel van der Kolk, a psychiatrist and renowned PTSD expert at Harvard Medical School whom we first met in Chapter Eight, is another champion of the stress-damages-the-brain theory. Van der Kolk coined the catchy phrase "The Body Keeps the Score" as a title for a book chapter in 1996. This chapter has been very popular and has been cited nearly 1,000 times in other scientific articles since it was published. The chapter is so influential that it was included in a collection of twenty-eight of the most influential papers on trauma.[8] Van der Kolk apparently believed it was such an important contribution that he reused "The Body Keeps the Score" phrase as the title for his autobiography[9] and again for his best-selling book.[10] The phrase appears consistent with his statements such as "The recognition that psychological trauma results in enduring biological changes goes back to the very earliest descriptions of the human trauma response."[11]

Is it really credible, though, that stress can damage brains? One must pause, step back from the enticing and dramatic narrative, and reflect on the bigger picture. Humans have been around for thousands of years. Humans have endured over that long time; one could even say our species has thrived despite enormous daily stressors and frequent major catastrophes. The enormously complex process of human development repeats itself with amazing precision and fidelity in every new human being that is born. One could argue that we appear to be designed to survive an enormous array of stressors, from viruses and bacteria to psychological stress and severe deprivation. The insults keep coming every day, yet human beings are born, grow, develop, and turn out pretty much the same way year after year. If the brain could not withstand these insults on an everyday basis, it would be too fragile to endure. It seems highly unlikely that the brain can be damaged so easily by such common occurrences as stress and trauma. I think because of that big-picture perspective, I was never seduced by the belief that stress damages the brain. In this bigger perspective, the notion that stress damages the brain is an extraordinary claim.

The stress-damages-the-brain belief has spread easily through the media and into the minds of the public and other professionals. In November of 2013, senators in the Wisconsin state legislature did an amazing thing. They introduced Senate Joint Resolution 59, which read in part:

> Whereas, chronic, unrelenting stress in early childhood caused by conditions such as extreme poverty, repeated abuse, neglect, severe maternal depression, parental substance abuse, and violence can be toxic to a child's developing brain . . .
>
> *Resolved by the senate, the assembly concurring,* That policy decisions enacted by the Wisconsin state legislature will acknowledge and take into account the principles of early childhood brain development and will, whenever possible, consider the concepts of toxic stress.[12]

The resolution passed unanimously. The Wisconsin legislature not only concluded that trauma such as repeated abuse caused brain damage; they went beyond the impact of traumatic stress. They included nontraumatic stress with such global and vaguely defined stressful conditions as "extreme poverty . . . neglect, severe maternal depression, parental substance abuse, and violence." In addition, they claimed these experiences "literally shape the physical architecture of a child's developing brain," which has impacts on all learning, health, and behavior.

The stress-damages-the-brain theory, therefore, is not just an academic question. Proponents of the theory have successfully proselytized the public, and the theory is now being used to influence how lawmakers make laws, which ultimately can impact how taxpayer dollars are spent.

The idea that stress damages the brain is a fantastic story. The story fits nicely with the human need for the narrative fallacy—a nice, clean, simple story with a clear hero and a clear villain. The English author Charles Dickens would love it, I suspect. Dickens found many ways to criticize the moral failings of society in his stories. His stories seem to convey that the world would be good if everyone would just act generously. Horrible things can happen to people, and it is the things that happen to them that matter. But with the right interventions, such as Ebenezer Scrooge being visited by three ghosts to show him the error of his ways, such adversities can be overcome. In other words, life events make people bad, but other life events can make them good. We can all be damaged or fixed at will.

The great astronomer Carl Sagan stated, "Extraordinary claims require extraordinary evidence." Despite the widespread belief in the stress-damages-the-brain theory, which is an extraordinary claim, there happens to be very little evidence in humans to support it.

Correlation Does Not Equal Causation (Revisited)

We saw in Chapters Nine and Ten that the vast majority of studies that examined parenting in relation to children's PTSD symptoms had a major design shortcoming in that they were cross-sectional study designs. They had the problem of trying to understand a whole loaf of bread by looking at just one slice. We have the same problem with respect to the vast majority of research studies that have found neurobiological differences in human subjects with trauma experiences and PTSD compared to subjects without trauma and PTSD. That is, the researchers assessed the subjects at only one point in time, and it was always after they had traumatic experiences. These single-slice assessments have limited power to tell us how things happened and have almost no power to address questions of causation. Relatively few of the neurobiological studies used a prospective repeated-measures design that assessed the neurobiology of subjects before they experienced traumas and then again after the traumas. The only way to truly know whether stress damages the human brain is to assess subjects before they experienced trauma and then again after they experienced trauma.

"The most splendid assumption still needs verification."

Jim Shepard

HPA Axis and Cortisol

Isaac Galatzer-Levy, PhD, a psychologist at Columbia University in New York City, and a team of researchers conducted one of the few studies in which individuals were assessed before they experienced traumas. They assessed 234 police recruits during their training before being exposed to dangers in the field and then assessed them more than four years after being exposed to dangers in the field.[13] The researchers measured cortisol reactivity in response to stressful video stimuli. They found that those police officers who developed more PTSD symptoms over those years were different from those who developed fewer or no PTSD symptoms before they were ever exposed to on-the-job trauma. Those who developed more PTSD symptoms had weak cortisol reactions to the video stimuli when they were in the training academy. In contrast, those recruits who developed fewer or no PTSD symptoms had shown big increases in cortisol following the video stimuli when they were in the training academy. The police recruits were different from each other before they were ever exposed to traumas, supporting the diathesis-stress theory.

In summary, Dr. Galatzer-Levy and his colleagues at Columbia University looked at two slices of the loaf of bread instead of one slice, and they found something completely different from what those who had been looking at only one slice found. There are other studies similar to Galatzer-Levy's, most of them relatively new, that have looked at other neurobiological systems and come to the same conclusion that individuals who develop PTSD are different prior to traumas compared to those who do not develop PTSD. With these newer studies, it is evident that the widely believed claim that stress damages the brain is far from consistent, and the evidence to support it is not yet extraordinary.

Wrapping Up with Some Balance

Everything in our bones seems to tell us that all men and women are created equal, notwithstanding, of course, obvious developmental disabilities. Therefore, if one of us ends up different from the rest of us, we automatically believe there must be something to blame. We saw the blame game played out in Chapter Nine in our discussion of how mothers have been blamed for autism, schizophrenia, and PTSD in their children. The stress-damages-the-brain theory is the blame game in a different disguise. The proponents of this theory have done a great job of tapping into that belief and frightening everyone who is willing to listen to them. The theories that the body keeps the score and that stress damages the brain talk about the issue in a rather one-sided fashion, seeming to assume that the human brain is a nearly defenseless target waiting to be bullied and pushed around by the environment. I know the authors of these theories don't think of the brain that simplistically—they can't be that naïve—but if you only read what they wrote, it could easily give you that impression. A problem I see is that as long as the experts are not writing about the issue in a more balanced fashion, then alternative explanations are not being studied.

It is worth remembering that humans are not *that* fragile. Human beings are built to be tough. An incredible number of things have to go right in developing humans in wombs for fetuses simply to survive. A single major thing goes wrong—an organ system fails to develop the right way—and a fetus dies. There are many organ systems, and hundreds of things within each organ system that have to develop the right way. All of those organ systems have to continue to function normally throughout a life span for the organism to survive. At the same time, there are an enormous number of insults and challenges coming at organisms every day, such as viruses, bacteria, improper diets, cuts, tissue and bone injuries, ingested toxins, and stress, to name a few. The human body has tremendous defenses, fail-safe mechanisms, and backup plans to handle most things that are thrown at it. If the body did not have these defenses, most humans would never survive or function very well. When you think of it that way, the human body has been built to take a beating.

I have never been seduced by the belief that stress damages the brain like I was by the blame-the-mother parenting theory, because I think I have always possessed a fundamental belief that humans were built to take a beating. Because humans have thrived over thousands of years despite a constant onslaught of daily stressors and frequent major catastrophes, it seems much more likely, on the whole, that we were designed to withstand trauma—not designed to be damaged by trauma.

The theory that stress damages the brain, if true, would be tragic for trauma victims and so dramatic that it makes one's heart ache. Like the light of a full moon, the stress-damages-the-brain theory provides a glow in the dark to see a path forward to help these unfortunate victims. The implications of the theory are soaring, and we want to believe in a simple story that has one thing to blame. If children have abnormal brains, and stress caused the abnormalities, then we could prevent abnormal brains by preventing stress and trauma. The prospect of being able to shape a person's brain does not come along every day.

Determining which theory is right—the neurotoxicity of stress theory or the diathesis-stress theory—is not just an academic battle between aspiring researchers. Which theory is right matters, for several important reasons. First, it influences how researchers do the next experiment. If a trauma researcher believes a hippocampus becomes abnormally small after being exposed to traumas, then that researcher is never going to do a study to investigate how a hippocampus can be small for other reasons. That researcher will never conduct the right experiment.

Second, which theory is right matters because it influences how researchers look for better treatments. If the trauma researcher believes trauma caused hippocampi to become smaller, then logically he would design a treatment study to investigate drugs that block the action of trauma that makes hippocampi smaller. But because he is working with the wrong theory, and traumas do not cause hippocampi to become abnormally small, his investigations on treatment will probably never work.

Third, which theory is right matters because it has influenced laypersons who have no particular expertise in neuroscience to believe the stress-damages-the-brain theory. As mentioned in this chapter, senators in the Wisconsin state legislature unanimously passed a resolution stating that experiences such as violence literally "shape the physical architecture of a child's developing brain and establish either a sturdy or a fragile foundation for all the learning, health, and behavior that follows." This belief has the force to alter how taxpayers' funds are spent and public policies are crafted.

Fourth, and most important in my mind, which theory is right matters because it affects what you believe about yourself and why you believe you are the way you are or about your children and why you believe they are the way they are. In Chapter Ten I described Alex, who had broken his leg in a soccer game. His father thought his son was weak, a failure in his eyes. Perhaps if his father had understood that Alex was a product of his neurobiology that existed before the injury rather than a piece of damaged goods caused by the injury, he might have been more sympathetic.

The theory that stress damages the brain does not appear to be true for all trauma victims, but it might be true for some, to some degree. It might be true to some degree only for everyone who develops PTSD and not for those who do not develop PTSD. It might only be true for a smaller proportion of those who develop PTSD because they have unique individual differences that make their bodies react differently than those of others who develop PTSD. It might be true only for those who undergo the most severe and intense forms of traumatic experiences. The theory is an extraordinary claim. If Charles Dickens were a neuroscientist, he could not have written a more compelling story. It must be paid attention to, because it is something we certainly do not want to be wrong about. The idea that stress damages the brain is an appealing and intuitive theory. But intuition is notoriously wrong.

The diathesis-stress theory appears much more likely to be true, or at least true relatively more often. If the diathesis-stress theory is true, then children may be born with problem-causing genes that cause smaller hippocampi and overactive amygdalae. Those smaller hippocampi and overactive amygdalae may even explain why individuals become exposed to traumas in the first place, and may explain why groups who develop PTSD and those who do not develop PTSD following traumas were never the same as each other in the first place.

In this bigger view of things, the belief that trauma and stress are toxic to the developing brain is a wildly extraordinary claim. It would be more productive if scientists spent their time trying to figure out how to harness those differences to improve prevention, early intervention, and treatment approaches, because trauma is not going away.

Recap

- The thoughts, feelings, and behaviors of PTSD symptoms have an underlying basis in neurobiology.
- Many differences in neurobiology have been discovered in individuals with PTSD compared to individuals without PTSD. These differences involve the autonomic nervous system, the HPA axis and cortisol, multiple brain centers, and other systems.
- There are two main theories to explain the existence of these neurobiological differences: the stress-damages-the-brain theory and the diathesis-stress theory. Both theories can adequately explain the data that are collected from cross-sectional studies. Despite this, and the fact that there are few prospective longitudinal studies that can untangle this question, the vast majority of experts appear to believe that the stress-damages-the-brain theory is true.
- It is extremely difficult to conduct the type of experiment in humans that could truly answer the question of whether or not stress damages the brain.
- More recent studies in humans with stronger study designs have shown that neurobiological differences that once were claimed to be caused by trauma instead appear to have existed prior to trauma experiences. The newer evidence consistently favors the diathesis-stress model.

For Parents to Do

- Maintain some perspective. Understand that neurobiological differences do exist in individuals with PTSD, but despite the one-sided writings from most experts and the bandwagon propaganda from journalists and politicians, there are very little well-controlled data in humans to conclude that trauma causes these neurobiological differences. It is probably good to be alarmed and consider that the stress-damages-the-brain theory could be true, but it is also good to be skeptical and not believe everything you read.

- Whichever theory is true, remember that it is abundantly clear that all people were not created equal in their capacities to deal with stress. A medium level of balanced compassion is probably the best practice to adopt as a parent.

Chapter Sixteen

Frequently Asked Questions

"There go my people. I must find out where they
are going so that I can lead them."
Alexandre Ledru-Rollin

With this book, I have attempted to cover the topics I think are most important for victims of trauma to know, but I cannot cover everything in one book. There are many more worthy topics that people have asked me about over the years. I have tried to answer those succinctly in this chapter. I encourage readers to send me additional questions at michael. scheeringa@gmail.com.

Cause-and-Effect Questions
Can stress and trauma be positive?
Of course they can. What doesn't kill you can make you stronger in several different ways. We use this concept during treatment as part of the cognitive restructuring component of CBT. For example, a teenage female who was raped may decide to start a rape-awareness program at her school to prevent this from happening to other girls. Also, we have found that many individuals feel a higher power has chosen them for these experiences for larger purposes in their lives.

These ideas have been around since the beginnings of psychotherapy, but they have gained traction lately among some trauma researchers as a concept called post-traumatic growth. Some specific examples include reoriented priorities about what is important in life, development of new interests, greater spirituality, and a better acceptance of life circumstances. Much more can be learned by looking up "post-traumatic growth" and "post-traumatic growth inventory" on the internet or visiting your local library.

Why did I/my child get PTSD but others who went through the same event didn't?

Most people who experience life-threatening events do not develop PTSD. Research across many different types of traumas indicates that about 70 percent of individuals do not develop long-lasting symptoms. This research has also shown that it doesn't really matter what type of trauma a person has experienced. Life-threatening trauma is all the same, although there is some evidence that sexual assault and burns may cause higher rates of PTSD than other types of trauma.

Researchers have found that individuals who tend to develop PTSD have a preexisting trait of emotional over-reactivity, in which they get intensely upset easily from relatively minor stressors and then stay upset for a long time. (If you try to look this up in the scientific literature, search under the term **neuroticism**.) Another common predictor is the degree of fear and panic individuals felt during the actual traumatic experiences. The short answer, though, of who develops PTSD is genes. Your risk for developing PTSD is probably largely determined by your genes and how you were wired at birth, and whether you have those risk factors for overreactivity. It is not your fault that you developed PTSD, and you have not done anything wrong. You were simply born with certain genes.

What do scientists think is the underlying biological mechanism of PTSD?

Scientists have some good ideas, but they still don't really know. The hard lesson neuroscience researchers have learned over the past thirty years is that there are no simple explanations and no single pathways for psychiatric disorders. In contrast to an illness such as diabetes where the problem can be traced back to the faulty production of insulin, we have not found any causes with that level of simplicity in psychiatry.

Researchers have zeroed in on autonomic reactivity, cortisol production, overactive amygdala, smaller hippocampus, overactive cingulate cortex, and underactive prefrontal cortex. It is tempting to fall into the trap of the narrative fallacy and believe that there is one pathway to the development of PTSD, but I believe there are probably hundreds of different pathways.

What is the youngest age at which you can get PTSD?

The short answer is that it appears impossible below nine months of age, appears doubtful but not well studied between nine months and three years of age, and is definitely possible by three years of age. The youngest case on record was a child who was thirty-four months old.[1] Other cases of younger children have been published, but the authors did not systematically describe their symptoms well enough to make definitive conclusions about their diagnoses. For a more in-depth review of individual case reports, I have collected and reviewed the earliest known cases of traumatized young children in a chapter I wrote for a textbook.[2]

The rate-limiting feature that seems to prevent the development of PTSD is that the cognitive capacities needed for long-term memories and language are not yet in place prior to three years of age. Between nine and thirty-six months of age, children can have some form of long-term memory for personal experiences, but they are still not able to develop the full complement of different types of symptoms for the diagnosis of PTSD. Symptoms in the nine- to thirty-six-month age range may be more accurately diagnosed as conditioning to painful stimuli or adjustment disorders.

At how young an age can children remember traumatic events?

There is not one type of memory. Researchers have described many types of memory, but boiled down to the most general and useful types, there are two major ones. The first type of memory is called **behavioral memory** (also called nondeclarative or implicit memory). An individual can act out the memory behaviorally, but cannot yet verbally recall the memory. Infants as young as six months of age show behavioral memory by playing with toys in a specific way that was shown to them twenty-four hours earlier,[3] but it is not clear whether they can retain those behavioral memories over the long term. The brain structures responsible for long-term memory come online around eight or nine months.[4]

The second type of memory, **autobiographical memory** (also called declarative or explicit memory), is the ability to verbally recall distinct personally experienced events. By no accident, this coincides with the burst of language between eighteen and thirty-six months. By around thirty-six months, when most young children are stringing together simple sentences, autobiographical memory becomes apparent in somewhat coherent narrative forms.[5,6]

If you think back on your own life and try to recall the earliest thing you can remember, it is usually from around the age of four or five years. People often tell me they have memories from when they were one or two years old. I will acknowledge that exceptions to the rule are always possible, but I think it is more likely those individuals overheard discussions of the events from family members and have come to believe these were in fact their own memories, similar to the case described in Chapter Fourteen of the sister who was two years, one month old when her older sister was eviscerated by the suction of a swimming pool drain. It was concluded that these were vicarious memories created in the girl's mind from overhearing family stories of the event.

Prevalence
How common is trauma?
In a large study of nearly 3,000 adults in the United States, 90 percent reported that they had experienced at least one life-threatening traumatic event in their lives.[7] In a large study of over 6,000 adolescents ages thirteen to seventeen years in the United States, 62 percent reported exposure to life-threatening experiences.[8]

How does the rate of PTSD in youths compare to that in adults?
In two large studies of thousands of adults in the United States, when measuring any point in their lives past or present, 8 percent had full PTSD.[9,10] In comparison, youths in the age range of thirteen to seventeen years reported a lifetime prevalence of PTSD of around 5 percent, with

PTSD being more common in females than males.[11] There are no good studies of large samples of younger children for comparison.

Assessment and Diagnosis

Labels suck. Why do we have to label kids with PTSD?

Labels only suck if you are in denial that you have problems. For individuals who are ready to accept that they are not perfect, life is not fair, and bad things happen, labels have an immensely beneficial power. For every patient I have seen who does not like labels, I have probably seen a hundred patients who are thankful that somebody finally put a name to the mysterious problems they have been struggling with. Many of those patients were angry with their previous doctors and clinicians who failed to provide the correct diagnosis, and those patients wasted years and money on the wrong treatments.

I have heard dozens of stories in my career from patients who had wandered aimlessly around the mental health field because their clinicians either refused to provide a label or gave them the wrong label. Labels provide communication. Labels help individuals feel they are not alone and that others struggle with the same things. Labels provide guidance on where to turn when lost.

You said that children six years and younger need special criteria for the diagnosis of PTSD. What about seven- to twelve-year-old children?

I believe, and the early evidence agrees with me, that seven- to twelve-year-old children also need special criteria to make accurate diagnoses of PTSD. For example, in our study published in 2017,[12] and in other studies by Iselin and colleagues[13] and by Meiser-Stedman and colleagues,[14] researchers have examined this question. When children could not meet the *DSM-IV* definition of PTSD, but they could be diagnosed by the PTSD criteria for children six years and younger, they were extremely symptomatic; they averaged six to seven symptoms of PTSD. Clinical treatment studies typically require only five PTSD symptoms for patients to be included in the studies. The field of PTSD research is in a funny place, and because of my work researchers in this field know more about

PTSD in very young children than they know about it in older children, which is the reverse of what usually happens in research.

Do you believe problems such as anxiety, angry outbursts, inattention, and impulsivity may be caused by adverse life experiences or trauma and might otherwise be incorrectly diagnosed as attention deficit hyperactivity disorder?

I have heard that speculation often. While that may happen sometimes, there are no data that I am aware of to support that it happens commonly. My own data on preschool children do not support that idea on a common scale. I think it is a good question that will be difficult to answer because if children are being misdiagnosed in the community, they are not going to be captured often in a research study.

What I think happens more often, and what I have seen regularly, is that academic or behavior problems in school have been the first indication of a problem, and people suspect ADHD, but it doesn't rise to the level of formally misdiagnosing the child as having ADHD. So my experience is that children are being incorrectly identified by other problems that bring them to treatment before everyone realizes that the main problem is PTSD.

How do I untangle other disorders from the trauma?

The majority of patients with PTSD have at least one other psychiatric problem such as depression or anxiety. It is tempting to blame trauma as the cause of the other disorders. By nature, humans always want something or someone to blame.

PTSD can sometimes be mistaken for ADHD because difficulty concentrating is one of the PTSD symptoms and is also one of the hallmarks of ADHD. How can we tell whether difficulty concentrating is due to true ADHD or is a symptom of PTSD? The best way to know is to gather historical information from parents who raised the children from birth and determine when the difficulty in concentrating began. If the symptom was present before the traumatic events, then one may assume that the symptom is part of true ADHD.

This best method is not always possible for several reasons. If children have been exposed to traumatic events since birth, then there is no period of time "before" traumatic events to ask about. Or, when children are placed in foster care, the foster parents do not know the children's prior histories.

When it is not possible to determine whether the symptom goes with ADHD or PTSD based on a timeline, the next-best thing is to interview caregivers about all of the other symptoms of ADHD and PTSD. There are eighteen symptoms of ADHD in the *DSM-5*. Do the children have any of the seventeen other ADHD symptoms? There are fifteen to twenty symptoms of PTSD in the *DSM-5*. Do the children have any of the other PTSD symptoms? If they have lots of ADHD symptoms and few PTSD symptoms, then they probably have ADHD and not PTSD, and vice versa.

Sometimes children have a bunch of symptoms of both ADHD and PTSD and it is not clear that one condition is present and not the other. In these cases, the strategy I advocate is to plow ahead and treat the children with PTSD as the working diagnosis. The children's responses to treatment can be diagnostic. If most of the symptoms improve with treatment for PTSD, then it is safe to conclude that the appearance of ADHD was due to overlapping symptoms from PTSD.

Sometimes, though, very hyperactive and inattentive children cannot pay attention and cooperate with psychotherapy, so they need to be treated first for ADHD with medication so that they are able to cooperate. In this case, it may take more steps to untangle the diagnosis puzzle. If the ADHD symptoms improve dramatically with the ADHD medication, then that is a good clue the child has true ADHD. If the ADHD symptoms do not improve or improve only partially with the ADHD medication, that is a clue the ADHD symptoms were overlapping symptoms from PTSD (assuming that the dose of ADHD medication was high enough to be effective).

Course

Won't my child get better with time?

No, not really. That sounds harsh, and it's not 100 percent true, but someone needs to tell you to get your child to treatment as soon as possible and quit stalling. While there are some studies showing that people improve over time, the improvements are only moderate. Some symptoms may go away or some symptoms may become less intense, but few people are ever totally cured of all of their PTSD symptoms. Other studies show that PTSD symptoms do not improve at all over time. For example, my research team and I followed a group of one- to six-year-old children for two years. There was no statistically significant improvement in their symptoms over that time.

What if we don't get treatment? What will happen?

The longitudinal research is quite clear that your children's PTSD symptoms either will not improve much or will not improve at all without treatment. PTSD is usually a chronic injury. One must accept the fact that it is like living with chronic pain or diabetes. It is a lifelong condition that must be managed. Ignore it at your children's risk.

It is also likely to have a cumulative effect. Living with the chronic fear reactions, anxiety, and sleep and concentration difficulties that never get better can wear a person down over the years. It is difficult for a person with PTSD to describe to a person who has never had PTSD what it is like to live with it. Most people never attempt to describe it to another. Everyone knows what depression and hyperactivity look like and feel like. Everybody has experienced these in some degree in his or her life. But most people have not had excessive fear reactions triggered by a reminder of an event that is not a real threat but triggers all the feelings of a real threat.

What will happen if another trauma happens?

If your child has made a substantial recovery from an earlier trauma and a new trauma occurs, it is likely that your child will develop PTSD symptoms again, just like he or she did following the first trauma. I'm not sure whether additional traumas make symptoms worse or not. There are some experts who believe strongly that multiple traumas lead to more severe symptoms and worse long-term developmental outcomes compared to single traumas or relatively fewer traumas. The evidence to support that does not, however, come from well-controlled studies. And there are data that directly contradict that notion.

Parenting

My wife/husband seems impatient and insensitive to our child's symptoms. Is she or he making our child worse?

See Chapters Nine and Ten on parenting. That's an enormously complicated subject that can only be answered on a case-by-case basis with more knowledge about the particular details. It is unlikely that insensitive parents make children's symptoms worse, but it is likely that insensitive parents may prevent children from getting better.

Interventions

Should I talk about the trauma with my child?

You should absolutely try to talk about the traumatic event and his or her reactions to it. See my Tips for Parents sheet in the Appendix for some suggestions on how to talk about it. Because people with PTSD naturally avoid talking and thinking about it, and because they often feel like no one can understand them because others didn't go through what they went through, they often will not bring up the topics on their own. You need to reach out and let your children know that you want to listen.

But also remember to not be pushy about it. If your children don't want to talk, let it drop. Forcing them to talk when they are not ready can be counterproductive.

If it's better to have forgotten the memories of trauma, why does therapy focus on talking about the memories?

People with PTSD symptoms have not forgotten and they can't forget, so the idea they can just forget about it is simply not possible. The memories are burned into their minds. Also, talking about their experiences in a therapy situation is different from talking about it with a friend or family member. In therapy, patients are talking about the memories with professional, licensed clinicians who are trained to handle these discussions. Sometimes talking about it with friends or family members can be helpful, but it depends a lot on the nature of those relationships. In addition, in evidence-based treatments for PTSD, patients are not asked to talk about their events in much detail until they are taught new coping skills to help them deal with their negative feelings.

What percentage of people who receive treatment get better?

When patients have received evidence-based treatment for PTSD, the vast majority show marked improvement. About 75 percent of people reduce the severity of their symptoms dramatically.

How much better do they get?

Most people reduce their symptom severity by 50 percent or more. For example, if they experienced nightmares ten times per month, a 50 percent reduction would be to have nightmares five or fewer times per month. Some symptoms will go away completely. Some symptoms will be reduced in intensity but will not completely disappear. Even with this very good degree of improvement, most people have some degree of persisting symptoms for their entire lives.

Who doesn't get better with treatment?

That is a question scientists are eagerly trying to figure out. If we knew who didn't get better with our standard treatment, we would be able to identify them earlier and try to design different treatments specifically for them. I am actively conducting research at my clinic to tackle this next generation of challenges.

Do the comorbid syndromes get better even when you focus on trauma in treatment?

Yes, yes, yes. We know people with PTSD have at least one other psychiatric syndrome such as depression or anxiety 70 to 90 percent of the time. When patients are treated with an evidence-based therapy for PTSD, these comorbid syndromes improve at the same time the PTSD improves. This has been shown over and over in studies.

Why do the comorbid syndromes get better when the treatments focus on the PTSD symptoms?

Following traumatic events, the core psychological injury appears to be PTSD, not depression, anxiety, or defiant behaviors. So, when the core psychological injury is healed, the related syndromes can also heal.

Why don't we have better treatments for PTSD?

We actually have pretty good treatments. The problem is that many clinicians refuse to use them.

But why don't we have better treatments? We have made a lot of progress in developing treatments, but progress seems slow. Let's put this into context. To build one car, Toyota uses hundreds of workers and robots. Before the car is ever built, though, they have teams of engineers creating new features and troubleshooting problems. Their research and development department comprises dozens of individuals who spend millions of dollars per year to try to correct the smallest flaw. In contrast, research on PTSD, like all other mental and medical disorders, is usually led by one principal investigator who devotes 30 to 50 percent of his week to the project, a handful of coinvestigators who don't know what's going on day to day, and low-level research assistants who do the daily work but have none of the clinical expertise needed to drive new discoveries. While the Toyota model of an army of workers and boatloads of cash sounds like a good idea, we are not funded like that. When they need to experiment, they can simply create the parts they need out of raw material. When clinical researchers need to experiment, they need live human beings who happen to have the conditions they need to study and who are willing to participate in research. Give me twenty million dollars, however, and I'll see what I can do.

My child's therapist says he is using CBT with my child. How do I know that?

You don't unless the therapist spends time with you to describe in detail what goes on during the therapy sessions. How much time therapists spend to explain what goes on in therapy is a direct reflection of each therapist's philosophy about how to involve parents and commitment to transparency.

Therapists may also have different interpretations of how much CBT they have to do for it to "count" as CBT. One therapist may do CBT by following a manualized twelve-session protocol very closely. Another therapist may do mostly nondirective psychodynamic play therapy and mix in a few CBT techniques once or twice a session and consider that

CBT (even though it clearly is not sufficient CBT). A third therapist may start out trying to follow a CBT protocol closely but then get sidetracked by other interesting issues after several sessions, a pattern that, again, would not count as CBT.

If you really intend to clean your house, it requires you to comprehensively dust ledges and tabletops, clean sinks and counters, clean showers and bathtubs, mop tile floors, vacuum carpets, and change bedsheets and towels. If a person vacuumed only a few of the carpets and cleaned just a few obvious spots in some sinks, that person might say he or she cleaned the house, but it would not really be a clean house.

My child's therapist says she is using EMDR with my child. How do I know that?

See the previous question. Also, eye movement desensitization and reprocessing (EMDR) therapy is a more complicated procedure than CBT, and it requires more thoroughness to really follow all of the steps in the EMDR manual. Excellent EMDR therapists who use this technique a lot can follow these steps well, but it is relatively harder for therapists who use it infrequently to follow all the steps.

My child's therapist is using play therapy with my child. How do I know if that is going to help?

The only data I have that play therapy effectively treats PTSD in children come from a handful of published reports of individual cases. There are no controlled group studies of play therapy. Due in large part to this absence of data, in professional reports of which therapies are evidence-based, play therapy is not considered an evidence-based treatment.

It is possible that play therapy can be effective to treat PTSD, but it should be delivered by a therapist who adapts the technique specifically for PTSD. This has to include children reengaging with their memories of their traumatic events at some point and processing, to some degree, their thoughts and feelings. They should also learn new skills to more positively cope with their distressing memories and feelings. If all of those are done, however, it begins to sound a lot like CBT.

I cannot think of a situation where play therapy would be recommended instead of CBT. Many people advocate using play therapy before attempting CBT for the more difficult and challenging cases. This approach uses play therapy as a warm-up or a preliminary phase of treatment to prepare children for more specific treatment later. If a child has difficulty engaging in CBT because of anxiety, disorganized thinking, poor social skills, or emotional dysregulation, he or she is going to have those same problems engaging in a meaningful way in play therapy. This staging of treatments may have worked for individual cases in the past, but it is not clear that the treatments had to be staged that way. What many advocates of play therapy forget is that many clinical skills, such as play therapy, can be used during CBT to help children cooperate with the CBT techniques.

I told my child's therapist that your book claims children must receive an evidence-based treatment for PTSD in order to get better. My therapist said you were wrong and that many people can improve with therapy that is not necessarily recognized as evidence-based. Whom should I believe?

Believe your child. Is your child getting better with whatever your therapist is doing? Technically, your therapist may be right. In every study of an evidence-based technique, there is always a subgroup of people who improve early in the treatment. They benefit quickly from relatively little intervention before the main techniques have ever been used with them, and we don't really know why. However, that does not appear to be the majority of people. There are also patients who can improve with a variety of different things such as writing a journal on their own, yoga, changing schools, and other things. However, that does not appear to be the majority of people with full-blown PTSD. If your child got better with therapy your therapist claimed was not evidence-based, it might be that he or she used components of evidence-based techniques, but either doesn't know it or doesn't want to admit it. The main point is that if your child is not improving after two to three months of therapy, it's time to start asking hard questions and looking around for something better.

What should I look for in a therapist?

Besides a therapist who uses CBT for PTSD, the likeability of the therapist is very important. Psychotherapy is perhaps the most personal type of treatment in all of medicine. In addition, it is a voluntary activity. Parents can drag children to counseling, but they can't make them talk. Therapists can't work magic, either, to make children cooperate who don't want to cooperate. The likeability of the therapist, however, can go a long way in encouraging cooperation, in my experience.

What makes a therapist likeable? Is the therapist friendly? Is she fun? Does she show respect? Can she adapt herself to different developmental levels of children? Is she a good listener? Does she know when to be quiet? Can she be quiet? Does she know the crucial difference between when to do something and when to do nothing? Does she have enough experience with children to know how to manage their behavior and maximize cooperation? These qualities are in a checklist I created in the Appendix that you can copy and complete on your therapists. I have found that most of these factors can't be taught. A person is either born with them or not.

Appendix A
How to Talk with Youths Following Traumas

- **Be willing to talk.** Try to talk with your children about what happened to them. Try to be calm and straightforward. Children often can tell when their parents are upset. Admit how you are feeling. If children see that parents can't talk openly, they may be reluctant to talk as well.
- Take your cues from your children. **If they don't want to talk about it, then let it drop.** People cope in different ways, and some children may do better when not pushed to talk. There is no "right" way to talk about these experiences.
- **Tell the truth as much as possible.** Children's imagination is usually worse than the truth. If you can't answer a question, let them know that, and say that you will try to figure out an answer for them.
- Don't forget about **siblings or children who weren't actually at the event**. They may also need to talk and may develop symptoms.
- **Even very young children can be affected.** Don't assume children are too young to remember.
- **Crying can be good.** Don't try to make them feel better and fix everything. That's unrealistic. You may just need to be there quietly while they express their feelings.
- Try to **avoid saying, "Everything will be okay."** Give children a bit more credit. A trauma happened; everything is not okay. The

children certainly do not feel okay, and your acceptance of that can be validating for them.

- **Don't worry too much** if they don't talk right away. They may bring it up on their own later.
- Do things to **increase their sense of safety**. This may include them sleeping with you, you staying home from work, or asking them directly what would help them feel safe.
- **Distraction can also be helpful** to keep children from ruminating excessively about the events. If they seem overly fixated on the traumas, do some fun things.
- If their trauma was from an event that has generated a lot of media coverage, **limit what they watch about the event** on TV and the internet if it disturbs them.
- **Become sensitized to your children's internal worlds.** Pay attention to reminders in the environment that seem to trigger their distress.
- Once triggers are identified, **help shield them from triggers**.
- **Don't retraumatize them.** Don't put them back in situations where the same types of traumas can happen to them again.
- **Don't be impatient** with their symptoms.
- **Don't blame them** for what happened.
- If their symptoms have lasted for more than one month, **get them to good treatment**.

Appendix B
Elements of Cognitive Behavioral Therapy for PTSD

Session	Activities
1	Psychoeducation about PTSD.
2	Develop simple behavior management plan to deal with oppositional and defiant behaviors.
3	Ways to better get in touch with one's feelings.
4	Teach patients to use relaxation techniques.
5	Have them begin recalling their traumatic memories and talk about their traumatic event(s) in detail for the first time.
6–10	Have them tell more and more detail about their trauma memories in order to make themselves anxious on purpose; they then use their new relaxation techniques to gain control over their anxious feelings.
11	Relapse prevention. Patients are taught to think about some times in the future when their symptoms are likely to be retriggered and preemptively validate for them that this is normal.
12	Review the narrative of what they have been through both in terms of their trauma and in terms of their recovery.

Youth PTSD Treatment by Michael S. Scheeringa, MD

Therapist Likeability Checklist

Based on your observations of meeting with a therapist, circle the number that seems to fit the best. Do not ask these questions directly of the therapist. These ratings are based on your observations.

Fill out the form either during the meeting or after you leave the office.

These can be subjective and difficult to rate. Because patients tend to be biased toward justifying their decision to pick a doctor or therapist, they usually overestimate their therapists' good qualities. So, if in doubt, choose the lower rating.

	No	Somewhat or Uncertain	Yes
1. Is the therapist friendly?	0	1	2
2. Is s/he fun?	0	1	2
3. Does s/he show respect?	0	1	2
4. Can s/he adapt her- or himself to different developmental levels of children?	0	1	2
5. Is s/he a good listener?	0	1	2
6. Does s/he know when to be quiet?	0	1	2
7. Can s/he be quiet?	0	1	2
8. Does s/he know the crucial difference between when to do something and when to do nothing?	0	1	2

9. Does s/he have enough experience with children to know how to manage their behavior and maximize cooperation?	0	1	2
10. Does s/he answer questions about treatment plans with respect toward you?	0	1	2
11. Does s/he provide answers in language and with logic that you can understand? (If you are in doubt, the answer is No).	0	1	2
12. Does your child like her/him?	0	1	2

Total Score: _____

A score below 10 suggests the therapist is less than likeable.

Michael Scheeringa, 2016

Chapter Notes

Chapter One Notes

1 American Psychiatric Association, *Diagnostic and Statistical Manual of Mental Disorders,* Third Edition (Washington, DC: American Psychiatric Association, 1980).

2 Alexander McFarlane, "Posttraumatic phenomena in a longitudinal study of children following a natural disaster," *Journal of the American Academy of Child and Adolescent Psychiatry* 26 (1987): 764–69.

3 Bonnie L. Green et al., "Children and disaster: Age, gender, and parental effects on PTSD symptoms," *Journal of the American Academy of Child & Adolescent Psychiatry* 30 (1991): 945–51.

4 Robert S. Pynoos et al., "Life threat and posttraumatic stress in school-age children," *Archives of General Psychiatry* 44 (1987): 1057–63.

5 J. David Kinzie, William H. Sack, Richard H. Angell, Spero Manson, and Ben Rath, "The psychiatric effects of massive trauma on Cambodian children: I. The children," *Journal of the American Academy of Child Psychiatry* 25 (1986): 370–76.

6 Lenore Terr, *Too Scared to Cry* (New York: Basic Books, 1990).

7 Elissa P. Benedek, in *Post-traumatic Stress Disorder in Children,* eds. Spencer Eth and Robert S. Pynoos (Washington, DC: American Psychiatric Publishing, Inc., 1985): 1–16.

8 Michael S. Scheeringa et al., "Predictive validity in a prospective follow-up of PTSD in preschool children," *Journal of the American Academy of Child and Adolescent Psychiatry* 44 (2005): 899–906.

9 Richard Meiser-Stedman et al., "The posttraumatic stress disorder diagnosis in preschool- and elementary school-age children exposed to motor vehicle accidents," *American Journal of Psychiatry* 165 (2008): 1326–37.

10 McFarlane, "Posttraumatic phenomena," 764–69.

11 Jon Shaw, Brooks Applegate, and Caryn Schorr, "Twenty-one-month follow-up study of school-age children exposed to Hurricane Andrew," *Journal of the American Academy of Child and Adolescent Psychiatry* 35 (1996): 359–64.

Chapter Two Notes

1 American Psychiatric Association, *Diagnostic and Statistical Manual of Mental Disorders,* Third Edition (Washington, DC: American Psychiatric Association, 1980).

2 World Health Organization, *The ICD-10 Classification of Mental and Behavioural Disorders: Clinical Descriptions and Diagnostic Guidelines* (Geneva: World Health Organization, 1992).

3   John E. Erichsen, *On Railway and Other Injuries of the Nervous System* (Philadelphia: Henry C. Lea, 1867).

4   Jacob M. Da Costa, "On irritable heart; a clinical study of a form of functional cardiac disorder and its consequences," *Journal of the American Medical Sciences* 61 (1871): 18–52.

5   Peter Gay, ed., *The Freud Reader* (New York: W. W. Norton & Company, 1989): 96–97.

6   American Psychiatric Association: Committee on Nomenclature and Statistics, *Diagnostic and Statistical Manual of Mental Disorders,* First Edition (Washington, DC: American Psychiatric Association, 1952).

7   American Psychiatric Association: Committee on Nomenclature and Statistics, *Diagnostic and Statistical Manual of Mental Disorders,* Second Edition (Washington, DC: American Psychiatric Association, 1968).

8   American Psychiatric Association, *Diagnostic and Statistical Manual,* Third Edition.

9   I. Lee Gislason and Justin D. Call, "Dog bite in infancy: Trauma and personality development," *Journal of the American Academy of Child and Adolescent Psychiatry* 21 (1982): 203–7.

10 George MacLean, "Psychic trauma and traumatic neurosis: Play therapy with a four-year-old boy," *Canadian Psychiatric Association Journal* 22 (1977): 71–75.

11 Judith A. Cohen and Anthony P. Mannarino, "A treatment outcome study for sexually abused preschool children: Initial findings," *Journal of the American Academy of Child and Adolescent Psychiatry* 35 (1996): 42–50.

12 Judith A. Cohen and Anthony P. Mannarino, "A treatment study for sexually abused preschool children: Outcome during a one-year follow-up," *Journal of the American Academy of Child and Adolescent Psychiatry* 36 (1997): 1228–35.

13 Alicia F. Lieberman, Patricia Van Horn, and Emily J. Ozer, "Preschooler witnesses of marital violence: Predictors and mediators of child behavior problems," *Development and Psychopathology* 17 (2005): 385–96.

14 Richard Meiser-Stedman et al., "The posttraumatic stress disorder diagnosis in preschool- and elementary school-age children exposed to motor vehicle accidents," *American Journal of Psychiatry* 165 (2008): 1326–37.

15 Michael S. Scheeringa et al., "New findings on alternative criteria for PTSD in preschool children," *Journal of the American Academy of Child and Adolescent Psychiatry* 42 (2003): 561–70.

16 Michael S. Scheeringa et al., "Predictive validity in a prospective follow-up of PTSD in preschool children,"*Journal of the American Academy of Child and Adolescent Psychiatry* 44 (2005): 899–906.

17 Michael S. Scheeringa and Charles H. Zeanah, "Reconsideration of harm's way: Onsets and comorbidity patterns in preschool children and their caregivers following Hurricane Katrina," *Journal of Clinical Child and Adolescent Psychology* 37 (2008): 508–18.

18 Nathaniel Laor et al., "Israeli preschoolers under Scud missile attacks," *Archives of General Psychiatry* 53 (1996): 416–23.

19 Nathaniel Laor et al., "Israeli preschool children under Scuds: A 30-month follow-up," *Journal of the American Academy of Child and Adolescent Psychiatry* 36 (1997): 349–56.

20 Scheeringa and Zeanah, "Reconsideration of harm's way," 508–18.

Chapter Three Notes

1   Stephen Joseph, "Life-events and post-traumatic stress in a sample of English adolescents," *Journal of Community & Applied Social Psychology* 10 (2000): 475–82.

2   Joseph, "Life-events and post-traumatic stress," 481.

3   Lawrence A. Palinkas, Michael A. Downs, John S. Petterson, and John Russell, "Social, cultural, and psychological impacts of the Exxon Valdez oil spill," *Human Organization* 52 (1993): 1–13.

4   Margaret W. Gerard and Rita Dukette, "Techniques for preventing separation trauma in child placement," *American Journal of Orthopsychiatry* 24 (1954): 111–27.

5   A. Margaret Eastman and Thomas J. Moran, "Multiple perspectives: Factors related to differential diagnosis of sex abuse and divorce trauma in children under six," *Child & Youth Services* 15 (1991): 159–75.

6   J. Alexander Bodkin, Harrison G. Pope, Michael J. Detke, and James I. Hudson, "Is PTSD caused by traumatic stress?" *Journal of Anxiety Disorders* 21 (2007): 176–82.

7   Michael J. Scott and Stephen G. Stradling, "Post-traumatic stress disorder without the trauma," *British Journal of Clinical Psychology* 33 (1994): 71–74.

8   Miranda Olff et al., "Impact of a foot and mouth disease crisis on post-traumatic symptoms in farmers," *The British Journal of Psychiatry* 186 (2005): 165–66.

9   Michael Mong, Kenji Noguchi, and Brenna Ladner, "Immediate psychological impact of the Deepwater Horizon oil spill: Symptoms of PTSD and coping skills," *Journal of Aggression, Maltreatment & Trauma* 21 (2012): 691–704.

10 Substance Abuse and Mental Health Administration, *Types of Trauma and Violence*, retrieved from https://www.samhsa.gov/trauma-violence/types, accessed April 8, 2017.

11 National Center for Child Traumatic Stress, *Types of Traumatic Stress*, retrieved from http://www.nctsn.org/trauma-types#q7, accessed April 8, 2017.

12 National Center for PTSD, *Violence and Abuse*, retrieved from https://www.ptsd.va.gov/public/types/violence/index.asp, accessed April 8, 2017.

Chapter Four Notes

1   Isaac R. Galatzer-Levy and Richard A. Bryant, "636,120 ways to have posttraumatic stress disorder," *Perspectives on Psychological Science* 8 (2013): 651–62.

2   Bridget M. Kuehn, "Military probes epidemic of suicide," *JAMA* 304 (2010): 1427–30.

3   Teresa L. Kramer et al., "The comorbidity of post-traumatic stress disorder and suicidality in Vietnam veterans," *Suicide and Life-Threatening Behavior* 24 (1994): 58–67.

4   Michelle D. Leichtman and Stephen J. Ceci, "The nature and development of children's event memory," in *Trauma and Memory: Clinical and Legal Controversies*, ed. Paul S. Applebaum (New York: Oxford University Press, 1997): 163.

5   Michael S. Scheeringa, Charles H. Zeanah, and Judith A. Cohen, "PTSD in children and adolescents: Toward an empirically based algorithm," *Depression and Anxiety* 28 (2011): 770–82.

6   Michael S. Scheeringa, unpublished data.

7   Michael S. Scheeringa et al., "Factors affecting the diagnosis and prediction of PTSD symptomatology in children and adolescents," *American Journal of Psychiatry* 163 (2006): 644–51.

8   Richard Meiser-Stedman et al., "The posttraumatic stress disorder diagnosis in preschool- and elementary school-age children exposed to motor vehicle accidents," *American Journal of Psychiatry* 165 (2008): 1326–37.

9   Greg Iselin et al., "Which method of posttraumatic stress disorder classification best predicts psychosocial function in children with traumatic brain injury?" *Journal of Anxiety Disorders* 24 (2010): 774–79.

Chapter Five Notes

1   Drew Miele and Edward J. O'Brien, "Underdiagnosis of posttraumatic stress disorder in at risk youth," *Journal of Traumatic Stress* 23 (2010): 591–98.

2   M. Van Zyl, Piet P. Oosthuien, and Soraya Seedat, "Posttraumatic stress disorder: Undiagnosed cases in a tertiary inpatient setting," *African Journal of Psychiatry* 11 (2008): 119–22.

3   William E. Copeland et al., "Traumatic events and posttraumatic stress in childhood," *Archives of General Psychiatry* 64 (2007): 577–84.

4   George MacLean, "Psychic trauma and traumatic neurosis: Play therapy with a four-year-old boy," *Canadian Psychiatric Association Journal* 22 (1977): 71–75.

5   Diane H. Schetky, "Preschoolers' responses to murder of their mothers by their fathers: A study of four cases," *Bulletin of the American Academy of Psychiatry and Law* 6 (1978): 45–57.

6   Kyle D. Pruett, "Home treatment for two infants who witnessed their mother's murder," *Journal of the American Academy of Child and Adolescent Psychiatry* 18 (1979): 647–57.

7   Mollie M. Wallick, "Desensitization therapy with a fearful two-year-old," *American Journal of Psychiatry* 136 (1979): 1325–26.

8   Theodore J. Gaensbauer, "Anaclitic depression in a three-and-one-half-month-old child," *American Journal of Psychiatry* 137 (1980): 841–42.

9   I. Lee Gislason and Justin D. Call, "Dog bite in infancy: Trauma and personality development," *Journal of the American Academy of Child and Adolescent Psychiatry* 21 (1982): 203–07.

10 Neil Senior, Toba Gladstone, and Barry Nurcombe, "Child snatching: A case report," *Journal of the American Academy of Child and Adolescent Psychiatry* 21 (1982): 579–83.

11 Jean Goodwin, "Post-traumatic symptoms in incest victims," in *Post-Traumatic Stress Disorder in Children*, eds. Spencer Eth and Robert S. Pynoos (Washington, DC: American Psychiatric Press, 1985): 162.

12 Lenore C. Terr, "What happens to early memories of trauma? A study of twenty children under age five at the time of documented traumatic events," *Journal of the American Academy of Child and Adolescent Psychiatry* 27 (1988): 96–104.

13 Max Sugar, "Toddlers' traumatic memories," *Infant Mental Health Journal* 13 (1992): 245–51.

14 Richard W. Jones and Linda W. Peterson, "Post-traumatic stress disorder in a child following an automobile accident," *The Journal of Family Practice* 36 (1993): 223–25.

15 Michael S. Scheeringa, "PTSD in children younger than the age of 13: Toward developmentally sensitive assessment and management," in *Assessment of Trauma in Youths: Understanding Issues of Age, Complexity, and Associated Variables*, ed. Kathleen Nader (New York: Routledge, 2014): 21–37.

16 J. David Kinzie, William H. Sack, Richard H. Angell, Spero Manson, and Ben Rath, "The psychiatric effects of massive trauma on Cambodian children: I. The children," *Journal of the American Academy of Child Psychiatry* 25 (1986): 370–76.

17 Robert S. Pynoos et al., "Life threat and posttraumatic stress in school-age children," *Archives of General Psychiatry* 44 (1987): 1057–63.

18 Copeland et al., "Traumatic events," 577–84.

19 Dean G. Kilpatrick et al., "Violence and risk of PTSD, major depression, substance abuse/dependence, and comorbidity: Results from the National Survey of Adolescents," *Journal of Consulting and Clinical Psychology* 71 (2003): 692–700.

20 Markus A. Landolt, Ulrich Schnyder, Thomas Maier, Verena Schoenbucher, and Meichun Mohler-Kuo, "Trauma exposure and posttraumatic stress disorder in adolescents: A national survey in Switzerland," *Journal of Traumatic Stress* 26 (2013): 209–16.

Chapter Six Notes

1 David Finkelhor et al., "Upset among youth in response to questions about exposure to violence, sexual assault and family maltreatment," *Child Abuse & Neglect* 38 (2014): 217–23.

2 Michael S. Scheeringa, Mary Jo Wright, John P. Hunt, and Charles H. Zeanah, "Factors affecting the diagnosis and prediction of PTSD symptomatology in children and adolescents," *American Journal of Psychiatry* 163 (2006): 644–51.

3 Harold S. Koplewicz et al., "Child and parent response to the 1993 World Trade Center bombing," *Journal of Traumatic Stress* 15 (2002): 77–85.

Chapter Seven Notes

1 Isaac R. Galatzer-Levy and Richard A. Bryant, "636,120 Ways to have posttraumatic stress disorder," *Perspectives on Psychological Science* 8, no. 6 (2013): 651–62.

2 Timothy A. Brown et al., "Current and lifetime comorbidity of the DSM-IV anxiety and mood disorders in a large clinical sample," *Journal of Abnormal Psychology* 110 (2001): 585–99.

3 Michael S. Scheeringa et al., "New findings on alternative criteria for PTSD in preschool children," *Journal of the American Academy of Child and Adolescent Psychiatry* 42 (2003): 561–70.

4 Robert L. Spitzer, M. B. First, and J. C. Wakefield, "Saving PTSD from itself in DSM-V," *Journal of Anxiety Disorders* 21 (2007): 233–41.

5 John D. Elhai et al., "Empirical examination of a proposed refinement to DSM-IV posttraumatic stress disorder symptom criteria using the National Comorbidity Survey Replication data," *Journal of Clinical Psychiatry* 69 (2008): 597–602.

Chapter Eight Notes

1 Peter S. Jensen, Penelope Knapp, and David A. Mrazek, *Toward a New Diagnostic System for Psychopathology: Moving Beyond the DSM* (New York: The Guilford Press, 2006).

2 Thomas A. Widiger, "A dimensional model of psychopathology," *Psychopathology* 38 (2005): 211–14.

3   Derek Summerfield, "The invention of posttraumatic stress disorder and the social usefulness of a psychiatric category," *British Medical Journal* 322 (2001): 95–98.

4   Sharon Begley, "DSM-5: Psychiatrists' 'Bible' Finally Unveiled," *The Huffington Post* (online May 16, 2013), http://www.huffingtonpost.com/2013/05/17/dsm-5-unveiled-changes-disorders-_n_3290212.html, accessed August 15, 2016.

5   Allen J. Frances, "DSM-5 and Diagnostic Inflation," *Psychology Today* blog (January 23, 2012 online), https://www.psychologytoday.com/blog/dsm5-in-distress/201201/dsm-5-and-diagnostic-inflation, accessed August 14, 2016.

6   Gary Greenberg, "Inside the battle to define mental illness," *Wired.com* (12/27/2010), http://www.wired.com/2010/12/ff_dsmv/, accessed August 13, 2016.

7   Allen J. Frances, *Saving Normal: An Insider's Revolt Against Out-of-Control Psychiatric Diagnosis, DSM-5, Big Pharma, and the Medicalization of Everyday Life* (New York: William Morrow, 2013).

8   Monica Hesse, "The bible of the mind turns the page," *Washington Post* (May 12, 2013), https://www.washingtonpost.com/lifestyle/style/the-bible-of-the-mind-turns-the-page/2013/05/12/17d8fc1c-b1b6-11e2-baf7-5bc2a9dc6f44_story.html, accessed August 15, 2016.

9   Robert M. McCarron, "The DSM-5 and the art of medicine: Certainly uncertain," *Annals of Internal Medicine* 159, no. 5 (2013): 360–61.

10   Shadia Kawa and James Giordano, "A brief historicity of the Diagnostic and Statistical Manual of Mental Disorders: Issues and implications for the future of psychiatric canon and practice," *Philosophy, Ethics, and Humanities in Medicine* 7 (2012): 1–9.

11   11 Michael B. First, "Mutually exclusive versus co-occurring diagnostic categories: The challenge of diagnostic comorbidity," *Psychopathology* 38 (2005): 206–10.

12   Ronald C. Kessler and Phillip S. Wang, "The descriptive epidemiology of commonly occurring mental disorders in the United States," *Annual Review of Public Health* 29 (2008): 115–29.

13   Judith L. Herman, "Complex PTSD: A syndrome in survivors of prolonged and repeated trauma," *Journal of Traumatic Stress* 5, no. 3 (1992): 377–91.

14   Ibid., 388.

15   Ibid., 379.

16   Ibid., 388.

17   Ibid., 385.

18   Google Scholar, accessed February 4, 2017.

19   Susan Roth, Elana Newman, David Pelcovitz, Bessel A. van der Kolk, and Francine S. Mandel, "Complex PTSD in victims exposed to sexual and physical abuse: Results from the DSM-IV field trial for posttraumatic stress disorder," *Journal of Traumatic Stress* 10, no. 4 (1997): 539–55.

20   Bessel A. van der Kolk, "Developmental trauma disorder: Toward a rational diagnosis for children with complex trauma histories," *Psychiatric Annals* 35, no. 5 (2005): 401–08.

21   National Center for PTSD, "Complex PTSD," http://www.ptsd.va.gov/professional/pages/complex-ptsd.asp, accessed April 30, 2013.

Chapter Nine Notes

1   Evan Thomas and Daniel Klaidman, "Blood Brothers," *Newsweek* 127, no. 17 (April 22, 1996): 28–34.

2   Leo Kanner, "Autistic disturbances of affective contact," *Nervous Child* 2 (1943): 217–50.

3   Leo Kanner, "Problems of nosology and psychodynamics in early childhood autism," American Journal of Orthopsychiatry 19 (1949): 416–26.

4   James C. Harris, "Neurotribes: The legacy of autism and the future of neurodiversity," *Journal of the American Academy of Child & Adolescent Psychiatry* 55, no. 8 (2016): 728–35.

5   Bruno Bettelheim, *The Empty Fortress: Infantile Autism and the Birth of the Self* (New York: The Free Press, 1967).

6   Ibid., 393.

7   Ron Grossman, "Genius or Fraud? Bettelheim's Biographers Can't Seem to Decide," *Chicago Tribune,* January 23, 1997.

8   Anne C. Roark, "Bettelheim plagiarized book ideas, scholar says: Authors: The late child psychologist is accused of 'wholesale borrowing' for study of fairy tales," *Los Angeles Times,* February 7, 1991.

9   Ron Grossman, "The Puzzle That Was Bruno Bettelheim," *Chicago Tribune,* November 11, 1990.

10   Theodore Lidz, Stephen Fleck, and Alice Cornelison, *Schizophrenia and the Family* (New York: International Universities Press, 1965): 291.

11   Ibid.

12   Michael S. Scheeringa and Charles H. Zeanah, "A relational perspective on PTSD in early childhood," *Journal of Traumatic Stress* 14 (2001): 799–815.

13   Lenore C. Terr, "What happens to early memories of trauma? A study of twenty children under age five at the time of documented traumatic events," *Journal of the American Academy of Child and Adolescent Psychiatry* 27 (1988): 96–104.

14   See above, n. 12.

15   Ibid.

16   Ibid.

17   Adam Morris, Crystal Gabert-Quillen, and Douglas L. Delahanty, "The association between parent PTSD/depression symptoms and child PTSD symptoms: A meta-analysis," *Journal of Pediatic Psychology* 37 (2012): 1076–88.

18   Ibid., 1082–83.

19   Ibid., 1084.

20   Internet Movie Database, "Kevin Costner," http://www.imdb.com/name/ nm0000126/bio?ref_=nm_ov_bio_sm, accessed May 26, 2014.

21   Jenessa L. Malin et al., "A family systems approach to examining young children's social development," in *Child Psychology: A Handbook of Contemporary Issues,* Third Edition, eds. Lawrence Balter and Catherine S. Tamis-LaMonda (New York: Routledge, 2016): 355–78.

Chapter Ten Notes

1   Judith Rich Harris, *The Nurture Assumption: Why Children Turn Out the Way They Do* (New York: Free Press, 1998).

2   Sharon Begley, "The parent trap," *Newsweek,* http://judithrichharris.info/tna/ newswk1.htm, accessed February 11, 2013.

3   Ibid.

4   Ibid.

5   Russell Banks, *The Sweet Hereafter* (New York: HarperCollins Publishers, 1991).

6 Michael S. Scheeringa and Charles H. Zeanah, "A relational perspective on PTSD in early childhood," *Journal of Traumatic Stress* 14, no. 4 (2001): 799–815.

7 Alytia A. Levendosky et al., "The impact of domestic violence on the maternal-child relationship and preschool-age children's functioning," *Journal of Family Psychology* 17 (2003): 275–87.

8 Harold S. Koplewicz et al., "Child and parent response to the 1993 World Trade Center bombing," *Journal of Traumatic Stress* 15 (2002): 77–85.

9 Michael S. Scheeringa, "Posttraumatic stress disorder," in *Handbook of Infant, Toddler, and Preschool Mental Health Assessment,* eds. Rebecca DelCarmen-Wiggins and Alice Carter (New York: Oxford University Press, 2004): 377–97.

10 Michael S. Scheeringa, Leann Myers, Frank W. Putnam, and Charles H. Zeanah, "Maternal factors as moderators or mediators of PTSD symptoms in preschool children: A two-year prospective study," *Journal of Family Violence* 30, no. 5 (2015): 633–42.

11 See above, n. 6.

12 Michael S. Scheeringa et al., "Trauma-focused cognitive-behavioral therapy for posttraumatic stress disorder in three- through six-year-old children: A randomized clinical trial," *Journal of Child Psychology and Psychiatry* 52 (2011): 853–60.

13 Michael S. Scheeringa, *Treating PTSD in Preschoolers: A Clinical Guide* (New York: The Guilford Press, 2016).

14 14 Michael S. Scheeringa et al., "Feasibility and effectiveness of cognitive-behavioral therapy for posttraumatic stress disorder in preschool children: Two case reports," *Journal of Traumatic Stress* 20 (2007): 631–36.

Chapter Eleven Notes

1 Vanessa E. Cobham and Brett M. McDermott, "Working with children and adolescents after the Queensland floods," in *Proceedings of the Australasian Conference on Traumatic Stress Studies* (Perth, Australia, 2012).

2 CATS Consortium, "Implementing CBT for traumatized children and adolescents after September 11: Lessons learned from the Child and Adolescent Trauma Treatment Services (CATS) Project," *Journal of Clinical Child and Adolescent Psychology* 36, no. 4 (2007): 581–92.

3 Daniel Herman, Chip Felton, and Ezra Susser, "Mental health needs in New York state following the September 11th attacks," *Journal of Urban Health* 79, no. 3 (2002): 322–31.

4 Andrea Allen, William R. Saltzman, Melissa J. Brymer, Assaf Oshri, and Wendy K. Silverman, "An empirically informed intervention for children following exposure to severe hurricanes," *The Behavior Therapist* 29, no. 6 (2006): 118–24.

5 Lisa H. Jaycox, Judith A. Cohen, Anthony P. Mannarino, et al., "Children's mental health care following Hurricane Katrina: A field trial of trauma-focused psychotherapies," *Journal of Traumatic Stress* 23, no. 2 (2010): 223–31.

6 Barbara Rothbaum, Edna Foa, and David S. Riggs, "A prospective examination of posttraumatic stress disorder in rape victims," *Journal of Traumatic Stress* 5, no. 3 (1992): 455–75.

7 NICE, "Post-traumatic stress disorder: The management of PTSD in adults and children in primary and secondary care," *National Institute for Clinical Excellence* (2005).

8   Alexander McFarlane, "Posttraumatic phenomena in a longitudinal study of children following a natural disaster," *Journal of the American Academy of Child and Adolescent Psychiatry* 26 (1987): 764–69.
9   Jon Shaw, Brooks Applegate, and Caryn Schorr, "Twenty-one-month follow-up study of school-age children exposed to Hurricane Andrew," *Journal of the American Academy of Child and Adolescent Psychiatry* 35 (1996): 359–64.
10 Michael S. Scheeringa et al., "Predictive validity in a prospective follow-up of PTSD in preschool children," *Journal of the American Academy of Child and Adolescent Psychiatry* 44 (2005): 899–906.

Chapter Twelve Notes

1   John S. March, "The future of psychotherapy for mentally ill children and adolescents," *Journal of Child Psychology and Psychiatry* 50, nos. 1–2 (2009), 173.
2   Judith A. Cohen, Anthony P. Mannarino, and Esther Deblinger, *Treating Trauma and Traumatic Grief in Children and Adolescents* (New York: The Guilford Press, 2006).
3   Scheeringa Lab website, http://www2.tulane.edu/som/departments/psychiatry/ScheeringaLab/index.cfm.
4   Michael S. Scheeringa, *Treating PTSD in Preschoolers: A Clinical Guide* (New York: The Guilford Press, 2016).
5   Lori A. Zoellner, Lee A. Fitzgibbons, and Edna B. Foa, "Cognitive-behavioral approaches to PTSD," in *Treating Psychological Trauma and PTSD,* eds. John D. Wilson, Matthew J. Friedman, and Jacob D. Lindy (New York: The Guilford Press, 2001): 159–82.
6   Michael S. Scheeringa and Carl F. Weems, "Randomized placebo-controlled D-cycloserine with cognitive behavior therapy for pediatric posttraumatic stress," *Journal of Child and Adolescent Psychopharmacology* 24, no. 2 (2014): 69–77.
7   Michael S. Scheeringa et al., "Trauma-focused cognitive-behavioral therapy for posttraumatic stress disorder in three- through six-year-old children: A randomized clinical trial," *Journal of Child Psychology and Psychiatry* 52, no. 8 (2011): 853–60.
8   See above, n. 6.

Chapter Thirteen Notes

1   Curtis McMillen et al., "Untangling the psychiatric comorbidity of posttraumatic stress disorder in a sample of flood survivors," *Comprehensive Psychiatry* 43, no. 6 (2002): 478–85.
2   Ibid., 478.
3   Michael S. Scheeringa and Charles H. Zeanah, "Reconsideration of harm's way: Onsets and comorbidity patterns of disorders in preschool children and their caregivers following Hurricane Katrina," *Journal of Clinical Child and Adolescent Psychology* 37, no. 3 (2008): 508–18.
4   Brad Stone, *The Everything Store: Jeff Bezos and the Age of Amazon* (New York: Little, Brown and Company, 2013).
5   Natalya S. Weber et al., "Psychiatric and general medical conditions comorbid with schizophrenia in the National Hospital Discharge Survey," *Psychiatric Services* 60, no. 8 (2009): 1059–67.

Chapter Fourteen Notes

1 Judith L. Herman, *Trauma and Recovery* (New York: Basic Books, 1992).
2 Eitan Schwarz, Janice M. Kowalski, and Richard J. McNally, "Malignant memories: Post-traumatic changes in memory in adults after a school shooting," *Journal of Traumatic Stress* 6, no. 4 (1993): 545–53.
3 Steven M. Southwick et al., "Consistency of memory for combat-related traumatic events in veterans of Operation Desert Storm," *American Journal of Psychiatry* 154, no. 2 (1997): 173–77.
4 Jessica M. Sales et al., "Stressing memory: Long-term relations among children's stress, recall, and psychological outcome following Hurricane Andrew," *Journal of Cognition and Development* 6, no. 4 (2005): 529–45.
5 Richard Meiser-Stedman, "The Trauma Memory Quality Questionnaire: Preliminary development and validation of a measure of trauma memory characteristics for children and adolescents," *Memory* 15, no. 3 (2007): 271–79.
6 Stephen J. Ceci et al., "The possible role of source misattributions in the creation of false beliefs among preschoolers," *International Journal of Clinical and Experimental Hypnosis* 42, no. 4 (1994): 304–20.
7 Lenore C. Terr, "What happens to early memories of trauma? A study of twenty children under age five at the time of documented traumatic events," *Journal of the American Academy of Child and Adolescent Psychiatry* 27 (1988): 96–104.
8 Diane H. Schetky, "Child victims in the legal system," in *Trauma and Memory: Clinical and Legal Controversies*, eds. Paul S. Applebaum, Lisa A. Uyehara, and Mark R. Elin (New York: Oxford University Press, 1997): 497.
9 Ibid., 498.
10 Lisa A. Uyehara, "Diagnosis, pathogenesis, and memories of childhood abuse," in *Trauma and Memory: Clinical and Legal Controversies*, eds. Paul S. Applebaum, Lisa A. Uyehara, and Mark R. Elin (New York: Oxford University Press, 1997): 410.
11 Ibid., 415.
12 Alexander C. MacFarlane, "The longitudinal course of posttraumatic morbidity: The range of outcomes and their predictions," *Journal of Nervous & Mental Disease* 176, no. 1 (1988): 30–39.
13 Lenore C. Terr, *Unchained Memories: True Stories of Traumatic Memories, Lost and Found* (New York: Basic Books, 1994): 1–60.
14 Elizabeth F. Loftus and Katherine Ketcham, *The Myth of Repressed Memory* (New York: St. Martin's Press, 1994).
15 Mary Curtius, "Man won't be retried in repressed memory case," *Los Angeles Times* (July 3, 1996).
16 David L. Corwin and Erna Olafson, "Videotaped discovery of a reportedly unrecallable memory of child sexual abuse: Comparison with a childhood interview videotaped 11 years before," *Child Maltreatment* 2 (1997): 91–112.
17 Elizabeth F. Loftus and Melvin J. Guyer, "Who abused Jane Doe? The hazards of the single case history, Part I," *The Skeptical Inquirer* 26, no. 3 (May/June 2002).
18 Michael S. Scheeringa et al., "Do children and adolescents have different types of trauma narratives and does it matter? Reliability and face validation for a narrative taxonomy," *Journal of Traumatic Stress* 30, no. 3 (2017): 323–27.
19 Richard P. Kluft, "The argument for the reality of delayed recall of trauma," in *Trauma and Memory: Clinical and Legal Controversies*, eds. Paul S. Applebaum, Lisa A. Uyehara, and Mark R. Elin (New York: Oxford University Press, 1997): 51.

Chapter Fifteen Notes

1   Terence M. Keane et al., "Utility of psychophysiological measurement in the diagnosis of posttraumatic stress disorder: Results from a Department of Veterans Affairs cooperative study," *Journal of Consulting and Clinical Psychology* 66, no. 6 (1998): 914–23.

2   Rachel Yehuda et al., "Lower urinary cortisol excretion in patients with posttraumatic stress disorder," *Journal of Nervous and Mental Disease* 178, no. 6 (1990): 366–69.

3   Roger K. Pitman and Scot P. Orr, "Twenty-four-hour urinary cortisol and catecholamine excretion in combat-related posttraumatic stress disorder," *Biological Psychiatry* 27, no. 2 (1990): 245–47.

4   Ellen R. Klaassens et al., "Adulthood trauma and HPA-axis functioning in healthy subjects and PTSD patients: A meta-analysis," *Psychoneuroendocrinology* 37, no. 3 (2012): 317–31.

5   Eric Vermetten et al., "Long-term treatment with paroxetine increases verbal declarative memory and hippocampal volume in posttraumatic stress disorder," *Biological Psychiatry* 54, no. 7 (2003): 693–702.

6   Negar Fani et al., "Increased neural response to trauma scripts in posttraumatic stress disorder following paroxetine treatment: A pilot study," *Neuroscience Letters* 491, no. 3 (2011): 196–201.

7   J. Douglas Bremner, "Hypotheses and controversies related to effects of stress on the hippocampus: An argument for stress-induced damage to the hippocampus in patients with posttraumatic stress disorder," *Hippocampus* 11, no. 2 (2001): 79.

8   Bessel A. van der Kolk, "The body keeps the score: Memory and the evolving psychobiology of posttraumatic stress," in *Essential Papers on Posttraumatic Stress Disorder*, ed. Mardi J. Horowitz (New York: New York University Press, 1999): 301–26.

9   Bessel A. van der Kolk, "The body keeps the score: Brief autobiography of Bessel van der Kolk," in *Mapping Trauma and Its Wake: Autobiographic Essays by Pioneer Trauma Scholars*, ed. Charles R. Figley (New York: Routledge, 2006): 211–26.

10 Bessel A. van der Kolk, *The Body Keeps the Score: Brain, Mind, and Body in the Healing of Trauma* (New York: Viking, 2014).

11 Bessel A. van der Kolk and Jose Saporta, "Biological response to psychic trauma," in *International Handbook of Traumatic Stress Symptoms*, eds. John P. Wilson and Beverly Raphael (New York: Plenum, 1993): 25.

12 *2013 Senate Joint Resolution 59,* http://docs.legis.wisconsin.gov/2013/related/proposals/sjr59, accessed November 18, 2013.

13 Isaac R. Galatzer-Levy et al., "Cortisol response to an experimental stress paradigm prospectively predicts long-term distress and resilience trajectories in response to active police service," *Journal of Psychiatric Research* 56 (2014): 36–42.

Chapter Sixteen Notes

1   Theodore J. Gaensbauer, "Traumatic stress disorder," in *DC: 0-3 Casebook,* eds. Alicia Lieberman, Serena Wieder, and Emily Fenichel (Washington, DC: Zero to Three, 1997): 31–46.

2   Michael S. Scheeringa, "Posttraumatic stress disorder," in *Handbook of Infant Mental Health,* Third Edition, ed. Charles H. Zeanah (New York: The Guilford Press, 2009): 345–61.

3   Rachael Collie and Harlene Hayne, "Deferred imitation by 6- and 9-month-old infants: More evidence for declarative memory," *Developmental Psychobiology* 35 (1999): 83–90.
4   Charles A. Nelson, "The ontogeny of human memory: A cognitive neuroscience perspective," *Developmental Psychology* 31 (1995): 723–38.
5   Robyn Fivush, "Children's recollections of traumatic and nontraumatic events," *Development and Psychopathology* 10 (1999): 699–716.
6   Lenore C. Terr, "What happens to early memories of trauma? A study of twenty children under age five at the time of documented traumatic events," *Journal of the American Academy of Child and Adolescent Psychiatry* 27, no. 1 (1988): 96–104.
7   Dean G. Kilpatrick et al., "National estimates of exposure to traumatic events and PTSD prevalence using *DSM-IV* and *DSM-5* criteria," *Journal of Traumatic Stress* 26, no. 5 (2013): 537–47.
8   Katie A. McLaughlin et al., "Trauma exposure and posttraumatic stress disorder in a national sample of adolescents," *Journal of the American Academy of Child & Adolescent Psychiatry* 52, no. 8 (2013): 815–30.
9   Ronald C. Kessler et al., "Posttraumatic stress disorder in the National Comorbidity Survey," *Archives of General Psychiatry* 52 (1995): 1048–60.
10 See above, n. 7.
11 See above, n. 8.
12 Amy J. Mikolajewski, Michael S. Scheeringa, and Carl F. Weems (in press), "Evaluating *DSM-5* posttraumatic stress disorder diagnostic criteria in older children and adolescents," *Journal of Child and Adolescent Psychopharmacology*.
13 Greg Iselin et al., "Which method of posttraumatic stress disorder classification best predicts psychosocial function in children with traumatic brain injury?" *Journal of Anxiety Disorders* 24 (2010): 774–79.
14 Richard Meiser-Stedman et al., "The posttraumatic stress disorder diagnosis in preschool- and elementary school-age children exposed to motor vehicle accidents," *American Journal of Psychiatry* 165 (2008): 1326–37.